Human Reality and the Social World

Human Reality and the Social World:

Ortega's Philosophy of History

Oliver W. Holmes

University of Massachusetts Press   Amherst 1975

Library of Congress Cataloging in Publication Data

Holmes, Oliver W   1938–
    Human reality and the social world.

    Bibliography: p.
    Includes index.
    1. Ortega y Gasset, José, 1883–1955. 2. History—
Philosophy. I. Title.
B4568.074H63   901   74-21238
ISBN 0-87023-173-1

To my mother and father

Contents

Preface

This essay attempts a systematic analysis of Ortega's philosophy of human reality, the social world, and history. The unified analysis of his philosophy drew heavily upon the traditions of historicism, phenomenology, and existentialism. Such was the influence of these philosophical traditions that Ortega became, at once, critic and representative of their respective positions, problems, and solutions.

The external historical connections among historicism, phenomenology, and existentialism, as philosophical movements, are not broached here, albeit these are the themes with which this study will be concerned. The internal essential philosophical relations, however, of these points of view are perceptible in the philosophical perspective of Ortega and, in this regard, are critical connections to consider in our analysis of his philosophical orientation. The picture of Ortega's philosophy of history that will emerge from these considerations will present his general intellectual development in the form of an analysis of his thought.

The enterprise of intellectual history is as varied as the intellectual historians writing it. The approach taken here is to inquire into the interrelationships of Ortega's social and intellectual experiences with the formation of his ideas. The inquiry here, then, is concerned specifically with the general coherence of Ortega's philosophy of human reality, society, and history, with identifying the fundamental features of his philosophical perspective to determine the underlying principle of uniformity.

It is important for our purposes to begin our inquiry with a discussion of the external events and circumstances that helped shape Ortega's experiences. In analyzing his philosophical point of view, one is immediately confronted with the essential question: what was Ortega's view of reality and how did he—if he in fact did—perceive its common principle of unity? In this context of identifying his philosophical description of the component characteristics that constitute reality, we are able also to discern the coherence of his ideas and how this coherence in thought systematizes the essential relations of the principle of variety with the principle of uniformity in reality in connection with man, society, and history.

I wish to express my profound gratitude to a number of people for their personal interest and their generous and valuable help in the course of the research and the writing of this study. I express particular gratitude to the Ortega family and specifically to Ortega's daughter, Soledad Ortega de Varela, and widow, Rosa Spottorno y Topete de Ortega, for their warm reception and for their overall assistance in my research. I am also grateful to Julián Marías and to Paulino Garagorri for giving generously of their time and for the opportunity of clarifying conversations concerning certain biographical details about Ortega. To Ramón Bela and Matilde Medina, of the Fulbright Commission in Spain, I want to give particular thanks for their help in making my research stay in Madrid a very pleasant and memorable experience.

I would also like to express my gratitude to the late Hermann L. Van Breda, O.F.M., who was the founder and director of the Husserl Archives at the University of Louvain, and to Iso Kern, for their kind reception and assistance, and for making available to me Husserl's unedited, unpublished manuscripts. These manuscripts were eventually edited by Iso Kern and published in the series *Husserliana,* also founded and directed by Father Van Breda.

In the course of preparing this study I have profited enormously from several discussions with friends and scholars. I am especially indebted to Leonard Krieger, who supervised an earlier version of this study and who has read the manuscript in its preliminary and final stages, for his probing comments, his constructive criticisms and suggestions, and his perceptive analyses. His authoritative grasp of the complex terrain of concepts and his critical insights have been of inestimable value. I am also very grateful to Karl J. Weintraub for his careful reading of and his critical comments on the earlier version of this work. Though we differ in the interpretation of certain facets of the study, we agree that no two investigations of similar subjects necessarily arrive at similar results. To Louis Gottschalk, who has been a source of encouragement throughout the course of the work, many thanks.

Toward the completion of this study, there were several friends and colleagues who read the manuscript and contributed support, to whom I wish to express particular thanks: David Bien, David Campbell, Thomas J. Cottle, François Furet, Charles Gibson, Raymond Grew, Michael Harper, David Pines, Geoffrey Russel, Paul

Seaver, Hannah Sokal, Sylvia Thrupp, Charles Tilly, Louise Tilly, Nicholas West, and Hayden V. White. In different ways, each has been helpful and each has provided encouragement when it was sorely needed; to each, I shall always be grateful.

This study could not have been completed without the generous assistance of a number of institutions. The research for the study began with the help of a Fulbright Scholar Fellowship to Spain; a fellowship from the Center for Advanced Study at the University of Illinois, Urbana, a Horace H. Rackham faculty fellowship from the University of Michigan, and faculty research grants from the department of history at Stanford University enabled me to expand and complete the writing of the manuscript.

Finally, there must also be some mention of those who made the publication of this work possible. I am most grateful to the staff of the University of Massachusetts Press for their collective assistance in bringing the work to print.

A word about the source material: I have used throughout Ortega's *Obras Completas*. While a number of his major works have been translated into English, the references made here to the original text are my own translations. With all said and done, I bear the sole responsibility for the limitations that may remain.

Human Reality and the Social World

Introduction

José Ortega y Gasset was born 9 May 1883, in an apartment overlooking Madrid's beautiful Retiro Park. José Ortega Munilla and Dolores Gasset Chinchilla thereby became the parents of their second of four children, three sons and a daughter; Eduardo was born in April of the preceding year, and, after young José, Rafaela in 1884 and Manuel in 1885.[1] Ortega Munilla, novelist and journalist, divided his time between creative writing and directing the daily newspaper *El Imparcial*, which had been founded by his father-in-law, Eduardo Gasset y Artime. This atmosphere of creative writing and journalism offered Ortega and his brothers the environmental factors that would attract them, as well, to essay and novel writing.

Many Spaniards believe that an abundance of sunshine is vital for both internal and external development. Apparently Ortega Munilla shared this view—all the more, perhaps, as a novelist—for he took the family to spend every fall and winter, between 1887 and 1893, in the quaint, Arabic-influenced city of Córdoba or in the sunny coastal city of Málaga, only returning to Madrid for the hot summer months to manage the more important administrative affairs of *El Imparcial*. Young Ortega was enrolled in the Jesuit-staffed Colegio de San Estan-

---

There is no complete written biography of Ortega, partly because Ortega did not compile a great deal of personal material, and partly because much of what was available was either destroyed or lost during the Spanish Civil War. The personal material that has been assembled here comes from Ortega's autobiographical anecdotes in his writings, his letters to Navarro Ledesma, and the biographical data compiled by the Ortega family.

For studies relating Ortega's background to his career, see: Julián Marias, *Ortega: Circunstancia y Vocacion*, vol. 1 (Madrid: Revista de Occidente, 1960); Robert McClintock, *Man and His Circumstances: Ortega as Educator* (New York: Teachers College Press, 1971); Ida Blanche De Puy, "The Basic Ideology of José Ortega y Gasset: The Conflict of Mission and Vocation" (Ph.D. diss., Stanford University, 1961); Joaquín Iriarte, *Ortega y Gasset: su Persona y su Doctrina* (Madrid: Editorial Razón y Fe, 1942).

islao de Miraflores del Palo in Málaga during this time and, at the age of nine, he began to learn Greek with Father Coloma at the Colegio and Latin under the private instruction of Don Ramón Minguella.[2] The Catholic Colegios were among the few institutions in which it was possible to pursue classical studies. In 1897, Ortega received his *bachillerato* from the Colegio and, during the following year, went on to study philosophy, letters, and law at the University of Salamanca. Ortega performed with distinction in completing his studies at Salamanca with the pleasing results of *notable* in world literature, and *sobresaliente* in Greek, history, and metaphysics.[3] Miguel de Unamuno, an eminent figure in Spanish literature, philosophy, and letters until his death in 1936, was one of Ortega's examiners at Salamanca. The following year, Ortega entered the Central University of Madrid and, in 1902, he received his *licenciatura* in philosophy and letters.

In 1904, the year prior to his departure for Germany, Ortega wrote his first article for *El Imparcial* on the Belgian poet Maurice Maeterlinck.[4] This article in the family newspaper was the first of several signs pointing toward an active career as a journalist and an essayist. This year was maturative for Ortega in other stages of his growth: it was the year that he became engaged to Rosa Spottorno y Topete, and it was the year in which he received his doctoral degree in philosophy and letters from the Central University of Madrid. Ortega wrote his thesis on "The Terrors of the Year One Thousand,"[5] revealing an early interest in a general interpretive approach to history. The thesis attempted to recapture the "historical climate" of eleventh-century France through a general description of the different modes of living among the nobility, clergy, vassals, and peasants. The two most important factors, for Ortega, in discussing any aspect of medieval life were "land" (the basic criterion of wealth) and the "sword" (which he viewed as the symbol of power). The relationships between lord and vassal, the church and nobility, landlord and peasant, were based upon the possession of, and the ability to hold, land. The thesis also described how continual wars among the nobility, which often resulted in higher rents and taxes, accompanied by the rises in the price of bread and the threat of plagues, made death an ever-present phenomenon in the precarious existence of eleventh-century man in France. This interpretation of man as an historical being, confronting the chances attenuating historical circumstances, was taken by Ortega to constitute an "historical epoch" and thereby to result in what he called a "sociological logarithm."[6] He did not carry his interpretation of the eleventh century beyond these broad generalizations. This general interpretive approach to history, however, with a view toward the sociological manifestations of an historical period, provided Ortega with the essential perspective that led him to write a systematic philosophy of history thirty years later.

In 1905, Ortega left Spain—"fleeing," he said, "the vulgarity of my country"[7]—for Germany, "to stuff myself with whatever I can get out of it."[8] His original goal was studying classical philology and philosophy, and this first trip to Germany became an eight-months stay at the University of Leipzig. Ortega's German was inadequate to study philology, but this linguistic deficiency did not deter his enthusiasm: he enrolled in the Indo-European language and linguistic courses of professors Brugmann and Meyer. Although the time he spent on philological studies distracted him from the philosophical training he had sought initially, Ortega was introduced to the works of Wilhelm von Humboldt, Renan, Taine, Schopenhauer, Nietzsche, and Darwin, and audited the anatomy, histology, physiology, and psychology courses of Wilhelm Wundt,[9] who, despite the fact that he had been appointed to the chair of philosophy, served as professor of physiology and psychology at Leipzig.[10]

Ortega's eight-months stay in Leipzig enabled him to discern certain fundamental differences between the Spanish and German world views. In one of several letters written from Leipzig to his close friend, the novelist and literary critic Francisco Navarro Ledesma, he alluded to an inclination on his part toward the German Protestant ethic of self-discipline and hard work as he criticized the "supineness" of the Mediterranean spirit of his native country. "I do not think," he wrote, "as they do today in Spain: 'we are here to lose time.' This is their [the Spaniards'] own foolishness . . . in order not to work."[11] This kind of inertia and inaction was only one manifestation of what Ortega saw as the Spanish problem. In another letter to Ledesma, he pointed out one way through which he became aware of the enormous cultural gap between Europe and Spain:

> Paco, it is necessary to reconstruct the history of Spain, all the way from the beginning. Here in the Pauline Library [at the University] there are a considerable number of books on the history of Spain. The little time that I have free, I read some of these works. I tell you Paco, it is necessary to produce a history of Spanish Civilization . . . a work that deserves a life all its own. This book could be the first solid block of a reconstruction. The four or five times that Germany has reconstructed its own history the work has been done under the inspiration of a new history book by some historian. Such a person is he who, from time to time, reunites mother and child, the spirit of race and people, and who establishes a line

of communication for them by means of the umbilical cord of his book. . . . I will clarify. France, Germany and England offer the normal type of historical life of a race: all those sheaves of ideas and ways of feeling that which is called French, German and English Civilization have been developed through time without a single grain, a single concept remaining unproductive among the cobblestones of the road. The harvests of civilization have passed leaving one another without hungry years, without blank centuries. With us . . . what fertile sheaves have not lain dormant for the past centuries? In the early part of the seventeenth century, the upper grindstone stopped; for four centuries these grains have been neither ground nor replanted. The fruition of these grains could restore the umbilical cord of historical continuity which had been severed with the political eclipse of Charles I [Charles V of the Holy Empire] . In order to be able to think of a serious renovation it is necessary, before nothingness fills that empty gap, to produce artificially, in one or two generations, four centuries of harvests. Only a legion of learned youths are able to do this, with the service of a squadron of archivists: That is what we are lacking and not country roads. . . . History, blessed history . . . Taine, Renan, Ranke, Ranner, Treitschke. That is what we lack![12]

A first-rate book on the history of Spanish civilization, however, was not the only thing Ortega saw lacking in Spain. A solid background in philosophy was also needed. Thus, while at Leipzig, Ortega made plans to return to Germany during the following year to realize his primary aim of studying German philosophy, which the psychologism of Wundt had apparently failed to fulfill; the place he chose was Berlin.[13] After completing his language and linguistic course, the sole obstacle remaining was the securing of financial assistance that would enable him to resume his studies in Germany. In August 1906, he left Leipzig for Madrid, where he soon received the good news that he had been granted a stipend for another year of study in Germany. Within a few weeks, he was in Berlin, where at this time Wilhelm Dilthey, Friedrich Paulsen, Eduard Meyer, Heinrich Wölfflin, Georg Simmel, Carl Stumpf, Max Planck, and Alois Riehl were all teaching. While in Berlin, however, Ortega attended only the lectures of Riehl.[14]

Ortega's stay at the University of Berlin was brief. Six months after his arrival, he left for the University of Marburg, where he began his philosophical studies, joining Nicolai Hartmann, Paul Scheffer, and Heinz Heimsoeth under the Neo-Kantian philosophers Hermann Cohen and Paul Natorp.[15] It was at Marburg that he found in Cohen and Natorp the necessary inspiration and direction to pursue his studies in philosophy.[16] The University of Marburg, with its approach to an inquiry into the logical foundation of the natural sciences and its emphasis on the epistemological and methodological facets of philosophy, provided Ortega with the kind of philosophical foundation and training that he had been seeking. The intellectual context of the Neo-Kantian atmosphere at the Marburg school—particularly its general reaction against metaphysical systems—provided Ortega with the essential point of view (supplementing the overall orientation of his doctoral thesis) that facilitated the development of his philosophy of man, society, and history.

In the fall of 1908, Ortega returned to Madrid and, in addition to his recent appointment to the staffs of the weekly newspapers *El Imparcial* and *Faro*, began to teach ethics, logic, and psychology at La Escuela Superior del Magisterio.[17] When he had departed for Germany in 1905, the dominant intellectual issue in Spain had been the regeneration of Spain and the fundamental question, "what is to be done: 'Hispanization or Europeanization?'" On his return, this question was the central theme of heated discussions, as the "Spanish problem" continued virtually to dominate the conversations of the intellectuals at Madrid's well-known literary club, El Ateneo; the only addition to those discussions was Ortega's literary polemical exchange with the historian Gabriel Maura y Gamazo in *Faro*.[18] Maura coined in *Faro* the designation "generation of 1898" for the group of young writers and social thinkers who came together to discuss the "degeneration" of Spain in the wake of Spain's ignominious defeat in the 1898 war with the United States.[19] It was Spain's last international conflict as a colonial power: the Treaty of Paris recognizing the quick and decisive victory of the United States required Spain to relinquish her rights to Cuba and yield Puerto Rico and the Philippines to the United States.[20]

The "generation of '98"—the term was popularized in the newspaper articles of the novelist Azorín, who considered himself a member of the group[21]—analyzed the "Spanish problem" and voiced their criticisms, reflections, and protests in their novels and in literary polemics. The impressive group, men who had come to maturity in the 1890s, included Azorín; the writer on political and philosophical subjects Ramiro de Maeztu; the poets Antonio Machado, Juan Ramón Jiménez, and Valle Inclán; and the novelists Ramón Pérez de Ayala, Pío Baroja, and Unanumo.[22] These writers distinguished themselves through their efforts to characterize, their desires to define the essence of "Spanishness" and to revitalize the media through which the Spanish language

was expressed. In 1898, at the age of fifteen, Ortega was too young
to take part in the early literary polemics and the intellectual discussions of the "generation of '98." However, in this contemporary and
problematic spirit he grew, and, once an adult, he made significant
reflections of his own on the "Spanish problem."

In addition to causing the formation of the "generation of '98," the
"national disaster" of 1898 also brought about an essential split within Spanish intellectual circles, between the "patriots" who clamored
for the regeneration of Spain "from within" and those who aspired
for continual cultural contact with Europe.[23] The manifestations of
this nascent feeling of patriotism became more conspicuous after
1898, whereas the spirit of a kind of cultural internationalism could
be traced back to the founding of La Institución Libre de Enseñanza
(Free Institute of Education) in 1876 by Francisco Giner de los Ríos
(1839-1915), who, in turn, had been very much under the influence
of a movement in the 1860s known as El Krausismo Español (Spanish
Krausism).[24] El Krausismo, for a select group of intellectuals, became
a means of remaining in contact with European thought. The movement had its beginning after Julián Sanz del Río (1814-69), a professor of philosophy at the Central University of Madrid, had returned
to Spain from Germany, where between 1843 and 1845 he was introduced to the doctrines of the German philosopher Karl Christian
Friedrich Krause (1781-1832) while studying at the University of
Heidelberg under the Krausian disciples Hermann von Leonhardi and
Karl David August Röder.[25] Krause called the fundamental view of
his philosophic system Panentheismus, or "All-in-God," and, for this
reason, considered his system of "Panentheism" to be basically different from the doctrines of theism and pantheism.[26] Although he attached the term panentheism to his philosophy, there appears to be little
difference between his viewpoint and pantheism. To Krause, God, the
Absolute Being, is disclosed in Nature, in Mind, and in Humanity. As
God is one with the world, Krause's system developed the idea that
there is a unity of Humanity and Nature that is based upon the totality of the Spiritualness of the Absolute Being. Krause's philosophy is
characterized by its spiritual mysticism and, perhaps, it was this religious quality of his system, as well as his ideas on secular universal
education, that drew Sanz del Río to his thought.[27] Having been very
much under the sway of the moral and religious philosophy of Krause,
Sanz del Río began a series of lectures in 1854 on his philosophic
doctrines. In 1860, Sanz del Río translated Krause's "Ideal for Humanity" (in which he proposed the formation of a League for Humanity and the Universal Educational Association), which, because
of opposition by influential reactionary Catholic prelates, was placed

on the *Index Expurgatorius* of the Vatican. The vindictive mood of
the Catholic Church in Spain followed Sanz del Río to the grave, literally, as he was denied ecclesiastical burial because of his secular
Krausist views; he was eventually buried in an unconsecrated ceme-
tery.[28] Through his lectures and informal conversations, Sanz del Río
had exercised an enormous influence on his students and disciples for
a decade and a half and thus initiated *El Krausismo Español.*

Giner de los Ríos was a student and a follower of Sanz del Río and
El Krausismo, as well as a supporter of the "radical-liberal" principles
of the abortive Revolution of 1868.[29] During 1868, he was elected to
a professorship of philosophy of law at La Universidad Central (University of Madrid). Subsequent to his admission to the faculty, Giner
de los Ríos expressed his sympathies with Sanz del Río, Salmerón,
and Fernando de Castro, who had been removed from their university
positions—"separated from their chairs," to use the words of Giner de
los Ríos—by the reactionary minister Manuel Orovio.[30] In 1875, Giner
de los Ríos lost his chair of philosophy of law at the Central University
of Madrid, along with Salmerón and a group of other professors who
had also been "separated from their chairs," for "radical" religious
and political convictions. It was under this set of circumstances that
La Institución Libre de Enseñanza was founded by Giner de los Ríos
and his colleagues in 1876, and it thereby took its rise as a protest
against state and clerical control of education.[31] Its aim was to be a
secular university, dedicated to the ideals of academic freedom—freedom from both church and state—and to place Spain in constant
touch with the mainstream of European thought.[32] This emphasis on
European contact by La Institución and its followers contributed to
the consciousness of cultural internationalism that had been set against
the isolationist tendencies of the "patriots." By the early 1900s, the
former approach had gained Ortega as an advocate of its precepts.

Thus, by the turn of the century, the best minds of Spain were split
into two major factions. These two groups were in accord with the
view that Spain was a "backward" nation—in the presence of a world
that was changing—but the difference between the two groups arose
over how modernization should be pursued. The "Hispanophiles"—
the "patriots"—extolled the approach of Spanishness and argued that
the regeneration of Spain should be sought from within the framework
of the nation, within all that had been, and could be said to be, Spanish. On the other hand, the "Hispanophols"—those who supported
foreign contact—maintained that only through the integration of European culture and values could Spain hope for a vital regeneration that
would bring the nation closer to the twentieth century. *El Krausismo,*
which was the closest contact to German thought that Spain could

claim at the time,[33] was not as influential on the younger students of Ortega's generation as it had been on the students of philosophy in the 1860s. For Ortega and the increasing number of Hispanophols, the ideals and principles which were eventually to contribute to the modernization of Spain had to be sought beyond the mysticism of *El Krausismo*; an effort had to be made, they reasoned, by Spanish intellectuals to broaden Spain's awareness of European thought.[34] It was in this intellectual setting that Ortega had departed for Germany in 1905, and it was in this context that his polemical literary exchange with Maura took place.

This dispute threw into sharp relief the fundamental differences between the majority of thinkers of the "generation of '98" and the rising young intellectuals of Ortega's generation with respect to the regeneration of Spain. Maura, an exponent of the Hispanophile point of view of the "generation of '98," argued that Ortega's Hispanophol attitude was unpatriotic. "Is Mr. Ortega y Gasset," he said, "one of the more highly esteemed representatives of the generation that is now approaching; a generation born, intellectually, immediately after the disaster, patriot without patriotism; optimist, but not candid, because the lessons of misfortune moderated in it [this generation] the possible exaltation of juvenile faith?"[35] In an edition of *Faro* that appeared two weeks later, Ortega responded to Maura:

> I do not know if my generation is patriotic, but it is not correct to characterize my thoughts as being so. Is a patriot he who places the country before everything else? Then I am not one; if I had to choose, at one time, between my country and prudence, there would be no doubt in my mind that I would follow the solicitation of the latter. My liberalism chooses it: Europe is more important to me than Spain, and Spain is only important to me if Europe is spiritually integrated within her.
>
> I am, on the other hand, a patriot because my Spanish nerves, with all the sentimental heritage, are the only means given to me to arrive in Europe. Neither sorrow nor melancholy is the cause of my being Spanish; it is more than this: I believe that Spain has a European cultural mission to fulfill; I see in this mission a country where there is more work to finish than in other countries, within this grand work of moral advancement.[36]

Ortega pursued the issue of the "Spanish problem" with his former professor of Greek at the University of Salamanca, Unamuno, reproaching the latter for preferring to "Africanize" Europe rather than "Europeanize" Spain.[37] For Ortega, the only effective means of tackling the "Spanish problem," thereby bridging the gap between "backward" Spain and "advanced" Europe, would be through the Europeanization of Spain,[38] albeit, one suspects, that by Europeanization Ortega meant the Germanization of Spain. "Facing Germany," he said, "is the other Germany, the one of yesterday and tomorrow, the one of all times and this Germany does not die; if Germany were to die, that would terminate, equally, the only possibilities that remain over Europe of a future worthy of being lived."[39]

A few years later, during the early 1920s, Spanish writers and intellectuals witnessed two sentimental ceremonies that demonstrated the difference between the younger and older generations of intellectuals in Spain. In 1920, at one ceremony, the Hispanophiles gathered around the tomb of the novelist José Mariano de Larra, who was greatly admired by the "patriotic" segment of the "generation of '98" and noted for his virulent attacks against foreign influence in Spain.[40] The other ceremonial occasion was a tribute of five minutes of silence by the younger, more European-oriented generation of Ortega, who met on 11 September 1923 in the Botanical Gardens of Madrid, in memory of the death of the French poet Stéphane Mallarmé.[41] These two occasions indicate the divergent tendencies of the two generations: a kind of romantic nationalism and negation in one; and in the other, a form of cultural internationalism aspiring to attain a European world view. Although Ortega did not attend La Institución Libre de Enseñanza, he and the students of his generation grew under its tradition and influence. Travel and study abroad had given them new and deeper insight into the "Spanish problem" and, through their efforts to propagate foreign culture and ideas, they returned to Spain as cultural citizens of the European countries. The tribute by this group of five minutes of silence to the memory of Mallarmé signaled the final flowering of the struggle for the Europeanization of Spain— as a group effort—before the outbreak of the Spanish Civil War.

In the fall of 1910, Ortega returned to Madrid after spending the summer months in Siguenza. Only two months had passed when Don Salmerón, professor of metaphysics at the Central University of Madrid, died.

In open competition, Ortega competed for the vacant chair of metaphysics and on 5 November was congratulated on receiving the professorship.[42] Six months earlier, on 7 April 1910, Ortega had married his fiancée, Rosa Spottorno y Topete, and the new appointment provided him with some means of financial support. In January 1911 he was granted another stipend, by the Ministry of Public Education, for further study and research in Germany. Accompanied by his wife,

Ortega returned to Marburg, where their first son, Miguel Germán, was born on 28 May in the same year.[43]

At the end of December 1911, Ortega returned to Madrid so that he could begin his teaching duties—in January of the following year—as professor of metaphysics at the Central University. Ortega occupied this chair of metaphysics for twenty-four years—with only two brief interruptions: once, in 1929, when he resigned to protest the encroachments on academic freedom during the dictatorship of Miguel Primo de Rivera; again, in 1931, when Ortega was one of the first members of the Constituent Cortes at the time of the second Spanish Republic —until his exile from Spain in 1936 at the outbreak of the Spanish Civil War.

When the First World War erupted, Ortega began to contribute his share to the "European cultural mission" of Spain through his lectures on some of the major trends within the mainstream of European thought. Such thinkers as Driesch, Weissmann, and von Uexküll in biology, and the economic and social thoughts of Scheler, Simmel, and Sombart, were introduced to Spanish university students for the first time. As his lectures and intellectual background may suggest, Ortega was a Germanophile. Nevertheless, he supported the Allies over the Germans, maintaining that it was essential to distinguish between the "ideals of German culture" and the "ambitions of Imperial Germany."[44]

In the summer of 1914 Ortega published his first book, *Meditations on Quixote*. The "prologue to the reader" of this book, like the several essays in the text itself, contains a variety of intellectual themes: from the nature of the novel and poetry, the epic, comedy, and tragedy, to general statements on philosophy. Ortega also discussed the Quixotic character of Cervantes' classic work in conjunction with its place in the tradition of Spain's past glory and with the possibility of providing the Spanish people with an impetus to strive toward greater accomplishments. In the prologue to these essays, he stated that his first book announced "several essays on various subjects of no very great consequence . . . but they all end by discussing Spanish 'circumstances' directly or indirectly."[45] These essays were presented as "salvations," for "the author who is writing them and those to whom they are addressed have their spiritual origin in the negation of a decrepit Spain."[46] In this context, the *Meditations* is a work directed toward the "cultural" and "spiritual" regeneration of Spain.

Ortega commented on an observation about Spain in Kant's *Anthropologie* in which Kant referred to Spain as the land of ancestors. The degeneration of Spain was viewed by Ortega as the nation's inability to go beyond the tradition of the past and this, he lamented, was "one of our terrible national diseases." He said: "[Spain] land of ancestors! Therefore, not ours, not the free property of present-day Spaniards. Those who have passed before continue ruling us and form an oligarchy of the dead that oppresses us. 'Know this'—says the servant in the Choephori—'the dead kill the living.'"[47] These words call to mind Nietzsche's criticism of the "disadvantages" of "monumental history" for "life" when the abuse of traditional historical facts can virtually lead one to cry: "Let the dead bury the—living."[48] Ortega envisioned his meditations hence as "an experiment" toward the realization of a "new Spain," a Spain that would go beyond the "reactionary propensities" of Spanish tradition in that the "people become every day less and less than they were meant to be."[49] He continued:

> Since this is the case with Spain, it has to appear to us as a perverse patriotism without perspective, without hierarchies, that accepts as Spanish whatever has been produced in our land, confusing the most inept degeneration with that which is essential to Spain.
>
> Is it not a cruel sarcasm that after three and a half centuries of misguided wandering, it is proposed to us to follow the national tradition? Tradition! The traditional reality in Spain precisely has consisted in the progressive annihilation of the possibility of Spain.
>
> . . . No, no we cannot follow tradition; on the contrary: we must go against tradition, much beyond tradition. From the traditional debris, it is urgent for us to press forward to save the primary substance of the race, the Hispanic module, that simple Spanish tremor before the chaos. What is customarily called Spain is not that, but exactly the downfall of that. In one huge, painful flame we would have to burn the inert traditional appearance, the Spain which has been, and then, among the well sifted ashes, we shall find, as an iridescent gem, the Spain that could have been.
>
> For this it will be necessary that we liberate ourselves from the superstition of the past. . . . Then, if there is courage and genius amongst us, we would be capable of making, with all integrity, the new Spanish experiment.
>
> But in the meantime, until someone arrives, let us be content with vague indications, more fervent than exact, trying to maintain ourselves at a respectful distance from the great novelist [Cervantes]; so that we do not say something a little delicate or extravagant in our attempt to approach him too closely.[50]

From this stance, Ortega continued the protracted debate over the regeneration of Spain, reviving the spirit of Joaquín Costa's slogan—which goes back to 1867—"break with the past: a double turn of the key on the tomb of El Cid."[51] Ortega considered his "criticism" of the Spanish predicament as "patriotism" and, through his paradoxical formulation of the notion that "the death of what is dead is life," appealed for an expansion of cultural consciousness that would not only go beyond the cultural tradition of the past, but would also extend past the traditional geographical boundaries of Spain into the mainstream of European culture. The essays attempted to provide "a pretext" and "an appeal for a wide ideological collaboration on national themes and nothing else." The "ideological collaboration" on "national themes" to which Ortega referred served the "cultural" function that he sought to relate to his compatriots and to Spain. The "intention" of "these ideas," he said, "is to serve a function much less serious than a scientific one: they will not stubbornly insist on being adopted by others, but merely wish to awaken in kindred minds kindred thoughts, even though they may be antagonistic."[52]

Ortega continued with his efforts to write about the prospects of a "new Spain," speaking out in 1921 in his book *Invertebrate Spain* against the movements in Spain toward "regionalism," "sectionalism," and "separatism." "Spanish social life," he wrote, "in our day offers an extreme example of this atrocious particularism. *Spain is today not so much a nation as a series of water-tight compartments.*" This tendency toward "particularism," he argued, is evidenced by the fact that, save for "a few fleeting moments, the whole of Spanish history has been the history of a long decay."[53] In order to get beyond "this historical invertebration," then, he clamored for the unity of the provinces and for the regenerative reconstruction of Spain. *The Theme of Our Time*, written two years later, is, in many ways, an elaboration of Ortega's appeal for the regeneration of Spain as in *Meditations* and in *Invertebrate Spain*; only, in this instance, he made an appeal to all Europeans to rebuild the cultural values of Europe as "the destiny of our generation."[54] His argument that "people who are under the obligation, by reason of their eminent intellectual qualities, of assuming responsibility for the conduct of our age, have no excuse for living, like the masses, on a derivative level,"[55] anticipated, in part, his later message to Europeans in his *The Revolt of the Masses*.

In December 1917, Ortega severed relations with the weekly *El Imparcial* (the result of an argument over his article of 17 June which had criticized the role of the army in politics); and, together with his brother Eduardo and a close friend, Nicolás Maria de Urgoti, founded the daily newspaper *El Sol*.[56] Five years later Ortega also assisted in setting up the publishing house Espasa Calpe, which remains one of the more important and well-known publishing concerns in Spain. This aggressive and innovative spirit of the young journalist and publisher eventually led to the founding of the *Revista de Occidente*, the first issue of which was published in July 1923.[57] In this first issue, Ortega put forward the statement of purpose:

> The *Revista de Occidente* would like to put itself to the service of that state of spirit which is characteristic of our epoch. For this reason, it is neither merely a literary repertory nor is it superciliously scientific. Turning our backs on all that is political, seeing that the political never aspires to understand things in general, this Journal will attempt to go forth offering to its readers the essential panorama of European and American [Hispano-American] life. Our information will have, then, an intensive and hierarchical character. It is not enough that a fact happens or that a book is published to oblige one to speak on them. Extensive information only serves to confound the spirit more, favoring the insignificant to the detriment of the select and the effective. Our Journal will reserve its attention for the themes which are truly important and will endeavor to treat them with the amplitude and rigor necessary for their fecund assimilation.
> ... Thus, we will be attentive to the matters of Spain, but, at the same time, we will bring to these pages the collaboration of all men of the Occident whose exemplary word signifies an interesting pulsation of the contemporary soul.[58]

From Marburg, Ortega received a letter from the cultural historian and literary critic Ernst Robert Curtius, noting that he, Max Scheler, and other intellectuals in Germany were already interested in the *Revista* as a literary journal:

> Through my respected friend, Max Scheler, whom I have just recently visited in Cologne, I had the occasion of reading the *Revista de Occidente* which has been of great interest to me. I am composing for the *Neuen Merkur* (of which I am sending you a copy) an article on French magazines and also would like to publish in the *Neuen Merkur* something on your magazine. For this reason, I would appreciate it very much if you could send me a copy of it. . . .[59]

This 1923 letter was the beginning of several years of correspondence between Curtius and Ortega that continued up to the year before the latter's death. Moreover, through the letters of Curtius, Ortega remained in contact with German culture, as Curtius often provided him with information on the latest developments and the most recent publications in German literature and philosophy.[60] Through the contributions of Ortega, Pío Baroja, Azorín, Eugenio d'Ors, Juan Ramón Jiménez, and Antonio Machado of Spain, and other prominent writers and thinkers in Europe, the *Revista de Occidente* enjoyed a wide reputation in Europe during its height of influence in the 1920s and '30s. As a magazine and publishing house, the *Revista de Occidente* is still in existence today under the directorship of Ortega's youngest son, José Ortega y Spottorno.

In his function as a member of the editorial staff of Espasa Calpe, Ortega was given the opportunity to continue in his self-assigned mission to expose Spain to European—primarily German—culture. Some of the first books to be translated from German by Espasa Calpe were done with the assistance of Ortega, and most of them he prefaced with prologues and introductions. In his "Prologue for Germans," written in 1934, Ortega mentioned that he had received "a world of ideas" from Germany as a student, and maintained that he had fulfilled his obligations through his efforts to introduce German ideas to the Spanish-speaking world in Spain and South America.[61] In various ways, his devoted efforts to "Europeanize" Spain justified this feeling. Earlier, in February 1923, he was one of the leading spirits behind inviting Albert Einstein to come to Spain. Einstein presented, in general form, a series of lectures of advanced studies on the subject "the basis of a general theory of relativity" at the Central Universities in Barcelona and Madrid and, at the special request of Ortega, at the Residencia de Estudiantes (Residential College for Students).[62]

Ortega's lectures on "What is Philosophy?" pointed to a turn in political events in Spain, concomitant with his active involvement, as well as to a shift in his philosophical concerns and ideas. In September 1923, Miguel Primo de Rivera established a military dictatorship, under King Alfonso XIII, which lasted until he was forced into exile— in December 1929—by the same generals who had placed him in power. During his six years' rule, Primo de Rivera exercised thorough control over the political life of Spain.[63] On 15 March 1929, he extended this dictatorial rule to the academic realm when he closed the Central University of Madrid and El Ateneo, by royal decree.[64] This gesture of dominance was viewed, by Ortega and most of his contemporaries, as an outrageous violation of academic freedom. By way of protest, Ortega, together with professors Luis Jiménez de Asúa and Felipe Sánchez Román, resigned his chair at the university. Having no classroom in which to expound his ideas, Ortega moved to the auditorium of the Ateneo, and to the Residential College for Students, to the Sala Rex and to the Infanta Beatriz Theatre, to present his lectures. Under these circumstances he presented the series "What is Philosophy?" An earlier version of the first part of these lectures had been given by Ortega in a group of presentations at the conference of the Friends of Art and at the Faculty of Philosophy and Letters in Buenos Aires. For seven months, he and his colleagues continued to lecture outside the Central University until 16 December 1929—after the defeat of Primo de Rivera—when King Alfonso XIII reappointed them to their chairs.[65] During this period of protest Ortega published his book *The Revolt of the Masses*, in which he discussed the situation of a "select minority" within a social and political framework where the "masses" (a term which is not employed as a class concept and which is taken primarily to mean the educated and uneducated majority who do not demand the standards of "quality" and "excellence" of themselves and who should always be led by an *elite*) are perpetually taking over the decision-making processes. A political figure characteristic of Primo de Rivera provided a concrete example of what Ortega called the "unqualified" "mass-man" who enters the political process without the essential qualities of leadership.

In conjunction with his political protests and his opposition to Primo de Rivera's encroachments on academic freedom, Ortega was dismayed over what he considered to be the "ineffectiveness of the Spanish monarchy." On 15 November 1930, in *El Sol*, he wrote an article entitled "The Mistake of Berenguer." General Damaso Berenguer, as the successor of Primo de Rivera, was another instance of the monarchy becoming more rather than less the instrument of the army. The ineffectual tendencies of the monarchy, combined with the successes of the Generals Primo de Rivera and Berenguer within its very structure, would, in fact, hasten its demise. "Spaniards," said Ortega, "your state no longer exists! Re-build it! *Delenda est monarchia* [the Monarchy must be destroyed]."[66] On 14 April 1931, this prophesy proved to be true as King Alfonso XIII hastily departed from Madrid for Paris, leaving Spain on the same day that the second Republic was proclaimed.[67]

In February 1931, prior to the actual collapse of the monarchy, Ortega, together with his close friend, the novelist Ramón Pérez de Ayala, and Doctor Marañón, organized a select number of intellectuals into a nonpolitical party grouping referred to as "La Agrupación al Servicio de la República" (In Service of the Republic). This action carried Ortega directly into politics for, through his association with "La Agrupación," he was elected to the Constituent Cortes of the Republic as a deputy for the province of León.[68] While performing his duties as a delegate to the Constituent Cortes, Ortega continued to reveal his involvement with the problem of the regeneration of Spain. He published a collection of political essays that had been presented previously in a series of newspaper articles in *El Sol* and *Crisol*, subsumed by the titles *The Rectification of the Republic* and *The Rendition of the Provinces and National Decency*, encouraging a spirit of solidarity in Spain (an ideal which he had set forth in *Invertebrate Spain*) with the view that political unity should become a self-conscious objective of the Republic.[69] The majority of his compatriots in the Cortes, however, did not share his view of political unity, as many of the delegates were inclined to feel more allegiance to their respective provinces than to the nation, a tendency which proved to be an important factor in leading to the Spanish Civil War.[70]

As a member of the Cortes, Ortega experienced the practical difficulties and problems inherent in the nature of political leadership. Manuel Azaña had been elected president of El Ateneo at this time, and his political following was a group of intellectuals who had continually opposed the ideas and leadership of Ortega. Ortega and his associates of "La Agrupación" never strove to make their group a powerful political party; while they were involved with the problems of Spain and felt politically committed to take part in the decision-making process of their country, they were not interested in the struggle of party politics, as were Azaña and his following.[71] The tensions of party politics resulted in what Ortega was to consider a "'sad and disagreeable Republic'"; he would have chosen to return to the "'joyous' days of April, 1931."[72] When incessant arguments and conflicts between the followers of Ortega and Azaña reached the point where communication was virtually impossible, in the fall of 1932, Ortega left active politics. Daunted but not distressed, he returned to his chair of metaphysics at the Central University of Madrid. Between the time of his return to the Central University and the outbreak of the Spanish Civil War, Ortega continued writing political articles in *El Sol*—very much in the role of the politician in opposition—criticizing the politicians he thought were primarily responsible for steering the Republic in the wrong direction.[73]

Ortega's writing activities did not isolate him from the Republic's political turmoil. Despite his criticisms of several of the regionalist politicians in the Cortes, Ortega supported the Republic in Spain. This political commitment to the Republic and his association with "La Agrupación" made him suspect to the communist faction of the left and the nationalist faction of the right. Thus, by July 1936, when the early phases of the Spanish Civil War had begun, Ortega, not knowing what to expect from his political enemies of the extreme left and right, had to make preparations for leaving Spain. On 31 August, with the assistance of the French Embassy, Ortega succeeded in leaving the country; he, his wife and three children, and his brother embarked on a French boat from Alicante for Marseilles.

From Marseilles he continued to Grenoble and remained there until his departure for Paris in November. During this period of self-imposed exile, Ortega passed most of his time writing, corresponding with his good friend in Bonn Ernst R. Curtius, lecturing, and traveling. In the spring months of 1938, he gave a series of lectures at the University of Leyden and in Oegstgeest, Holland, residing there until September when he returned to Paris. In the following month, he was taken seriously ill and had to undergo a gallbladder operation. The operation put a brake on his activities for a few months as he convalesced, quietly, in Paris. By February 1939, when he felt strong enough to travel, Ortega and his wife left Paris for a three-months stay in Portugal, and in that year the Spanish Civil War came to an end. Ortega, however, was still both unwilling and unable to return to Spain. On 21 April 1939, while still in Portugal, he received word that his mother had died in a small town (Puente Genil) near Córdoba, and on 12 November, in the following year, Ortega's sister, Rafaela, died; the unity of the family was such that it must have been difficult for Ortega not to be able to return to attend the funeral.[74]

In August 1939, after returning to Paris for a brief stay, Ortega and his wife departed for Buenos Aires. He remained in Argentina during the major part of the Second World War, lecturing at the University of Buenos Aires (his third and final trip to Argentina—the first and second trips were made in 1916 and 1928), until the middle of March in 1942, when he and his wife left for Lisbon. It was during his stay in Argentina that Ortega began to prepare his ideas on *Man and People* for publication. Finally, in August 1945, for no apparent reason other than the desire to be with his family, Ortega left some of his favorite locations along the sunny coast of Portugal and returned to his native country, the first time since the outbreak of the Spanish Civil War.[75] He stayed for the remainder of the summer in Zumaya, for the abundance of sunshine and tranquility that it offered, before returning to Madrid in October. Ortega's return to Spain in 1945 marked the end of nine years " in exile." To many of his Republican compatriots in exile, however, it appeared that, by returning to Franco-Spain, he had "sold out."[76] From a different perspective, the supporters of Franco considered him a former enemy and distrusted him for his prior affiliation with the Republic. Because he was viewed with disfavor, Ortega was not permitted to return to teach at the government-controlled university. Thus, in 1948, with the assistance of his former student and disciple, Julián Marías, Ortega established the Instituto de Humanidades, where he succeeded in attracting many students and liberal intellectuals to his lectures.

The designation "Humanities Institute," in a sense, was a symbolic institutionalization of Ortega's intellectual endeavors throughout his philosophical career. In a letter to Walter P. Paepcke, who had recently helped establish the newly formed Aspen Institute for Humanistic Studies, Ortega outlined his conception of what constituted an Institute of Humanities. "I understand by Humanities," Ortega wrote in 1949,

> not only the traditional humanities—which are summarized in the study of Greece and Rome—but all the disciplines which specifically study the human fact, I include—and even principally—their more present-day problems. . . . Observe that even in Europe we feel the need of attending, *more* and in *new ways*, to the problems of the fact "Man." Hence, among many other symptoms, the foundation of my *Instituto de Humanidades*.[77]

The Instituto de Humanidades was never permitted to function smoothly, as the government constantly intervened to control its administration. By the fall of 1950, Ortega and his followers had no alternative other than to end the activities of the Institute.[78]

Between 1949 and 1955, Ortega averted the pressures of the Spanish government by attending and presenting lectures abroad. Repeating the traveling activities of his youth, Ortega reactivated his cultural interests in conferences and lectures outside Spain. In early July 1949, Ortega and his good friend Ernst Curtius accepted an invitation to join Dr. Albert Schweitzer and several other eminent guests in attending the bicentennial celebration of Goethe's birth in Aspen, Colorado, under the auspices and direction of Robert M. Hutchins and the University of Chicago.[79] This event marked the opening of the Aspen Institute for Humanistic Studies and the annual summer Music Festival, both of which remain active cultural centers in Aspen. Six weeks later, after his first and only trip to the United States, Ortega and his wife and eldest son, Miguel, went to Hamburg, on 28 August, to take part in another bicentennial ceremony commemorating the birth of Goethe. While in Germany, he returned to the "Neo-Kantian citadel" of his youth, the University of Marburg, to receive an honorary doctorate.[80]

During the period from 1950 to 1952, Ortega spent some time traveling and lecturing at various cities in Germany.[81] In 1953, he left Munich for sojourns in England and Scotland and lectured at the universities of London and Glasgow before returning to his favorite retreat—Germany. In the following year, he took another trip to England to speak in the nonacademic atmosphere of a "Board of Management" conference in Torquay. By February 1954, Ortega returned to Munich to enjoy "Fasching"—the Bavarian-style carnival—with his friends and family. He passed the following summer months quietly in Spain, at Fuenterrabia, not far from the Spanish-French border. In the months of May and June 1955, Ortega resumed traveling and went to present what proved to be his last series of lectures in Venice. Because of unfortunate and unforeseeable circumstances, he missed the opportunity to meet Arnold Toynbee, as the latter had arrived in Madrid to give a lecture, at El Ateneo, while Ortega was lecturing in Venice. Ortega, as well as Toynbee, would liked to have discussed the former's interpretation of *Universal History* in person.[82]

In September, after what was to be his last trip outside Spain, Ortega returned to Madrid. On a gray and chilly day in autumn, in his apartment on the sixth floor at Monte Esquina 28, Ortega died. His widow still resides in this apartment; and the date on Ortega's desk calendar remains fastened to the day that he passed away—18 October 1955.

Chapter I

Ortega's Heritage and Intellectual Development

The preceding biographical sketch has outlined some of the fundamental factors that were central in Ortega's career and in his political activities. The active experiences of the man have been related to the active formulations of his ideas. The circumstances surrounding Ortega's experiences assist in tracing the different currents in his thought and in understanding the important tendencies in his internal intellectual development that will be our primary concern.

To understand Ortega's intellectual development and the systematic formulation of his philosophy of history, we must turn attention, for the moment, to the brand of Neo-Kantianism that Cohen and Natorp brought to bear at Marburg, and to the European intellectual traditions that were germane in fostering his ideational outlook. Ortega dissociated himself from any particular school of thought, yet he would have been the first to admit that a philosopher's ideas become linked with previous philosophical traditions. His attitude toward this intrinsic aspect of thought is evident when he remarked later: "In our present philosophical posture, and in the doctrine that is produced by it, we view and take into account a substantial portion of previous thought on themes relating to our discipline. This is tantamount to saying that past philosophies are our collaborators, that they survive and are present in our own philosophy."[1] The most important and obvious connection, then, between the intellectual currents in Europe and the thought of Ortega was the influence, in general, of German philosophy, and of his studies at the University of Marburg in particular. The Neo-Kantian movement at Marburg reflected a particular trend in German and European Neo-Idealism around the turn of the century, in addition to illustrating the extent to which intellectual tensions and philosophical debates took place in Germany during this time.

As we review the 1860s, when the Neo-Kantians were preparing their respective points of view, we find that German philosophy was in full retreat from the post-Kantian idealism of the first half of the century. When we refer to post-Kantian idealism, the reference indicates the position of the systematic speculative philosophies of Fichte, Hegel, and Schelling—although the philosophies of Krause, Schleiermacher, and Schopenhauer may also be considered exemplary of the viewpoints of speculative idealists. Idealism means here the view that ideas possess the key to the interpretation and to the understanding of reality and that the mind and spiritual values are fundamental in the world as a whole. During the second half of the nineteenth century, intellectual currents began to flow in another direction, away from speculative metaphysics and system-building, whether it was the systematic dialectical idealism of Fichte and Hegel, or the systematic dialectical materialism of Marx and Engels, toward mathematics and the natural sciences. Some philosophers hoped that the model of inquiry in all spheres of knowledge would follow the procedures which were adopted by such empirical disciplines as mathematics and the physical sciences. Some borrowed the positivism of Comte or the empiricism of John Stuart Mill.[2] Others went back, beyond Hegel, to Kant and began a careful reexamination of his epistemology and his analysis of the cognitive process. In the 1860s, thus, a *Kantbewegung* was manifest. For although the idealism of the Neo-Hegelians was making some headway in England in the philosophies of T. H. Green,[3] F. H. Bradley, and Bernard Bosanquet (and, in Italy, in the early philosophies of Benedetto Croce and Giovanni Gentile), the Neo-Kantian movement was more predominant and pervasive toward the end of the nineteenth century as both philosophically minded scientists and critically minded philosophers were engaged, variously, in the revival of Kant's critical philosophy.

The variety of disciplines and the range of thinkers involved with the Kantian revival not only reflected the diverse nature of the epistemological rifts in Germany and in Europe, but also revealed the broad influence which was wielded by Kant in the intellectual atmosphere of this period. The intention here is not to discuss in detail Kant's philosophy, and the task is not to demonstrate the full extent to which his influence had taken effect. We are concerned, rather, with the general relationship between Kant's critical philosophy and the Neo-Kantian movement as a whole.

Otto Liebmann is generally credited with having been the first to have raised the cry of "back to Kant" in his *Kant und die Epigonen,* in 1865.[4] This summons was still audible to the group of German philosophers at the University of Marburg and to the Southwest

German or Baden School, associated with Hermann Cohen, Paul
Natorp, Wilhelm Windelband, and Heinrich Rickert, particularly between the 1870s and 1920.[5] The Neo-Kantian ambience at these
schools coincided with the general philosophic reaction in Germany
against the systematic speculative tradition of idealism and the meta-
scientific tendencies of naturalism and the physical sciences.

This philosophic reaction to speculative philosophical systems—
idealistic or positivistic—was as much a component part of the Neo-
Kantian movement as it was an integral part of the philosophies of
Cohen and Natorp.[6] Between 1885 and 1912 both men occupied
chairs of philosophy, in Marburg,[7] and emphasized the approach and
the general position taken by Kant through their inquiries into the
methodological and epistemological differences between the physical
sciences and the social sciences.[8]

The transcendental and logical position of Cohen's philosophy
sought to refute the naturalistic psychophysical explanations of sensible reality and the process of human consciousness in the Neo-
Kantianism of some of the German thinkers during this period, particularly Helmholtz and Lange. Naturalism, in this connection, means
that point of view which professes to demonstrate that knowledge
and consciousness are dependent on the material features of nature.
This point of view in the 1890s was a response to speculative metaphysical philosophy in general and to "subjective" idealism in particular. Some of the philosophically minded natural scientists and critical theorists expressed concern over epistemological questions of the
nature of knowledge and called for a return to Kant. Hermann von
Helmholtz, one of the most important scientists in Germany at this
time, approached epistemology through the physical sciences and argued that his scientific studies of the specific energies of the senses
had important implications for an empirical theory of perception as
embodying a system of unknown objects that interact with our sensory organs.[9] This theory made it possible for Helmholtz to contend
the contingency of the perception of space upon our physiological
constitution. Like Helmholtz, Friedrich A. Lange maintained that the
revelation of our knowledge of sensible reality rests in the interaction
between the human organism and any reality that may be considered
as unknown. The experience of the world of physical objects is determined by this interaction among men but the human organism itself
is only an object of experience, and can only be understood by physiology and psychology.[10] Thus, insofar as reality can be known,
physical materialism prepares one for the journey along the road to
certainty most likely pursued, as these natural scientists argued on
the side of science in their effort to combat speculative metaphysics.

Cohen was in sympathy with the antimetaphysical objectives of these and other like-minded thinkers, but he repudiated the notion that the approach and true access to Kant and to external reality could be found only through the methodology of physico-psychological analysis, without taking the results of experimental psychology as having some bearing on a priori knowledge.[11] Neither a metaphysical system nor a physico-psychological method, according to him, adequately explicates or presents a new theory of objective experience. For Cohen, a theory of experience is constructed by independent logical principles and, in order to discover and to establish these principles, the principles of mathematics, logic, and mathematical physics must, first and foremost, be the ultimate aim of the philosopher as it was the aim of Kant.[12] Cohen put forth the claim that epistemology and psychology cannot be conjoined, for psychology, as an empirical science, deals with the empirical self as a phenomenon amidst phenomena, whereas epistemology embodies the science of reason itself and the "facts" of science, dealing with the a priori principles on which the possibility of all phenomena depends. Psychology is logically dependent on epistemology, not the reverse. Epistemology sets forth and "deduces" those principles without which neither psychology nor any other empirical science can proceed.[13]

The fundamental form of mathematics and logic, then, for Cohen, cannot be ascertained by the methodology of physico-psychological induction. Induction can never lead to truth and universal validity, as can logic. Logic, for him, is the logic of knowledge, truth, and thought, and thought accepts nothing as "given" which cannot be true of anything that claims to be independent of it, as was the claim of the psycho-physical materialists.[14] In Cohen's *Logik der reinen Erkenntnis,* the theme of Parmenides' notion that "thinking and being are one thing" is discernible throughout and is a theme which is repeated in varying degrees in his *Ethik des reinen Willens* and in his *Aesthetik des reinen Gefühls.*[15] For Cohen, there is no gap between thought and reality, since thought is the core and very foundation of science and reality. He based his *Logik* on "the principle of origin" and, according to this principle, held the view that there is no being, objectivity, or "nature of things" which does not originate in thought.[16] Cohen undoubtedly felt bound to dispose of the notion of the unknowable object and to insist on finding the object somehow within experience, even at the expense of adopting some form of speculative idealism.

Through this position, Cohen argued that his "transcendental method" could dispense with the notion of independent "givens" in knowledge. He maintained that the logic of differential calculus and

mathematical physics best served the knowability and the understanding of the fundamental principles of reality of empirical objects,
and that Newtonian science demonstrated the possibility of an a
priori knowledge of nature and physical objects by way of mathematical concepts of space and time.[17] Kant would not disagree with the
proposition of the possibility of postulating universal and lawful
principles of physical objects provided that empirical and rational
principles be well coordinated. For a priori principles are the conditions under which one conceives the ordered system of nature. The
"laws of nature" and all concepts of objects are specifications of the
a priori forms: thus the "objective reality" of phenomena consists in
their conformity to the laws of the system as constituted.

The principles of constraint, for Kant, are reciprocal.[18] But to
Cohen, the "facts" of science are completely determined by thought.
Hence, things-in-themselves, for him, are not things and do not exist;
things-in-themselves do not exist because they are only concepts
which are aimed at limiting the methodology of the complete determination of things as they are and as they are known by logic and
mathematical physics. In his three works—*Kants Theorie der Erfahr-
ung*, 1871; *Kants Begrundung der Ethik*, 1877; and *Kants Begrundung der Aesthetik*, 1889—Cohen criticized Kant's notion of the independent "givens" of the categories and laws of things-in-themselves
and contended that the lawful character of nature, derived from the
mathematical logic of pure thought, is calculated independently of
the perception of the senses.[19] In these works and by the agency of
his "transcendental method," Cohen attempted to break through the
barrier that Kant placed between a priori and empirical knowledge
by way of the latter's distinction between sensibility as receptivity and
understanding as spontaneous activity. Thus, Cohen's Neo-Kantianism
went not only "back" to Kant but "beyond" him. Going beyond
Kant, he rejected the constraining concept of a noumenal world, the
thing-in-itself, standing behind the world of phenomena. The laws of
nature cannot be understood as categories by which the mind organ-
izes the sense data it receives. Rather, the understanding of these laws
is derived from the realm of pure thought alone, independently of
raw sense data. In this context, Cohen appeared far more radically an
idealist than Kant, for Cohen recognized only thought-consciousness
as real. Having retired from the University of Marburg in 1912, and
being subsequently disappointed that the faculty refused to pass his
chair over to the man of his choice—Ernst Cassirer—Cohen departed
for Berlin. Natorp remained in Marburg and in his *Allgemeine Psych-
ologie nach Kritische Methode*, 1912, attempted to bridge the gap between the objective world of phenomena and the subjective world of

the nonphenomenal self that possessed knowledge of the world of
empirical phenomena. In this work, Natorp made an effort to apply
Cohen's "transcendental method" to psychology rather than leave
the study of it to the physical sciences. Natorp realized that some of
the panlogistic doctrines of Cohen resembled the post-Kantian idealism of Fichte, Hegel, and Schelling.[20] He posited the view that the
empirical self and empirical objects are not necessarily independent
realms of phenomena, for the ego cannot be an object in nature. The
objective and subjective realms of the world, according to Natorp, are
not two realms that are diametrically opposed to each other, or to
the situation in which one is subsumed by the other. Rather, they are
two different directions of knowledge—both objective and subjective
—in which each begins from the same phenomenon utilizing the transcendental method of objectivication and unification.[21]

These features of Cohen's thought and Natorp's attempt to combine his writings with those of Cohen provided Ortega with the bulk
of his philosophical training in Germany. Neo-Kantianism in general
and Cohen in particular had a broad influence on the intellectual development of Ortega. Cohen was Ortega's primary mentor during the
latter's stay at the University of Marburg. Ortega recalled this fact in
his "Prologue for Germans" when he referred to Cohen, in retrospect,
as "my teacher."[22] Some of the critical influence of Marburg Neo-
Kantianism is perceptible in Ortega's thought. His general philosophical position can be characterized as an attempt to distinguish philosophy from the assumptions and the assertions—whether idealistic or
positivistic—of speculative metaphysics. Ortega rejected speculative
metaphysical systems and, like Cohen, rejected the approach to epistemology of the natural sciences, with its naturalistic and psycho-
physical explanations of sensible reality of the "subjective" idealists.
Although Ortega would not proceed as far as Cohen to postulate the
"facts" of science as being completely determined by thought, there
is a kind of Neo-Kantian metaphysics in his fundamental philosophic
point of view. For rather than posit pure thought solely as real,
Ortega replaced Cohen's logic with his notion of "human life." That
is, Ortega's generalized view of existence contains human life in place
of human logic as the underlying unifying principle of reality. Ortega's major writings were concerned with the idea of life as the
"dynamic dialogue between the individual and the world"; he was not
concerned, as Cohen was, with assigning to external experiences a
reality that is contingent upon the principles of logic and mathematical physics. "The structure of life as futurition," he later wrote, "is
the most persistent *leit motiv* of my writings, inspired certainly by
questions—raised by the logic of Cohen—which are very remote from

the vital problem to which I apply it."[23] This distinction drawn by
Ortega between his vitalistic point of view and Cohen's all-embracing
logic suggests that Ortega's experience at Marburg brought him closer
to a critical than to an absolute Neo-Kantianism. The critical approach to philosophical problems was an important factor in the influence of Ortega's thought and in the philosophical training that he
received at Marburg. In his "Reflections on Kant's Centenary,"
Ortega, in retrospect, metaphorically referred to his struggle with
Kant and Neo-Kantian philosophy as having taken place in a "Kantian
prison,"[24] and, in his "Prologue for Germans," he acknowledged his
experience at the University of Marburg as having been an important
factor in influencing his intellectual development. "In this city," he
said, "I passed the equinox of my youth; to it I owe half, at least, of
my hopes and almost all my discipline."[25]

The emphasis placed on the vital world of life took Ortega a step
beyond the Neo-Kantian transcendental logicality of Cohen. Ortega
combined his idea of "human life" with emphasis on history as constituting the vital dynamics of its expression, and this viewpoint
brought him closer to the humanistic side of the *Naturwissenschaften-
Geisteswissenschaften* distinction made by the German Southwest or
Baden School and Wilhelm Dilthey than to Cohen's Neo-Kantianism.

The striking similarities in the historicist focus of Windelband,
Rickert, and Dilthey, the early historical thought of Croce, and the
historical thought of Ortega suggest that the latter was both directly
and indirectly influenced by their ideas. Where the historical ideas of
Windelband and Rickert reflected those European intellectual currents
which were parallel to Ortega's intellectual development, and where
Dilthey had been acknowledged by Ortega as having influenced directly his intellectual focus, Croce's early historical ideas also appear
to have had an influence on the historical thought of Ortega. In this
context, then, we are concerned with the general trend of historicism
and its relationship to Ortega.

In his rectorial address of 1894 at the University of Strasbourg, on
"History and Natural Science," Windelband contributed to the Neo-
Kantian epistemological discussion by drawing a distinction between
knowledge that is derived from the natural sciences and knowledge
that is drawn from historical studies or the cultural sciences.
Windelband modified the viewpoint of reality as pure thought that
had been posed by Cohen and the Marburg School with his notion
that the epistemological problem of empirical reality is a problem in
axiology, not one in logic.[26]

Windelband was concerned more with questions of values than with
problems in logic and drew attention to the methodological distinc-

tion between the natural sciences as "nomothetic" and historical studies as "idiographic." In this sense, the Baden School attempted to apply Neo-Kantianism to the realm of cultural and historical consciousness; for the "nomothetic" or lawgiving factor of the natural sciences, according to Windelband, reveals their study of facts without any reference to value, whereas the historical studies are "idiographic," reconstructing the unique, the individual, and deal with those features in reality which have value and meaning.

Rickert shared with Windelband the view of the importance of the criterion of values and meaning, and the notion of distinguishing between natural scientific knowledge and historical knowledge. The espousal of these points of view was expressed in his *Die Grenzen der Naturwissenshaftlichen Begriffsbildung,* 1902, and in *Kulturwissenschaft und Naturwissenschaft.*[27]

For Rickert[28] the identifying characteristic of the form of knowledge that one derives from the natural sciences rests on its use of lawful principles. The natural scientists approached reality with the view that objects in the world operate and are determined by universal laws, and the function of these general concepts attempts to overcome the multiplicity and variety of things in external reality. The general conceptualization and the application of such lawful principles to objective reality is a kind of denial, Rickert argued, of the concreteness and the uniqueness in the reality of the individual. The cultural sciences or historical studies, on the other hand, investigate and observe the very individuality and the uniqueness in reality that are not included in generalized lawful principles. Historical knowledge does not aim at the general conceptualization of things but at grasping the concreteness and the individual concept of things so that the function of history, as characterized by its interest in the particular and in the unique, differs primarily from the natural sciences. "Empirical reality becomes nature," he said, "when we regard it with reference to the general *(das Allgemeine),* it becomes history when we regard it with reference to the particular and individual *(das Besondere und Individuelle)*."[29] From this point of view, Rickert, like Windelband, maintained that the fundamental difference between history (the cultural sciences) or historical studies and the natural sciences is one in methodology, not one in subject matter. While the natural sciences aim at discovering laws, according to Rickert, the *Kulturwissenschaften,* through comparative methods, study and analyze human and social phénomena under the influence of aesthetic, ethical, and intellectual values.

Wilhelm Dilthey, in his *Einleitung in die Geisteswissenschaften* (1883), put forward, eleven years earlier than Windelband, his view on the primary methodological difference between the natural sciences and the historical studies or the cultural sciences. Where Rickert preferred to distinguish these disciplines by establishing the *Naturwissenschaften-Kulturwissenschaften* dichotomy, Dilthey preferred the term *Geisteswissenschaften*[30] to designate the realm of the nonphysical sciences. Windelband, Rickert, and the students of the Baden School preferred to discuss the study of human and social phenomena as historical studies (*Geschichtswissenschaften*) or cultural studies (*Kulturwissenschaften*).[31] Dilthey's notion of the "humanistic," "social," or "cultural" sciences (*Geisteswissenschaften*), on the other hand, made room in his theory for the complexity and the variety in the subject matter of the "sciences" of the human mind. Dilthey thought that the proper grouping of categories could not be done solely by method but had to include subject matter, and it is in this proper grouping that all the human studies stand together in contrast with the sciences of nature. Such subtle distinctions indicate the difficulties involved in translating these words from German to English. The connotation of these terms is not exactly equivalent, for the *Kulturwissenschaften* or *Geschichtswissenschaften* of Windelband and Rickert are not concerned with psychological processes, whereas Dilthey's concept of *Geisteswissenschaften* does include psychology. The position of Dilthey can be distinguished from that of Windelband and Rickert in that Dilthey considered a classification of disciplines in terms of their subject matter to be more fundamental than a classification by methodology.[32]

One of the important characteristics of Dilthey's *Weltanschauung*, as an interpretation—*hermeneutic*—of history and life, which distinguishes his position from that of Rickert, is his philosophy of life. Life is the fundamental reality. "Life," he said, "is the fundamental fact which must serve as the starting point of philosophy. It is that which is known from within, it is that behind which one cannot go. Life can not be brought before the judgment seat of reason."[33] In his concept of life, in his notion of lived experiences, and not in abstract logical principles, lies the root and essence of reality and all knowledge. In this visible, vital realm, and not in subjective lawful principles Dilthey found the basis of reality through which thought processes emerge from immediate experience and return to the lived experience for verification.[34] Thought and life, in this connection, are inseparable. Since there is nothing behind nor beyond life itself, for Dilthey, the lived experience is the foundation of all knowledge. That is, to experience human life is to perceive its distinctive complexities and the multiple individual lives which constitute human and social phenomena. This is historical reality, and the way of knowing this reality comes from within; it must be perceived through the process of *das Verstehen,* or "understanding."[35] In this context, "understanding" is used in the sense of sympathetic intuition, as discerning and knowing the reality of human life from within; and this can be done through the autobiography, the biography, and the general historical situation in which human life experiences itself. "Mind," Dilthey said, "understands only what it has created. Nature, the object of natural science, embraces that reality which is produced independently of the activity of the mind. Everything upon which man by acting has set his stamp forms the object of the human studies."[36]

In his essay, "Wilhelm Dilthey and the Idea of Life," Ortega mentioned the importance of the influence of Dilthey in his intellectual development. Twenty-seven years after his studies in Berlin, he wrote of his misfortune of not having been exposed earlier, as a student, to the ideas of Dilthey:

> I became acquainted with Dilthey's work as late as 1929, and it took me four more years before I knew it sufficiently well. This ignorance, I do not hesitate to maintain, has caused me to lose about ten years of my life—ten years, in the first place, of intellectual development, but that, of course, means an equal loss in all other dimensions of life. . . . When I studied in Berlin in 1906, none of the philosophical chairs of the university was occupied by an outstanding scholar. Dilthey *happened* to have given up lecturing in the university building a few years before and admitted to the courses he held in his home only a few specially prepared students. Thus *chance* had it that I did not come in touch with him.[37]

By the late 1920s and the early 1930s, however, Ortega did incorporate the idea of human life into his philosophic point of view. The *Lebensphilosophie* of Dilthey is not only a denial of the notion of an abstract transcendental reality; he considered life, also, to be more than mere biological organism. His concept of life is not biological. In this sense, Ortega's notion of human life is quite similar. For Ortega, "my life"—in the "biographical" not in the "biological" sense—is the question of what to do with it and that of what happens to me as I find myself "shipwrecked" in the precarious sea of "circumstances."[38] Man, from this point of view, saves himself by sinking into the inner depths of his being as he makes an effort to hold on to consciousness and to the very essence of his life. "To live," he said, "is to deal with the world, aim at it, act in it, be occupied with it."[39] For Dilthey, life is realized empirically within the experiential process of consciousness, as lived experience, which gives the experience of the individual life and reality. Dilthey's position, like Bergson's, contains the vitalist viewpoint that our experience of the life of our own minds is a direct experience of that life, as it exists, and therefore cannot be perceived as some mechanistic physiological explanation of human organism or as some subjective neo-idealistic logical principle. The emphasis on the active, dynamic, and historical dimension of human and social phenomena, as realized within the lived experiences of life, reveals the vitalization of philosophy and the historicization of life perspective that is reflective of historicism and the attitude that historical knowledge is unique to the realm of human affairs.

This historicism is the perspective perceived in Ortega's notion of the "dynamic dialogue" in the "drama" of the life-world of the individual. Historicism is not used here as an absolute systematic point of view in which historical prediction and determinism are its form of methodology.[40] Rather, the term "historicism" means that historical knowledge deals with an explanation or an evaluation through history because the subject matter of history is human life in its multiplicity and totality. Furthermore, the term signifies here both "historism" (in the German sense of *Historismus* in connection with Windelband, Rickert, Dilthey, Meinecke—via Herder—Mannheim, and Troeltsch), and "historicism" (in the Italian sense of *Storicismo* as formulated by Benedetto Croce).[41] Historicism, understood as an outlook on the world (*Weltanschauung*), emphasizes the historical quality of human existence; as an interpretation of history and life, it concerns itself with concepts of individuality and with individual development. Historicism seeks to describe and to interpret the unsystematic variety of the reality of society and history, for the concept of individuality not only embraces individual persons but also includes the variety of historical forms, such as different peoples, customs, cultures, institutions, nation-states, and the like; and the concept of development includes the historical process—at a particular time and place—within which individuality manifests itself not by any abstract, general laws or principles but by the living expressions of the multiplicity of these unique historical forms. Individuality, the "fact of change,"[42] and the historical process, the *Weltanschauung* of historicism, combine to maintain a sort of historical relativism. This signification of historical phenomena entails the sense in which historical knowledge and reality are explained by Dilthey:

> The historical consciousness of the finitude of every historical phenomenon, every human or social state, of the relativity of every sort of belief, is the last step toward the liberation of man. With it, man attains the sovereign power to wring from

> every experience its content, to surrender wholly to it with-
> out prepossession. . . . Every beauty, every sanctity, every
> sacrifice, re-lived and expounded, opens up perspectives
> which disclose a reality. . . . And, in contrast with the rela-
> tivity, the continuity of the creative force makes itself felt as
> the central historical fact.[43]

The historicist orientation of Croce contributed to the shift from
the historicization of life to the historicization of philosophy. Ortega's view that "historical thinking proceeds with respect to human
phenomena," which is combined with his notion of the vital dimensions of "historical reason," reveals some of the affinities in their historical thought. Croce and Ortega both viewed human life as embodying an essentially historical process within which the realm of human
reality is perceived and understood. Historical knowledge is found in
the flow of the historical process and it is knowledge of this very process that provides an essential understanding of human reality. Where
history, for Croce, consists in the "inseparable syntheses of individual
and universal," history, for Ortega, embodies the "inexorable chain"
of human experiences and is constituted by the synthetic function of
"historical reason." Traversing from philosophy to history and then
back again to philosophy, Croce presented his systematic "**Philosophy of the Spirit**" as absolute historicism. He formulated his systematic treatment of the "Philosophy of the Spirit" in four volumes[44]
and devoted one volume of this general position to historical thought.

Reality, for Croce, is what he calls the "spirit,"[45] and the whole of
reality, or the "spirit," has two forms: namely, the theoretical and
the practical. In this context, Croce made a fundamental distinction
between the level of human activity which is theoretical and that
which is practical. By theoretical (or mental) activity, Croce meant
the realms of intuitive and conceptual knowledge. "Knowledge," he
said, "has two forms: it is either intuitive knowledge or logical knowledge; knowledge obtained through the imagination or knowledge obtained through the intellect; knowledge of the individual or knowledge of the universal; of individual things or relations between them:
it is, in fact, productive either of images or concepts."[46]

It is essential to distinguish among the various manifestations of
knowledge, and knowledge, for him, first appears through intuition.[47]
In this sense, Croce rejected the empiricist argument that knowledge
is derived solely from sense perception (and ratiocination). He differentiated between knowing an object from within (intuitive perception) and knowing it from without (sense perception), although both,
he argued further, are important for understanding reality. Sensory

perception presents us with the material content of empirical reality, whereas intuitive perception reveals the reality of the "spirit." He said:

> Matter, in its abstraction, is mechanism, passivity; it is what the spirit of man suffers, but does not produce. Without it no human knowledge or activity is possible; but mere matter produces animality, whatever is brutal and impulsive in man, not the spiritual dominion, which is humanity. . . . It is in such moments as these that we best perceive the profound difference between matter and form. . . . Matter, clothed and conquered by form, produces concrete form. It is the matter, the content, which differentiates one of our intuitions from another: the form is constant: it is spiritual activity while matter is changeable. Without matter spiritual activity would not forsake its abstractness to become concrete and real activity, this or that spiritual content, this or that definite intuition.[48]

This being the case, Croce, like Kant, maintained the viewpoint that sensory perception cannot exist without intuition (or imagination) as the latter cannot exist without the former and, therefore, though he distinguished between intuition and sensory perception, both appear concomitantly. While sensory perception and intuition are differentiated by Croce, he attributed more importance to intuition as a reflection of reality. For intuition is a representation of spirituality (the higher and truer form of reality), while sensory perception represents the impression received from material reality (or the lower form). Within this neo-idealistic point of view, intuition takes precedence over the perception of the senses as the latter form merely becomes the occasion for its expression and thereby unifies the external and internal forms of knowledge. "Intuition," he said, "is the undifferentiated unity of the perception of the real and of the simple image of the possible. In our intuitions we do not oppose ourselves as empirical beings to external reality, but we simply objectify our impressions, whatever they be."[49]

This notion of intuition is combined with the other factor of theoretical activity which, for Croce, is conceptual thought. Intuitive knowledge is distinct, but not separate, from conceptual knowledge. The relation between intuition and sensory perception, then, is directly parallel to the relation between intuition and concepts:

> Concepts are not possible without intuitions, just as intuition itself is impossible without the matter of impressions. Intui-

tions are: this river, this lake, this brook, this rain, this glass of water; the concept is: water, not this or that appearance and particular examples of water, but water in general, in whatever time or place it be realized; the material or infinite intuitions, but of one single constant concept.[50]

It appears, from this position, as an approximation, that intuition provides us with knowledge of the subject to which the concept furnishes the predicates. Knowledge of conceptual elements is characterized by the judgment of perception. That is, in order to perceive objects or events in reality, it is essential to think, and, to think, it is essential to perceive. Hence, Croce viewed intuition as an important factor in all conceptual judgments, for the process of thought synthesizes the aesthetic and logical modes of cognition.

History, in this connection, provides the important function of synthesizing the theoretical and the practical levels of human activity, of synthesizing the universal and the particular, thought and action. From the point of view of these levels of human activity historical knowledge provides information about what actually happened on particular occasions, at a particular place and under a clearly specified period of time. History deals not only with concrete individual developments and concepts of individuality, but also deals with the "universal." For Croce, individuality is the historical process within which there is an advance toward the universal and, in this context, the general is identified with what the individual experiences directly. The historical process is the expression of the "inseparable syntheses of individual and universal" and, as such, establishes for Croce the "identity of philosophy with history."[51] Any philosophical problem, when restored to the historical context that gave rise to the question we attempt to answer, he viewed as identical with historical synthetic judgments. As the synthesis of the individual and the universal, history possesses the most complete form of knowledge. Indeed, for Croce, "history is thought."[52] From the theoretical perspective, thought establishes connections between sensory-perception, intuition, and concepts, whereas history synthesizes the aesthetic, logical, and practical levels of human activity. Theoretic activity consists of knowledge while practical activity is characterized by volition, and thereby within this perspective knowledge is the precondition of action.[53] History, as the synthesis of the theoretical and the practical levels of human activity, goes on in the actions and in the minds of individuals and thus, for Croce, true knowledge and synthesis is historical. In this connection, Croce, like Dilthey, and subsequently Ortega, maintained that man can understand best what he has created, both in thought and in action.[54]

Ortega's return to Marburg in 1911 signaled another turn in his intellectual interests and in his philosophical development—an introduction to phenomenology. Ortega's interest in phenomenology began as a cordial, congenial acquaintanceship and developed into an ambiguous, ambivalent relationship. Certain concepts pertaining to phenomenological analysis eventually were to permeate Ortega's systematic statement on reality, being, and society. But this is not to say that he was a phenomenologist in the strict sense of the term— merely that some of the basic assumptions of phenomenology are perceptible in his mature works of the 1930s. General background on the genesis and development of the essential features that underlie these assumptions therefore merits some attention.

During the early 1900s, a group of German philosophers, principally of the universities of Göttingen and Munich, began to write a series of philosophical studies that were associated with the philosophical movement known as phenomenology.[55] These essays and volumes of phenomenological studies, mostly between 1913 and the 1930s, were published in the *Jahrbuch für Philosophie und Phänomenologische Forschung*. The editor-in-chief of the *Jahrbuch* was Edmund Husserl, and such thinkers as Oskar Becker, Moritz Geiger, Alexander Pfänder, Martin Heidegger, Max Scheler, and Adolf Reinach were coeditors at one time or another during this period.[56] These thinkers differed not only in philosophical interests and as philosophical personalities, but also in their interpretations of phenomenological analysis. Phenomenology is a term that is used often in a variety of philosophical (and psychological) contexts and with varying connotations. In 1929, Husserl remarked: "The term [phenomenology] has become popular. It seems that today every author who undertakes to give the world a philosophical reform wants to introduce his ideas under the title of phenomenology."[57] The term phenomenology here means the descriptive study of "phenomena"—that is, the reality of objects and events, as they appear in "immediate awareness" of the essence of experience as it is apprehended intuitively—as a philosophical basis and methodology, and purports to provide us with an accurate explanation and understanding of the fundamental structure of phenomena. Although they differed in their later interpretation of phenomenology, the German thinkers who were associated with the earlier phases of the phenomenological movement were in general agreement on this sense of the term:

> It is not a system that the editors share. What unites them is the common conviction that it is only by a return to the primary sources of direct intuition and to insights into essential structures derived from them . . . that we shall be able to put

to use the great traditions of philosophy with their concepts
and problems; only thus shall we be in a position to clarify
such concepts intuitively, to restate the problems of an intuitive basis, and thus, eventually, to solve them, at least in principle.[58]

This interpretation of phenomenology was initiated by Husserl and
since he was the central figure and creator, general discussion of the
fundamental features of the movement will focus on Husserl's interpretation of phenomenology with a view toward clarifying its connection with Ortega's philosophy of man, society, and history.

Husserl's philosophical standpoint attempted to present a presuppositionless description of the fundamental structure of "phenomena"
and of the essential structure of cognitive consciousness. The function
of phenomenology, for him, is to avert the speculative metaphysical
assertions of his generation and thereby to establish philosophy as a
"rigorous science."[59] In order to establish and to maintain its "scientific" character, philosophy must be presented as presuppositionless,
and, from this point of view, no statements or concepts can be accepted as philosophical truths without careful scrutiny and examina-
tion. The philosopher, according to Husserl, must seek clarity and understanding.[60]

The general theme of the phenomenological program, according to
Husserl, is intentionality; that is, he characterized the peculiarity of
consciousness as *consciousness of something.*[61] This interest in the
basic character of intentionality was taken up by Husserl from the
man under whom he studied philosophy in Vienna after turning aside
mathematics: namely, Franz Brentano.[62] For Husserl, objects are conceived as entities which are *intentionally constituted.* In experiencing
an act, a person—the subject—becomes aware of an object to the extent that Husserl characterized the act as *consciousness of something.*
The position that all acts are directed does not suggest that there is
always some object toward which an act is directed. For Husserl, a
noema is associated with every act. When there exists no object of
which one thinks, therefore, and a person conceives of a unicorn, his
(or her) act of thinking embodies a noema although it has no object.
By dint of its noema, however, such an act is directed. To be directed
simply means to have a noema. Husserl's notion of the noema, therefore, performed an important role in his theories of intentionality,
intersubjectivity perception and, in effect, his phenomenology. What
Husserl wanted to create with his program of phenomenology was a
new, radically different science of philosophy—"the science of Phe-

nomenology," that would "embrace all knowledge."

In the lecture of 1907, Husserl maintained that the term "phenomenology" "denotes a science, a system of scientific disciplines." It "also and above all denotes a method and an attitude of mind, the specifically *philosophical attitude* of mind, the specifically *philosophical method.*"[63] The philosophical method of this "attitude" has to confront the immanent data of the "acts of consciousness" as acts of the subject and as objective correlates to these acts.[64] What Husserl called "immanent seeing" incorporated the notion of meaning "in the intentional."[65] For to intend something is to use a word that signifies it, which contains "the meaning" of it, and the reference may be adduced symbolically: as concept or as precept.[66] Viewed in this way, one of the aims of Husserl's phenomenological method was to construe a philosophy of "essences" that would provide for experiences and descriptions of the phenomena of consciousness in order "to cognize pure phenomena scientifically."[67]

For Husserl, the transcendental, or phenomenological, reduction does not refer to trans-phenomenal entities, rather its aim is to reach back "to the things" (*Zu den Sachen*), to begin with phenomena and return to the reflective process of the ego's consciousness of "immediate data." The phenomenological reduction is the reflection process within which the transition from the natural attitude (observation of the natural world of objects) to the transcendental attitude (the "transcendental ego" or the realm of "pure consciousness") takes place.[68] The potentiality of realizing the phenomenological dimensions of the "transcendental ego" is evidenced when the individual ego discovers that whatever is in the world exists only as an object, toward which its actions are directed, and therefore as an integral ingredient of our consciousness. In this way, the transcendental reduction may be interpreted as performing the function of unveiling hidden intentional acts that project transcendental objects; for phenomenological analysis, as "intentional analysis," is analysis that describes the manner in which these intentional functions are operative in conjunction with each other.[69] Phenomenology, in this sense, is characterized as the description of a realm of being that serves as the ultimate basis of the world of lived experience.

It is in the later writings of Husserl (notably most of the unedited, unpublished manuscripts which contain his writings between 1921 and 1935;[70] his *Cartesian Meditations,* which was based on the lectures he gave at the Sorbonne in 1929, and his last major work, published posthumously, *The Crisis of European Sciences and Transcendental Phenomenology*) that the extension of his philosophy of phenomenology to include the ideas of intersubjectivity and of the life-world (*Lebenswelt*) is located.[71] In the *Cartesian Meditations*, Husserl attempted to desubjectivize the solipsism of the phenomenological reduction through his notion of a world of intersubjective communities. The world, for him, is no longer viewed as being what it is said to be, how it is constituted by the transcendental ego.[72] Rather, the objects of the world are experienced through the intersubjective community of individuals (or alter egos).[73] To Husserl the alter egos are constituted by the transcendental ego as equal percipients in an intersubjective community. The function of this intersubjective community, then, is to avert the condition of solipsism, as the world of lived experience is "objective" and is accessible to every living individual in the here-and-now and is therefore considered to be a more fundamental realm of verifiability in the constitution of the world.[74] The study of our experience of this life-world, thus, is delivered as the primary objective of phenomenology.

While studying at Marburg in 1911, Ortega recalled in his later writing, the students of Cohen and Natorp were deeply immersed in Neo-Kantian idealism.[75] Ortega, Hartmann, Heimsoeth, and Scheffer, members of this group of students, often discussed amongst themselves their agreements, disagreements, and dissatisfaction with the Neo-Kantianism of their teachers. The critical spirit of their intellectual "spontaneity,"[76] as a reaction to all the reading that they had to do in Marburg on Kant, Parmenides, and ancient philosophy in general, revealed the aspirations of this "group of young men" to proceed past the point of Neo-Kantian idealism and "to row toward" what Ortega called "the imaginary coast"; but "the success" of this venture "was improbable."[77] "However," Ortega recounted, "fate had presented us the gift of a prodigious instrument: phenomenology."[78] He continued:

> That group of young men had never been, in the strict sense of the term, Neo-Kantian. Nor had we given ourselves entirely over to phenomenology. Our desire for system prevented us from doing so. Phenomenology, because of its own consistency, is incapable of arriving at a systematic form or shape. Its inestimable value lies in the "fine structure" of fleshy tissues that it can offer to the architecture of a system. Thus, phenomenology was not a philosophy for us: it was . . . a piece of good luck.[79]

This "common awakening" of the group, however, also was "the signal" of its "separation." In 1911, they challenged, collectively, as a group of students, the positions of their teachers; on leaving Marburg, they had to pursue as individual thinkers whatever "pieces" of "good luck" they could find in phenomenology, and to put together whichever "fine structure" of a system of thought was attainable from it.

After 1911, there is some evidence that both Ortega and Hartmann did pursue particular interests of phenomenology. In 1912, Ortega began to study phenomenology "seriously"[80] and in 1913, he recollected, the *Jahrbuch für Philosophie und Phänomenologische Forschung*, Husserl's *Ideen*, and *The Ethics* of Scheler were published.[81] That June, Ortega wrote a long review of Heinrich Hoffmann's dissertation, *Studies on the Concept of Sensation*, which had been presented to the University of Göttingen during the same year.[82] In this essay on the descriptive psychology of one of the lesser-known students of the Göttingen Circle,[83] Ortega mentioned that "the influence—each time greater—of 'phenomenology' on psychology tends to separate in the latter, in the most fundamental and salubrious manner, description from explanation."[84] Three of the five sections of the review elaborated certain aspects of the "phenomenology" of Husserl as formulated in the *Ideen*. Ortega's response to the question "what is phenomenology?"[85] was to characterize phenomenology, in a general sense, as the "pure description of essences."[86] In view of this general description of phenomenology, Ortega made the point of distinguishing the "essential *individual intuition*" of Husserl's "pure description" of "essence" in the *Ideen*[87] from what he designated as the "mistaken" "definition" of phenomenology as a "descriptive psychology" that might be interpreted by some in Husserl's *Logische Untersuchungen*. For Husserl "was touching on a new territory of problems" that even he, as the "proper investigator, was not able to grasp at a glance."[88] Psychological statements, according to Ortega, must be distinguished from the "purely descriptive" statements of phenomenology on the grounds that psychology deals with facts and its statements, therefore, are empirical; whereas phenomenology, as formulated in a "clearer formula" in the *Ideen* of Husserl, deals with "consciousness," "human consciousness."[89] Through this formulation, he contended, it "is very clear that the new science [phenomenology] is not psychology, if by psychology we understand, according to the use of the term, a descriptive empirical science or a metaphysical science."[90] Husserl made a distinction between a general descriptive study (whether empirical or nonempirical) that might precede any attempt to provide an explanation of phenomena, and phenomenology that is presented as a descriptive manner in which one philosophizes without presuppositions and without empirical statements. The phenomenological reduction, in the *Ideen*, is the principal theme of this "new science" as it is the reflective process of "consciousness," and this "consciousness" is "consciousness of" perceptions of the "natural world." Husserl's position, thus, for Ortega, "reduces" phenomena, not as trans-phenomenal entities, but as entities in the "natural posture" of our world:[91]

There is a "natural manner" of carrying out the acts of consciousness, whatever they may be. That natural manner is characterized by the executive value which those acts have. Thus the "natural posture" in the act of perception consists in accepting as existing in truth before us a thing belonging to an ambit of things which we consider as effectively real and which we call "world." . . . Let us suppose, now, that at the point of having carried out our consciousness, as it were, in *good faith,* naturally, an act of perception turns back on itself, and instead of *living* in the contemplation of the sensible object, it occupies itself in contemplating its own perception. This perception, with all its executive consequences, with all its affirmation that there is something real before it, will remain, we might say, suspended; its efficacy will not be definitive; it will only be efficacy as a *phenomenon.* Note that this reflection of the consciousness upon its acts: (1) does not disturb them: perception is what it was before, only that—as Husserl says very graphically—now it is placed in parentheses [brackets]; (2) it does not pretend to explain them, but merely sees them, just as perception does not explain the object, but presents it in perfect passivity.

Well then, all the acts of consciousness and all the objects of those acts can be placed in parentheses [brackets]. The whole "natural" world, or science insofar as it is a system of judgments carried out in a "natural manner," remains reduced to *phenomenon.* And here phenomenon does not mean what it does in Kant, for example, something that suggests another substantial something behind it. Phenomenon here is simply the virtual character that everything acquires when in its natural executive value one passes to contemplate it in a spectacular and descriptive posture, without giving it a definite character.

That pure description is phenomenology.[92]

This sympathetic discussion of Husserl's *Ideen* expressed Ortega's enthusiastic and optimistic hopes in the potential of phenomenology as a significant philosophical movement—with or without a system—albeit Husserl's new approach apparently did not take a significant turn in the articulation of his own phenomenological perspective at this time.

Subsequent to this essay of 1912, on the other hand, the influence of the language of phenomenology is discernible in the works of Ortega in the usage of such terms as "apodictic appearance," philosophy as "a science,"[93] and philosophy "as a science without supposition."[94] "Since 1914," Ortega remarked in his work *The Idea of Principle in Leibnitz and The Evolution of Deductive Theory,* which was published posthumously in 1958, "reflection on the phenomenon 'human life' is the basis of all my thought. At that time I formulated it—in order to expound Husserl's phenomenology during various courses— correcting, in an essential manner, the description of the phenomenon 'consciousness of . . .' which, as is known, constituted, at that time, the basis of his doctrine."[95] In 1925, he wrote a short section in his essay "The Dehumanization of Art" entitled "A Few Drops of Phenomenology," in which he discussed the "perspectivism" motif of "diverse," " 'lived' realities."[96] The different perspectives of the perception of an "identical event" illuminate for us, he maintained, the fact that "one and the same reality may split into many diverse realities when it is beheld from different points of view."[97] Ortega perceived, in this sense, the "human point of view" as that "reality" in which "we 'live' situations, persons, things."[98] To establish "distance" between ourselves and reality as a manner of understanding these very "realities"—which is "by no means absolute"—we "must put ourselves into the place" of "another person" and "situation" in order that we may distinguish between the world ("persons, things, and situations") which is "given to us" as " 'lived' reality," and that which is "given to us" in the form of " 'observed' reality."[99]

It was during this very year that Ortega presented the phenomenology of Husserl to his students at the University of Madrid,[100] wherein he projected "a program" of study of the "restatement of the problem of Being" for "a series of publications."[101] Specifically, Ortega addressed himself to the possible adoption of a systematic method within which the "problem of Being" could have been resolved for him at this development of his thought. "In 1925," he said, "I stated my theme—some of my students would be able to remember—saying literally:

> 1st, It is necessary to renew, from its roots, the traditional problem of Being; 2nd, this has to be done with the phenomenological method insofar and only insofar as this means *synthetic* or *intuitive thinking,* and not merely conceptual-abstract thinking as is the traditional logical way of thinking; 3rd,

but it is necessary to integrate the phenomenological method, adapting to it a dimension of *systematic thinking,* which, as is known, it does not possess; 4th, and finally, in order that a systematic phenomenological thinking may be possible, it is necessary to start out from a phenomenon which may be a system *by* and *in itself.* This systematic phenomenon is human life and from its reflection and analysis one must set out. In this manner, I abandoned Phenomenology at the very moment of accepting it. Instead of withdrawing from consciousness, as has been done since Descartes, we become firm in the radical reality which is for every one his [or her] life.[102]

Ortega's ambivalence toward the adoption of the phenomenological method, by 1925, became apparent in his search for a coherent method of analysis. He was willing to retain the "synthetic" (or "intuitive") function of phenomenological analysis provided that this function is, in turn, integrated into the systematic "phenomenon" of "human life." Through this connection, the phenomenological method of analysis and the analysis of human life performed interchangeable functions for Ortega in the systematic apprehension of the "traditional problem of Being." This is the positive side of the ambivalence which moves him to approach and to accept phenomenology. But on the other side of the ambivalence, he avoided phenomenology where the emphasis appears to be more "abstract" and in the tradition of idealism. Ortega's response to Husserl's *Formale und Transzendentale Logik* pointed to his criticism of this tendency in phenomenology.

Many of the members of the phenomenological movement (and other European thinkers who were not necessarily members of this movement, but who were influenced in one way or another by the ideas of the movement) were dissatisfied with the solipsistic standpoint of Husserl's transcendental phenomenology in his *Formale und Transzendentale Logik* (1929). Ortega was one of these European thinkers, although he did not express explicitly any dissatisfaction with the solipsistic implications of the transcendental idealism in this work until twelve years later. In his *Notes on Thinking* (1941), Ortega found Husserl's approach to the problem of "the genesis of reason" to be "tantamount to being absolute" when Husserl expounded his "genetic phenomenology" as "consciousness of" reality, designating "consciousness of itself" as being "immediate to itself."[103] He criticized further the analysis and definitions of reason given by Husserl in *Formale und Transzendentale Logik* as not incorporating "the themes of humanity, life, and the functional character of reason."[104] According to Ortega, in this connection, "The phenomenological attitude as formulated in *Formale und Transzendentale Logik* is diametrically opposed to the attitude that I call living reason."[105] He was opposed to this tendency toward transcendental idealism in *Formale und Transzendentale Logik* but was not to reject, completely, phenomenology.

To be sure, Ortega's ambivalence toward phenomenology was manifest throughout this section of the article. For after he learned of Husserl's *Crisis of European Sciences and Transcendental Phenomenology,* Ortega did not argue that his later general position and that of phenomenology were "diametrically opposed." Indeed, in a long footnote at the conclusion of *Notes on Thinking,* Ortega invited a comparison between himself and Husserl. In the *Crisis,* Husserl's earlier account of the "genesis of reason" as the manifestation of "consciousness of itself," and as the essential relation in consciousness between "intentionality" and self-evident fulfillment, shifted to general discussions on "the a priori of history,"[106] on the " 'genesis' " of "the concepts of 'history,' " on "historical 'explanation,' " and on "grounding" the fact that "the insights of principle are *historical.*"[107] Ortega found this kind of "historical reflection" on the "historical manner of being"[108] compatible with his own notion of "historical reason" presented in *History as a System* (and he also pointed out that he arrived at this position independently of Husserl), which, therefore, is not opposed to the different direction of "reason" and "genetic phenomenology" taken by the new dimensions of Husserl in the *Crisis.*

> At the time of reading the proofs of this essay, I happened to see that in 1935 Husserl gave a course of lectures at the University of Prague under the title, *The Crisis of European Sciences and Transcendental Phenomenology,* the beginning of which had been published in the journal *Philosophia,* I, 1936, Belgrade. In it the great philosopher develops in a little more detail the content of the ideas cited by me in the early pages of these notes . . . in this study phenomenology leaps to views that I never believed could have sprung from it. Personally, this leap of the phenomenological doctrine has been extremely satisfactory for me because it consists in nothing less than a resort to "historical reason." It is important to observe that before the appearance of those pages of Husserl in *Philosophia* and much before the appearance of their continuation in the *Revue Internationale de Philosophie,* Brussels, 1939, which is where explicit resort to *Vernunft in der Geschichte* [reason in history] is made, my study on *History as a System* (1935) had already been published in England.[109]

Therefore, Husserl's later works *Cartesian Meditations* and *Crisis,* which were attempts to resolve the difficulties inherent in transcendental phenomenology and which were more representative as explicit statements of his phenomenological philosophy, were not diametrically opposed to "the themes" of "human life" or to the importance of postulating the epistemological and the ontological function of the experience of human life. Clearly, Husserl's idea of *Lebenswelt* was the kind of notion that Ortega discussed in his own philosophy of "human life." But this is not to deny that there were further differences between the two thinkers. Ortega took issue with a small point on the role of the notion "analogical transposition" in regard to the "Other," which was made in the fifth meditation of Husserl's *Cartesian Meditations*, yet this point was not considered by Ortega to be diametrically opposed to his notion of human life. "Husserl," he said at one point in his *Man and People* (1939), "was the first who clearly defined the radical and not merely psychological problem that I call 'The Appearance of the Other.' Husserl's development of the problem, is, in my opinion, much less successful than his definition of it, although there are many admirable discoveries in his development."[110] This kind of discussion of the differences of opinion on the development of a particular philosophical problem does not suggest that there was not some sharing of viewpoints or that Ortega was not influenced, intellectually, by Husserl. For although Ortega disagreed with Husserl's notion of "analogical transposition," he did view the latter's phenomenological thought as having been "the greatest influence of this last half-century."[111] The notions of the "appearance of the other"—that is, the other's presence both as an object (i.e., the physical structure of its body) and as a subject (i.e., as an alter ego that experiences the same world that is experienced by the "I")—and "life experience" also were viewed by Ortega as the procedure of analysis to avert solipsism and the "enclosure of the I within itself."[112] There is no direct evidence (in the form of acknowledgment) of Ortega having shared any particular phenomenological perspective with Husserl, but he did discuss such phenomenological notions as actions which are directed toward objects when the "I" encounters its environment; ego/alter ego interaction in the world of intersubjective communities as the realm of lived experiences; and the position of entering the transcendental attitude of phenomenological reduction in order to apprehend the alter ego, which are notions similar to those discussed by Husserl.[113]

From the viewpoint of this characterization of phenomenology, Ortega reached back to "I am I and my circumstances" as his starting point of analysis. For Ortega the individual ego's consciousness of self is through the awareness of both its physiological features and behavioral gestures and those of "others" in reciprocal human interaction, a consciousness of self that proceeds through self-analysis of the inner essence of the being of the "I" and the "I's" awareness of other selves as similar beings in the "circumstances" of intersubjective human activity of social relations, the "circumstances" of the world of lived experience. In short, he attempted to characterize the nature of an individual's experience of his world and himself; there is an attempt to distinguish between the facts that one's relationship to an organism is different from one's relation to a person qua being and that one's actions toward an organism are different from the way that one acts toward a person. "Living," he said, "is to reach outside of oneself, devoted, ontologically, to what is *other,* be it called world or circumstances."[114] So that although the label of "phenomenologist" is not being attached to Ortega in this context, it is maintained here that there is a discernible influence of points of view which reflect a phenomenological analysis in the philosophy of Ortega.

It is also maintained here that Ortega probably became increasingly interested in some of the viewpoints that are expressed in phenomenological analysis through his contact with the thought of Max Scheler. Through Ernst Curtius, Ortega became friends with Scheler between 1923 and 1928,[115] and this factor, perhaps, may be offered as an explanation of how he came into more direct contact with Scheler's interpretation of phenomenological analysis and with Scheler's non-phenomenological perspective of the hierarchy and the external order of values. This contact probably left Ortega with a favorable impression, for he conveyed positive thoughts about the importance of Scheler as a European thinker, as he did with Dilthey and Husserl. In his short obituary article, "Max Scheler: An Intoxicate of Essences," Ortega projected a positive image of Scheler as a philosopher. In this article, written in 1928, Ortega claimed that "the first man of genius, Adam of the new paradise [phenomenology] and as Hebraic Adam, was Scheler."[116] According to Ortega, "The death of Scheler left Europe without the best mind that it possessed. . . ."[117] Scheler was one of the four original coeditors of the essays and volumes on phenomenological studies which were published in the *Jahrbuch.*[118] In his impressive work on ethics, *Der Formalismus in der Ethik und die materiale Wertethik* (1913 and 1916), Scheler developed a doctrine of moral values and a hierarchy of norms which are based on "value-facts" that may be perceived by every individual. The eternal order of these values and their hierarchy, however, Scheler explained, are perceived from different points of view by individuals who live in different societies.[119] The writings subsequent to Scheler's

Ethik built upon the foundation of his phenomenology to develop other works on philosophical anthropology, sociology of knowledge, and a speculative sociology of religion.[120] In particular, Scheler gave emphasis in his writings to the description and analysis of the way man apprehends the world and himself, the perspective of human intersubjectivity, which he interprets as a form of social interaction, and his elitist, antiegalitarian notion of a kind of hierarchy of forms and values that are based on relating a "type of thought" to a "type of society"—viewpoints discussed at length in one context or another in the later writings of Ortega. The major works of Scheler that deal with these viewpoints, *Ressentiment* and *The Nature of Sympathy,* published in 1912 and 1913 respectively, *Die Wissensformen und die Gesellschaft,* 1926, and *The Place of Man in the Universe,* 1928, undoubtedly had an impact on Ortega's thought before Scheler's death in 1928. There is no explicit evidence that Scheler had a direct influence on Ortega (the latter did not acknowledge any such influence by Scheler in his thought as he did with Dilthey), but the affinities in thought between the two philosophers are clearly perceptible.[121]

The similarities in the strands of thought in Neo-Kantianism and in the Kantian components of phenomenology—in conjunction with the broad influences of both movements in Ortega's intellectual development—are such that it is conceivable that both Cohen and Natorp were instrumental in introducing Ortega to the earlier ideas of Husserl, as there is a perceptible link between the Neo-Kantianism of the Marburg School and the early philosophy of Husserl. Like Kant, Husserl was also interested in a fundamental understanding of objects as they appear to us by appealing for a return "to the things" (*Zu den Sachen*).[122] His phenomenological analysis contributed new and deeper insights into the realms of epistemology, logic, mathematics, and the sciences in general. These realms of knowledge were of major concern to the Neo-Kantians in Marburg as well. Cohen's panlogistic rejection of psychologism was somewhat similar to Husserl's critique of the assumptions that underlie the connection of logic and psychology in the latter's *Logische Untersuchungen* (1900–1901);[123] and Natorp's coupling of psychology and panlogism was similar to Husserl's *Ideen zu einer reinen Phänomenologie und phänomenologischen Philosophie* (1913).[124] In this context, we are able to discern another interesting link between the Neo-Kantianism of Marburg and the phenomenological movement in the philosophies of Nicolai Hartmann and Ortega. The philosophy of Hartmann (Natorp's student and successor to his chair at Marburg) is generally associated with the phenomenology of the "phenomenologists,"[125] and the later philosophy of Ortega (who was primarily a student of Cohen) also reflects some of the influences of the general ideas of phenomenology.[126] At least two members of the young Marburg group continued in their search for a systematic statement of their philosophical positions. Where Hartmann began to develop his version of phenomenology by 1921, in his *Outlines to a Metaphysics of Knowledge,*[127] Ortega did not begin to take in, systematically, some of the general assumptions of phenomenology until the 1930s.

In an edition of his works (1932), Ortega said: " 'I am I and my circumstances.' This expression, which appears in my first book and which condenses in final volume my philosophic thought, does not only mean the doctrine that my work expounds and proposes, but means that my work is an executive case of the same doctrine. My work is, by its essence and its presence, circumstantial. This is precisely what the cited phrase declares."[128] The conceptual frame of his intellectual development expands from the central hypothesis that "man," his "circumstances," and "life" are categories that are to be distinguished from those of "pure reason" and "physico-mathematical reason." There are, thus, perceptible lines connecting his early and his later ideas so that as we are able to locate the earlier bases of Ortega's later positions, we will attain the essential philosophic relations in his thought. For in analyzing these lines that delineate Ortega's philosophic works, we follow the logic of his internal intellectual development.

In so far as Ortega attempted to "awaken" the spirits of "kindred thoughts" in his first book, the alternate thrust of his "ideological" "appeal" projected "general" philosophical "considerations" and "observations" of which he commented: "although for the author the doctrines are scientific convictions, he does not expect the reader to accept them as truths."[129] "I only offer *modi res considerandi,*" he said, "possible new ways of looking at things."[130] Nor did he view these general considerations as consisting in a philosophy; philosophy and therefore "erudition," he claimed, are "pure synthesis" and "these *Meditations,* free from erudition . . . are propelled by philosophical desires."[131] These essays exhibit, for him, a gesture toward a different perspective of "things" and, for this reason, one should not "expect too much from them."[132] The *Meditations* do not constitute a philosophy, for "philosophy," according to him, "is a science."[133] They are, instead, "simply essays," and the "essay is a science minus the explicit proof."[134] "For the writer," he added, "it is permissible for him to eliminate from his work all apodictic appearance, leaving the verification merely in ellipse. . . ."[135]

Despite these disclaimers and his dissociating the general discussion of the *Meditations* from what he would consider as the formulation of a general coherent standpoint, Ortega did view these essays as "propelling" philosophical aspirations. According to some commentators, the nucleus of Ortega's basic philosophical principle—the notion that human life is the ultimate reality—is formulated in the *Meditations* through the instrumentality of his well-known expression, "I am I and my circumstances."[136] A close and more critical reading of the *Meditations* and Ortega's later writings reveals that albeit "I am I and my circumstances" appeared in this early work, it is not until his later works that we begin to perceive a systematic elaboration of "I am I and my circumstances"—subsequently put forward by Ortega—as an analytical and ontological statement in his general philosophic point of view. On the other hand, while Ortega did not discuss **systematically** the ontological features of "man" and his "circumstances" at this point in his intellectual development, he did convey certain key terms which may be identified in their subsequent systematic expression in the 1930s. "Man reaches the maximum of his capacity," he said there, "when he acquires complete consciousness of his circumstances. Through them he communicates with the universe."[137] In the *Meditations,* Ortega employed the term "circumstance" in the sense of one's environment and, in this context, it may be viewed as revealing the basis upon which to develop a philosophic position:

> Circumstance! *Circum-stantia!* That is, the silent things which are all around us. Very close, very close to us they raise their silent features with a gesture of humility and eagerness as if they needed our acceptance for their offering, and at the same time, were ashamed of the apparent simplicity of their donation. We walk blindly among them, our gaze fixed on remote enterprises, projected upon the conquest of distant schematic cities.[138]

"Circumstance" and "individual life" and "the immediate," for Ortega, are "different names for the same thing."[139] These terms represent "those parts of life from which their inner spirit, their *logos,* has not yet been extracted. Since spirit and *logos* are nothing but 'meaning,' connection, and unity, all that is individual, immediate, and circumstantial appears to be accidental and meaningless."[140] To "extract" a sense of connectedness, then, we must seek " 'to save the appearances,' the phenomena"; that is, we must "search for the meaning of what surrounds us."[141] For "I am I and my circumstances, and if I do not save it, I do not save myself. . . . In short: the reabsorption of circumstances is the concrete destiny of man."[142] In the *Meditations,* then, Ortega spun off these loose threads of expressions that he would eventually weave into a tighter and more coherent pattern in his mature work. The passing reference to such terminology as "circumstance," "apodictic appearance," "uneasiness," "preoccupation," "insecurity" and "culture," and "philosophy" as "a science" we may view as constituting, in embryonic form, the fundamental basis of his general philosophical viewpoint.

In the *Meditations,* Ortega also engaged in a general discussion of the synthetic function of conceptual categories, revealing some of the influence that his critical Neo-Kantian training at Marburg had upon him. These general comments can be characterized as an attempt to distinguish between what he considered the appropriate and inappropriate uses of reason in the assertion of speculative assumptions that one posits in regard to knowledge of certain facts of reality. Like Kant and some of the Neo-Kantians, Ortega maintained that it is not possible to obtain knowledge of the external world through the faculty of reason alone and thereby rejected all such attempts in the quest of certainty and knowledge. By the same token, the experience of mere sense perception does not deliver knowledge and understanding for, in the absence of some synthetic interpretation, sense experience is nothing but raw data. "Experience," for Kant, "is beyond all doubt, the first product to which our understanding gives rise, in working up the raw material of sensible impressions."[143] "Nevertheless," he added, "it is by no means the sole field to which our understanding is confined."[144] In this conceptual range, Kant explained, if our sensory perceptions were not arranged within what he called a "system of a priori knowledge from mere concepts," knowledge of an objective world and the pure a priori intuition of space and time in terms of rational principles would be impossible.[145] Hence, without synthetic a priori knowledge of space and time and the corresponding categories of the understanding, there would be a manifold of fluctuating "raw material" with little, if any, knowledge of the external world of nature.

To Ortega, "all knowledge of facts," as "isolated" data, "is, to be precise, incomprehensive and can be justified only when used in the service of a theory."[146] Our capacity to comprehend the connectedness in the external world is served best "in the synthesis of facts," for "this unity of facts" is "not found in themselves" but is found "in the mind of an individual. . . ."[147] Ortega elaborated this point further:

> Without the concept we would not know where an object begins or ends; that is, the objects as impressions are volatile and slip away, they slip out of our hands; we do not possess them. On tying the objects together, the concept fixes them and de-

livers them to us as prisoners; . . . impressions escape us if we
do not bind them with reason. . . .

The concept will never give to us what the impression im-
parts, that is, the flesh of things. But this is not to yield to an
inadequateness of the concept, except that the concept does
not claim such a function. The impression will never give to
us what the concept gives to us, namely: the form, the physical and moral sense of things. . . .

We feel today very far from the Hegelian dogma, which
makes of thought the ultimate substance of all reality. The
world is too wide and too rich for thought to assume the responsibility for all that occurs [in the world]. But on de-
throning reason, let us take care to put it in its place. Not
everything is thought, but without thought we do not possess
anything fully.

This is the prerequisite that the concept offers us over the
impression; each concept is literally an organ with which we
capture things. Vision is a complete vision only by means of
the concept; sensation gives us only the diffuse and pliable
matter of each object; it gives us the impression of things, not
the things themselves.[148]

Hence while Ortega viewed reason, or "the concept," as constituting
"the real instrument" for "the perception and the apprehension of
things," he also thought that the serviceability of the faculty of reason
had its limitations. In this connection, he set forth that "reason cannot and should not aspire to replace life."[149] It was at this point in
the *Meditations* that Ortega initiated a notion that would eventually
develop into one of the principal themes of his mature writings. In
those later works, rather than characterize "reason" and "life" as
categories that are pitted against each other, Ortega dissolved the
"reason-life" dichotomy by positing them as coexisting categories.
That is, "reason" and "life," for him, must interpenetrate each other,
and Ortega put forward this position from the point of view of his notion of "vital" and "historical reason." This is the position that would
assist in taking him beyond the influence of Neo-Kantianism. To proceed past this point, with "vital reason," Ortega planted the seed of
this notion in the fresh soil of his next major work, *The Theme of
Our Time*. In the climate of this work, "vital reason" takes on a fuller
life as the germinating factor in the thought of Ortega.

In this early work of 1923, Ortega claimed that the "theme of our
time" consists of reducing "pure reason" to "vital reason." His discussion of "life," however, is not presented as an ontological analysis of

the mode of being, which is the characterization of man that he exhibits in his later writings. In *The Theme,* rather, Ortega interpreted "life" more in the sense of the "organic," concrete, "biological" than in the biographical and in the ontological sense of the essense of man's being and the inner-outer experience of life and "circumstances." Ortega's general philosophical viewpoint is not characterized here as that of a vitalist or of a biologic philosopher; nonetheless, his interpretation of life as "biological organism" gives the appearance of the position of vitalism. Vitalism, in its broad philosophical sense, is a general description of life as a living organism whereby the principles of biology, chemistry, and physics are considered to be applicable to an understanding of "biological organisms" and of organic changes. In 1921, Ortega wrote short articles on Hans Driesch's *Die Philosophie des Organischen* (1908) and Jakob Uexküll's *Umwelt und Innenwelt der Tiere* (1911),[150] and it is conceivable that the tendency toward the use of biological language in *The Theme* may have been the result of this earlier interest in these philosophical biologists.

On the other hand, Ortega's characterization of generational changes as being explicable in naturalistic terms is an interpretation which resembles that of Bergson.[151] "A generation," Ortega said, "is a human variety in the strict sense that naturalists give to this term. Its members come into the world endowed with certain typical characteristics which lend them a common physiognomy, distinguishing them from the previous generation."[152] The "body" of "historical reality," or "the historical organism," as he put it, "like all other biological sciences," "exhibits a complete hierarchy in its anatomy, an orderly succession of subordinate parts and an equally successive interdependence between the various classes of facts."[153] Ortega's picturing of "each generation by means of the images of a biological projectile launched into space at a definite moment and with pre-determined force and direction," in a variety of ways, would appear to limit the vital—used here in the sense of experiencing life and not in the sense of "biological physiognomy"—spontaneous, and historical dimension of his later concept of human life and of the generation.

From the nonbiological perspective of *The Theme,* he took a different approach. Through this approach, Ortega addressed himself to the more crucial philosophical question of "the theme of our time," namely: "the problem" of " 'the' truth."[154] It is "this question of truth," he explained, which "will take us directly to the very root of the theme of our time."[155] For Ortega, it is "the problem of truth" which has "divided the men of the generations anterior to our own into two antagonistic tendencies: relativism and rationalism."[156] As each of these viewpoints "renounces what the other retains," he rejected both modes of thinking as establishing extreme philosophical positions. "Our own spirit," he said, "is alien to both of these positions: when we attempt to assume either of them we feel that we are suffering from mutilation."[157] In these philosophical orientations as epistemological possibilities toward an understanding of reality and the problem of truth, Ortega's response was: "Neither rationalist absolutism, which saves reason and nullifies life, nor relativism, which saves life but dissolves reason, are possibilities."[158]

The general principles of knowledge that are based upon what Ortega labeled the "absolute sovereignty" of rationalism with its abstract principles, and the "skepticism" of relativism (which "opposes all speculative theory"), are viewed by him as being "alien" to his general conceptual framework, since each position "is equally narrow and arbitrary."[159] From this stance, Ortega was interested in establishing "the limits of reason" and, as such, did not reject the theoretical function of reason; he was against what he considered to be the "abuse of reason" as articulated in the "arbitrary," "abstract," "pure intellection" of rationalism. His rejection of rationalism and relativism was epistemological and metaphysical and he expressed his dissatisfaction with their arbitrary bases of truth. But to deny one's thought of reason would be as "narrow" and as "arbitrary" as rationalism and relativism. *"Reason,"* thus, *"is solely a form and function of life."*[160] The "spontaneous" nature of life, for him, "does not require any fixed content," for "life exists simply for the purpose of being lived."[161] This purpose is served best, he argued, with his notion of "vital reason" wherein "pure reason" is reduced to "vital reason" as "reason" and "life" are one. On the other hand, as the term "vital" or "vital sensibility" was employed by Ortega in *The Theme* in the sense of "biological spontaneity," he presented the notion of "vital reason" as a kind of critique of "pure reason." Ortega perceived the problems confronting philosophy, at this point, to consist in problems of epistemology. His particular philosophical enterprise, here, pertained to a "critique of knowledge" with the broader implications of a *Critique of Vital Reason.*[162]

It was through this perspective that Ortega staked his claim that the "mission of the present generation" consists in its "energetic attempt to regulate the world from the point of view of life. . . ."[163] As the "theme of our time," for him, reflected the absolutist tendencies of rationalism and the skeptical inclinations of relativism, he proposed his "doctrine of the point of view" as a "third view of the process of knowledge, which is a perfect synthesis of the other two."[164] The "only false perspective is the one which claims to be the one and only perspective."[165] The "abstract point of view" of the absolutist standpoint of rationalism "deals only in abstractions," he contended, whereas, "*every life is a point of view directed upon the universe.*"[166] This "perspectivist" dimension, then, promises to perform the function of unifying reality. For "*perspective*" is, at once, "*one of the component parts of reality*" and "its organizing element,"[167] and, thereby, Ortega claimed that "all knowledge is knowledge from a definite point of view."[168] The distinction between that which is manifold in reality and that which is uniform did not fully satisfy Ortega's sensibilities and quest for fundamental truths which are knowable through a systematic interpretation of reality. He argued that "the *vital, historical, perspectivist dimension, . . .* the doctrine of the point of view requires a system to contain a properly articulated statement of the vital perspective from which it has proceeded, permitting, in this way, its own articulation with those of other systems. . . . *Pure reason has to be supplanted by a vital type of reason in which its pure form may become localized and acquire mobility and mental power of transformation.*"[169] Thus Ortega found it essential, at this point, to express his preference for a coherent epistemology that would account for knowledge of both the particular and the general. In his later works, when he extended his ontological analysis of human existence, human life, and society, we eventually witness the formulation of the systematic expression of his general philosophical point of view.

A year after the publication of *The Theme,* Ortega, apparently sensing that his notion of "vital reason" might be misrepresented, found it necessary to clarify his position. If the speculative metaphysical positions of "vitalism" and "rationalism" were read into this notion—the positions that he did not attribute to "vital reason"—clearer distinctions must be made between these positions and his own ideas. The reduction of "pure reason" to "vital reason," for him, served rather the purpose of the juxtaposition of the terms "reason" and "vital" with the combined attempt to distinguish between and to balance off the general and the particular.[170] Thus, by 1924, Ortega proceeded to confirm and to clarify his position on this issue in his article, appropriately entitled, "Neither Vitalism nor Rationalism."[171]

Ortega maintained, in this essay, that the term "vitalism" comprises two modes of thought: "biological vitalism" or "biologism," as the modality of the biological sciences, and the narrow sense of "philosophical vitalism" that takes the position of establishing the "opposition between theory [or reason] and life."[172] Ortega disclaimed both vitalistic positions. In the first instance, he opposed biological theory because of its tendency to reduce "organic phenomena to physical-chemical principles,"[173] under the veiled argument of "vital force" and "entelechy." He argued that the aim of his vitalistic perspective was to emphasize the distinct features of organic phenomena, not to superimpose the principles of physical and chemical forces on it, thereby denying the specific qualities of biological forces. Ortega attempted therefore to make clear that his position was opposed to the "entelechy" of Driesch and Oskar Hertwig.[174] He characterized "philosophical vitalism" in three ways. In the first instance of "philosophical vitalism" Ortega argued against those thinkers who attempt to "convert philosophy into a simple chapter of biology," by referring to a theory of knowledge which is a biological process, particularly in the style of the "empirical-criticism" of Avenarius or in the manner of Mach and "beatific pragmatism."[175] The second point reveals where he did not fully accept a method of knowledge which restrains reason's capacity to provide us with knowledge and an understanding of life. Ortega rejected, here, Bergson's insight of "intuition" wherein the division which is made between "instinct" and "intellect" is fundamental in his (Bergson's) philosophy. This position "makes, then, a method of knowledge out of life [that is] opposite to the rational methods."[176] The third position would not subordinate reason to life and, while affirming the central focus of life in philosophy, would attest to the importance of the ability of reason to penetrate its meaning. This position came closest to that of Ortega. "My ideology," he said, "does not go against reason, in as much as it doesn't admit another method of theoretical knowledge other than itself: it [my ideology] goes only against rationalism."[177] In short, for Ortega, "reason and theory are synonymous."[178]

In "Neither Vitalism nor Rationalism," reiterating his reaction against rationalism of *The Theme,* Ortega was not only against the absolutist tendencies of rationalism with its manner of "legislating," and the idealistic inclination that "characterizes rationalism" as "the arbitrary supposition" which believes that "things—real or ideal—are comported as our ideas";[179] he was also rejecting the "universal," the "ought to be," and the intellectual construction of "ideals" of rationalism that eventually results in what he considered to be "anti-theoretical" and "anti-contemplative" and "anti-rational" mental activity.[180] Reason, for Ortega, on the other hand, provides the philosophical function of theoretical understanding. "To reason," he said, "is, then, to go from an object—thing or thought—to its principle."[181] The function of principle in reason would provide us with the theoretical understanding that philosophers strive to attain in that it "penetrates" the "object of analysis" and thus "makes it transparent."[182]

On attempting to distinguish reason from "vitalism" and "rationalism" Ortega took up this theme of the function of reason in thought that was continued in his article on Kant in 1929. In this essay on

"Pure Philosophy" (which had been presented as an addendum to his earlier essay of 1924, "Reflections on the Centenary of Kant"), Ortega stated, in accordance with Kant, that the function of the rational faculty is not solely the cognitive apprehension of objects. Rather it seeks to apprehend the "what" and the "essence" of objects; and the manifold manifestations of these conditions of the possibility of the experience of the objects of experience, in turn, will provide a possible content for conceptual thought.[183] Reason orders these objects in space and in time and furnishes the concepts by means of which we understand experience. This quest for the "whats" and the "essences" of objects led Ortega to ask the broader ontological question: "What is Being?"[184] The "traditional position of idealism"—"being is thinking"—he finds unacceptable. "Before Kant," he said, "this old formula means that there is no reality other than thought, but that thought is *in-itself*, that thought is the 'thing' in true existence."[185] The "'I' of Descartes" is a specific example for Ortega of the position of the "I" as *the* mode of being "*in-itself*" in reality.[186] Kant, in the *Critique of Pure Reason* and the *Critique of Practical Reason*, according to Ortega, outlined cogent arguments against such subjectivism. Consequently, Ortega explained, "being is not itself *in-itself*, but the relation to a theorizing subject; it is a [being] for-another and, first of all, a [being] *for-me*."[187] Though Kant contended that we cannot possess knowledge of "things-in-themselves," Ortega maintained that the "subjective idealism" of the "Neo-Kantian" revived "what is living and what is dead" in Kantianism.[188] In responding to the call "back to Kant," Ortega argued, the Neo-Kantians enhanced rather than impaired "subjective idealism" by straying past the boundaries and the limits of pure thought. "I emphasize that foundation of Kantian ideology," he said, "as the most alive today in it, because I believe that the theme of our time in philosophy coincides with it."[189]

By addressing himself to these issues, in a tone which he considered to be within the spirit of Kant's critical philosophy, Ortega wanted to draw a clear line between those realms of knowledge which are objective and those which are subjective. In this manner, he felt he had to go beyond the "theorizing subject" and, therefore, beyond the subjectivism of his Neo-Kantian contemporaries, to the basic standpoint of the subject itself as the "element of the life of a man."[190] For "this subject is human life or man as vital reason. The life of man is at its root occupying itself with the things of the world, not with itself."[191] "The *moi-même* of Descartes," he added, "that only realizes itself, is an abstraction. The *je ne suis qu'une chose qui pense* is false."[192] In this connection, Ortega contended, "My thought is a partial function of 'my life' that cannot be disintegrated from the rest

. . . because on existing I do not exist only as I, but 'I am a thing that is preoccupied with the others, like it or not.'" . . . I am not them [other things], they are not I (anti-idealism), but nor am I without them, without world, nor are they or are there them [other things] without me for whom their being and the possessing of them can have meaning (anti-realism)."[193] Thus, for Ortega, "*Cogito quia vivo* [I think because I live]."[194]

It is at this point in Ortega's career that a shift is observed in his philosophical concerns from the problem of thought and knowledge to the problem of being and knowledge. In his writings after 1929, Ortega's ontological analysis of man began to assume a more systematic form. When Ortega pursued the problem of being, at this time of his writings, it was not at all surprising that he would initiate this philosophical concern with several essays on the more general question: "What is philosophy?" Perhaps the question "What is philosophy?" was similar, for Ortega, to the questions "What is science?" and "What is knowledge?"

In *What Is Philosophy?* (essays assembled from a series of lectures presented in 1929), Ortega characterized philosophy as "knowledge of the Universe."[195] "By 'Universe,'" he said, "I understand formally 'everything there is' . . . . all there is."[196] The "truths" of philosophical knowledge, however, are different from the "scientific truths" of mathematics and the natural sciences.[197] One differentiating characteristic between philosophy and science, for him, is that science is organized factual knowledge based on the method of observation and experimentation, but the method of philosophy is not. Another distinguishing factor is that factual statements are, at best, only contingently true, for any matter of fact may have been other than it is, whereas philosophical statements are considered necessarily to be true.[198] Although philosophy has always existed traditionally somewhat ambiguously on the peripheries of science, the practical function of "pure mathematics" and the physical sciences[199] is not performed by philosophy, Ortega claimed, for "philosophy is not a science."[200]

Ever since the seventeenth century, according to Ortega, the empirical truths of the physical sciences were combined with the a priori truths of mathematics and, thereby, the science of physics possessed "two qualities" that were "admirable": namely, "its exactness, and the fact that it is governed by a double criterion of certitude, rational deduction on the one hand, and on the other, confirmation by the senses."[201] "Magnificent" though these "qualities" may be, he contended, they are not a sufficient justification "to ensure that there is no more perfect form of knowledge in the world, no higher type of truth than physical truth and the science of physics."[202]

This kind of absolutist positivistic approach[203] to our knowledge of reality was no more acceptable to him than the subjectivism of Descartes' "indubitable, . . . *cogito, ergo sum*" for "reason ought not to be proud" any more than the empirical statements of the natural sciences.[204] To Ortega "modern philosophy" began with Descartes, but he also accused the "father of modernity" of making knowledge of the world less certain after projecting subjective idealism into the realm of philosophy.[205]

Ortega proceeded along this line of thought in an effort to supercede the traditional Cartesian dualism of external reality and consciousness, of subject and object. "Thanks" to Kant's argument against this "highly problematic" duality, he proclaimed, it is established that "we take external reality and put it within the mind."[206] For "without objects, there is no subject";[207] "things are no more than the 'contents of consciousness.'"[208] Therefore, philosophy has to be freed both from "this system of idealism"[209] and from "the imperialism of physics."[210]

Philosophy differs from mathematics and the natural sciences not only in its methodological approach to knowledge, but also in its subject matter. Whenever one poses the question, "What is philosophy?" Ortega's reply is that "philosophy is knowledge of the Universe, or of everything there is in reality."[211] The subject matter of mathematics is "ideas" and that of the physical sciences, "things"; whereas the subject matter of philosophy is not only "ideas" and "things" but also, and more importantly, "human life."[212] Thus, he said:

> We suppose that the physicist—and by the same token the mathematician, or the historian, or the artist, or the politician —on observing the limits of his craft, may fall back deeply within himself. Then he finds that he himself is not only a physicist, but that physics is only one among an innumerable series of things which he does in his life as man. The physicist, at the bottom of his being, in his deepest stratum, turns out to be a man, he is a human life. And this human life has the inevitable condition of relating itself constantly to an integral world, to the Universe.[213]

The philosophy of human life, then, for Ortega comes closest to any knowledge of reality in that it acknowledges the limitation of our knowledge of physical things, and makes no assumptions of identical certitude, as is the case with Descartes. Rather, the philosopher of human life extends the notion of man as a being that thinks and perceives matter to include the "living fact" that man is a being-that-lives-in-the-world. In this sense, the philosophy of human life becomes the critique of scientific and other modes of thought. Thinking, for Ortega, is truly philosophical when it turns back on itself for critical scrutiny. When thought turns back and examines itself it perceives the fact that thought and reality must fit one another and, thereby, philosophy is no longer viewed by him as the direct study of thought and ideas but, rather, as the study of thought and ideas through the study of "being."[214]

"Thus, every theory of knowledge," he said, "would have been an ontology"; that is to say, "a doctrine concerned on the one hand with what being is, and on the other with what the thinking about it (a being or a particular thing) is, and then making a comparison between the two."[215] When philosophy centers on man, the "structural identity" of "being" and "thinking" is demonstrated. Within this notional frame of reference, Ortega aligned himself with Kant's position in the *Critique of Pure Reason:* " 'The conditions of the possibility of experience (read thought), *are the same* as the conditions of the possibility of the objects (read being or reality).' "[216] "Only in this manner," he claimed, "can one seriously attack the problem of knowledge. . . ."[217] Ortega proceeded beyond this Kantian position, however, to include a general philosophical anthropology with an ontological focus on "being" as his general criticism of the limits of human thought. For him, as already indicated, "I think because I live."

It is during this period that Ortega formulated, in a systematic fashion, his general philosophic standpoint—positing human life as the ultimate reality—which contains philosophy within history, in his book *En Torno a Galileo* (1933), by way of his theory of generations, and in his essay on *History as a System* (1935). The "concept of being" or "human life," for Ortega, "is the very root of philosophy," and, therefore "any reform of the idea of being means a radical reform in philosophy."[218] At this point, he abandoned the "biological organism" content of his earlier notion of "life" in *The Theme* to incorporate a concept of life—"the life of each one of us"—as a being-that-lives-in-the-world. "Biologists," he said, "use the word 'life' in order to designate the phenomena of organic beings . . . but . . . when we say we live, and talk about 'our life,' the life of every one of us, we give this word a meaning which is more immediate, broader and more decisive."[219] In this "broader" connection, Ortega's concept of human life comprised a dimension which was similar to the *Fundamentalontologie* of Heidegger's *Daseinsanalyse*. Ortega's analysis of human existence and human life characterized "I am I and my circumstances" as the interchangeable interaction of the "I" and "the world." That is, "I am always with myself . . . the world is always linked with me and my being is a being with the world."[220] Ortega wanted to liberate the "I" from the "internal prison" of "subjectivism" and proposed that we "save ourselves in the world," in "that vital horizon."[221] This sense of being as having been "thrown into" the "world"[222] further characterizees the "authentic reality"[223] of life as "finding oneself face to face with the world" and "inside the world."[224] To "escape from idealism," then, "life includes both the subject [the conscious self] and the world."[225] Living is "*finding oneself* in the world." Hence:

> Life always finds itself in certain circumstances, in an arrangement surrounding it—*circum*—filled with things and other people. One does not live in a world which is vague, except that the vital world is circumstance [the things and the people around one], it is this world, here and now.[226]

We have indicated that by the late 1920s and the early 1930s, the idea of human life gradually evolved as an explicit statement in Ortega's basic philosophic standpoint. It was during this time that he "became acquainted with Dilthey's works."[227] Ortega viewed Dilthey as being one of the "first discoverers" of "the new great Idea of life."[228] After the posthumous publication of Dilthey's *Gesammelte Schriften,* in 1928, and Ortega's subsequent "acquaintance" with Dilthey's philosophical work, we begin to witness the eventual unfolding of a general systematic statement of human life in the thought of Ortega. The position put forward here, therefore, is that in addition to the influences of historicism and phenomenology, Ortega also integrated existentialism into his general philosophical outlook. During this period of his intellectual development, Ortega incorporated the idea of human life into his fundamental philosophic point of view, and the discernible transition from "vital reason" to "historical reason" took place in his thought. That is, once human life was established as the basis of his philosophical standpoint, the terms "vital reason" and "historical reason" became interchangeable terms for Ortega. Though he spoke of a "parallelism" between the ideas of Dilthey and his own, during the period 1914 to 1929, and although it is true that he discussed the notion of "vital reason" prior to the early 1930s, there was no such discussion of "historical reason" in the manner in which one is familiar with its usage in his mature writings of the 1930s. After his *What Is Philosophy?* and his essay on Dilthey, in these writings, "life" and "reason" and "vital reason"—or "living reason"—and "historical reason" were fundamental concepts in the fusion of his systematic analysis of man, society, and history. So that, to acknowledge with Ortega, the thought of Dilthey does appear to have played an important role in the intellectual development of Ortega.

In 1933, Ortega acknowledged in his essay "Wilhelm Dilthey and the Idea of Life" the importance of Dilthey in the development of his thought. Ortega even ventured to designate Dilthey "the most important philosopher of the second half of the nineteenth century."[229] Through the influence of the basic idea of Dilthey's *Lebensphiloso-phie*, Ortega was able to link his ontological point of view with his existentialist and historicist viewpoints. A perspective within which a connection of common emphasis placed upon the actions and the creations of the individual, the facticity and the uniqueness of individual human existence, is perceptible. Through a connection of this sort, "the significance of life," as Dilthey said, "lies in its shaping and its development."[230] To describe the "unique quality of life," and, for Dilthey, "on the basis of life itself, types of behavior arise, such as perceiving evaluating and the setting of purposes, with countless nuances merging into each other. In the course of life they form systematic connections which embrace and determine all activity and development."[231] Changes in the circumstances of the individual contribute significantly toward developmental changes in the "life-relationship" of the "I."

> Thus the life peculiar to man shows distinctive characteristics in its individual aspect, such as relations, attitudes, conduct, the shaping of things and people and the suffering caused by them. On the stable basis from which the differentiated processes arise there is nothing which does not contain a vital relationship to the I. As everything is related to it the state of the I changes constantly according to the things and people around it. There is not a person or a thing which is only an object to me; for me it involves pressure or advancement, the goal of some striving or a restriction of my will, importance, demand for consideration, inner closeness or resistance, distance or strangeness. Through the life relationship, either transitory or permanent, these people and things bring me happiness, expand my existence or heighten my powers; or they confine the scope of my life, exercise pressure on me and drain my strength.[232]

Existentialism, in a variety of ways, is an outgrowth of *Lebensphiloso-phie* and phenomenology, and it seems that Ortega, with the assistance of the historicist viewpoint of the "unique individual" and of "human life" as the ultimate reality, may have pursued the path which had been directed by Heidegger.[233]

In the works of the 1930s, Ortega posited "human life" as the ultimate reality and, from this standpoint, connected the philosophic point of view of an historicist with that of existential phenomenology. The existentialist perspective of Ortega is very close to the *Fundamentalontologie* or *existentiale Analytik* in Heidegger's *Sein und Zeit*.[234] Ortega's notions of "life as a happening" and the insecurity of "human life" in the face of "death," his analysis of the ontological distinction between "human life" and "things," between "being" and "authentic being," are strikingly similar to ideas which had been formulated by Heidegger in 1927. In *What Is Philosophy?* he aligned his philosophical position with that of Heidegger and the "new philosophy" of "being," "existence," and "human life":

> These common words, finding oneself, world, occupying oneself, are now technical words in this new philosophy. One would be able to talk for a long time on each one of them, but I will limit myself to observe that this definition, "to live is to find oneself in a world," like all the principal ideas in these lectures, is already in my published work. It is important to me to observe this, especially, with regard to the idea of existence, for which I claim chronological priority. For that very reason I am pleased to acknowledge that the person who has gone deepest into the analysis of life is the new German philosopher, Martin Heidegger.
> . . . To live is to find oneself in the world. Heidegger, in a very recent work of genius, has made us take notice of all the enormous significance of these words.[235]

Ortega was quite sensitive to comments made on the affinities between his work and Heidegger's, which, in part, explains his efforts to trace the originality of his formulations to his *Meditations*. Apart from a general discussion in his *Idea of Principle in Leibnitz and the Evolution of Deductive Theory*[236] and an essay, "Martin Heidegger and the Language of the Philosophers,"[237] Ortega referred to Heidegger only in passing in a long footnote in his essay, "Goethe from Within" (published in 1932),[238] and in an article in the daily newspaper *El Sol* in 1931.[239] The thrust of his statements centered on the contention that his ontological notion of "I am I and my circumstances"—the crux of Ortega's philosophy of human life as the ultimate reality—had anticipated Heidegger's ontology and philosophy of existence in *Sein und Zeit* by thirteen years in his *Meditations*. As discussed previously, however, Ortega did not develop this position into a systematic philosophic standpoint before this stage of his intellectual progress. In August 1951, Ortega was invited to attend a conference, along with Heidegger, which was given by architects and scientists in Darmstadt to discuss "Man and Space." This brief meeting apparently was quite pleasant, as neither philosopher raised the sensitive issue of originality or of the similarities in their thought during the course of their private conversations.[240] Whatever the context in which this controversy over Ortega's intellectual indebtedness to Heidegger may have been initiated, it was during the decisive period of the 1930s when he turned to the systematic formulation of the philosophy of *Lebensphilosophie,* and it was also in this period that Ortega's explicit postulation of the notion "I am I and my circumstances," as "radical reality," reflected the influence of existential and phenomenological points of view in his philosophy of existence, man, and society.

Where Ortega's general ontological position does bear some similarities to Heidegger's *existentiale Analytik,* and his idea of human life some affinities with Dilthey's *Lebensphilosophie,* there are also some differences between these philosophies and Ortega's fundamental philosophical position. The important difference to point out is that Ortega proceeded beyond the distinctive positions of *Daseinsanalyse* and *Lebensanalyse* by incorporating the two concepts. For Ortega, that is, the "analysis of being" and the "analysis of human life" constituted, at once, the systematic analysis of the existence of man in his "lived-relations" and his "being-in-the-world."

In *En Torno a Galileo,* Ortega maintained in regard to his theory of generation that there, finally, was the opportunity to "expound my idea more thoroughly."[241] Apart from the very short shrift that he gave to the notion of generation in *Meditations*[242] and in *What Is Philosophy?,*[243] *The Theme* was his only major work that made a serious attempt to discuss it as a theory of distinct changes prior to *En Torno a Galileo.* In the latter work, Ortega denounced Wilhelm Pinder's criticism of his "few paragraphs" in *The Theme* that dealt with the concept of generation by claiming that Pinder "did not understand" those paragraphs "very well" as he (Ortega) "did not develop the thought sufficiently."[244] Ortega referred to the concept of the generation as "the most important conception in history"; we have already mentioned that it is presented in *The Theme* more as a concept of changes in our "biological physiognomy."

It is in his works *En Torno a Galileo,*[245] *History As a System,*[246] and *Man and People,*[247] written in 1933, 1934, and 1939 respectively, that Ortega launched forward the systematic formulation of these viewpoints. Ortega imbued the precepts of the critical philosophy of his earlier writings with the principles of his subsequent metaphysical philosophy. In these mature works his ontological distinction between "being" and "things," "human life" and "the physical body," and his description of the intersubjectivity of the "I" and "others" in the social world, combined with his theory of generations and the historicity of man and society, contributed toward broadening and advancing Ortega's general philosophical standpoint. Through a philosophical spectrum, Ortega's concept of generation—which he was quick to point out was different from the idea of generation which had been developed by Pinder[248]—is characterized as a social world in which the "circumstances" of the "I" and "others" are experiences in the vivid present and thereby as the social world through which the historical past is made accessible to the "I" and its "contemporaries." Ortega's theory of generations (formulated in *En Torno a Galileo*), and his ideas of "historical reason" and history as the "systematic science of the present" (presented in his *History As a System*), are connected with his ontological perspective of reality, man, and society (as postulated in *The Revolt of the Masses* and *Man and People*) into a general philosophy of man, society, and history. The substantive content of his general philosophical schema combined the diverse (but not necessarily incompatible) currents of existentialism, phenomenology, and historicism. Viewed in its broadest perspective, Ortega's philosophic focus shifted from a social theory analysis of "mass society" to *Lebensphilosophie* and then to an existentialist phenomenological philosophy of human reality, time, intersubjectivity, and history; all of which are systematized into a philosophy of man, society, and history. In *En Torno a Galileo,* the concept of the generation was put forward as a fundamental concept in history and as a method of understanding historical changes. Ortega's treatment of this concept in these works was increasingly coherent in analysis as he employed the concept of the generation in conjunction with his notion of the experience of human life and our perceptual experience of occurrences in time and in space. Human life is understood here as being "historical life."[249]

History As a System connected Ortega's theory of the generation with his notion of "vital" and "historical reason." The temporal dimensions of man and his "circumstances" (as manifested by the changes in his life) and the flow of time in history (in the form of generational changes in the historical process) were synthesized in this notion of "historical reason." To Ortega "life" and "reason" are interpenetrable and, as such, "reason" (or thought) as "human life" is historical.[250] Through this connection philosophy was identified with history, for he characterized human life as being both an historical reality and a philosophical reality. Where the ontological issue of the essence of man's being was postulated, philosophically, as consisting in living, historicity was formulated as that which constituted the basic ingredient of human reality. Hence, "vital reason," for Ortega, penetrates and delivers a basic understanding of the individual factors of man's being and reality, and "historical reason" synthesizes these individual factors into a systematic analysis of human existence and human life.

The crucial links in Ortega's "complete" systematic analysis of man, society, and history of the 1930s are to be found in his well-known work *The Revolt of the Masses*[251] and in *Man and People*. The connection between philosophy, history, and human reality was contained in Ortega's conception of social reality and, in this sense, *The Revolt of the Masses* is an important forerunner of his subsequent sociological analyses wherein his social categories are philosophical concepts and his ontological categories develop into social concepts. In this work, which was published in 1930, Ortega constructed an analysis of social reality based on his description of the intersubjectivity of individual interaction in "mass society." Ortega's description of a "mass society" in which the "creative select minorities" are pitted against the "masses" is elitist, antiegalitarian, and is a form of philosophical sociology through his analysis of social relations and human interaction. This viewpoint is somewhat similar to the *ressentiment* that was discussed by Scheler (and which, in turn, is similar to the *ressentiment* of Nietzsche, to whom, as to Bergson, Dilthey, and Husserl, Scheler's thought is indebted in various respects).[252] In *The Revolt of the Masses,* Ortega's analysis of human interaction is more a social than a philosophical analysis of reality. It is in *En Torno a Galileo, History As a System*, and *Man and People* that a somewhat systematic philosophy of man, society, and history, is perceptible, reflecting the influences of existentialism, historicism, and phenomenology, which supplemented and expanded the analysis of his social theory of "mass society" and "mass" versus "select man" in *The Revolt of the Masses*. In this conceptual frame, Ortega's "mass man" analysis, constituting social theory, related to his ontological analysis of human life as being-in-the-world. In his "Prologue for French," written in 1930 after *The Revolt of the Masses*, Ortega made a passing reference to his preparation of *Man and People* and to it as an important philosophical link between his earlier ideas of "mass-man" in *The Revolt of the Masses* and his later writings on man:

> It would be from this alone that one might hope, with some vague possibility, for the solution to the tremendous problem posed by the present masses.
>
> This essay does not attempt, even at a great distance, anything resembling this. As these last words make clear, it is only a first approximation of the problem of man of the present. In order to speak on the problem more seriously and profoundly one would have no alternative but to put on a diving

suit and descend to the farthest depth of man. This is the task that one must undertake, without pretensions, but with determination, and it is what I have attempted in my next book, to appear under the title *Man and People*.

Once we have taken into consideration this human type dominant today, and that I have called the mass-man, the more fruitful and dramatic questions arise. . . .[253]

Thus, in order to place *The Revolt of the Masses* in a broader perspective, it is essential to connect Ortega's later existentialist-phenomenological and historicist points of view with his social analysis of "mass man" and the "select minorities"; and through this connection it becomes evident that in addition to Husserl and Scheler, the influences (whether direct or indirect) of Dilthey and Heidegger are visible in Ortega's philosophical development.

In 1937, while he was preparing *Man and People,* Ortega mentioned in a letter to Ernst Curtius how anxious he was to complete the systematic exposition of his philosophy of man, society, and history:

In reality, my situation is vexatious; because it has been four years that objectivities ought to have been out of me, the two great volumes of thought which represent my two titles: *Man and People* and *Dawn of Historical Reason.* They are all a philosophic system that is boiling inside of me, the result of all my life and all that which is there—inside of me—ready in all its details.[254]

Ortega viewed his notion of society, as expounded in *Man and People* as "developing" he said, "my entire social doctrine."[255]

The posthumous publication of this work, however, was not the completed version of the conception of one ultimate "objective" of his theoretical perspective of the "state," "the law," "nation, ultranation," and "Humanity."[256] Ortega was overtaken by death before he was able to complete, in *Man and People,* what he had originally envisioned as a *"study of the general structure of human life."*[257] The work on *The Idea of Principle in Leibnitz* began in "the spring and early summer of 1947" and continued until the early 1950s.[258] The theme of the book,[259] a kind of "teleological-historical reflection" upon the origins of a critical scientific and a philosophical "way of thinking," was not completed and, thus, it cannot be regarded as a finished work.[260] In his lectures of 1948–49 on Toynbee's *Study of History,* he reiterated his "objective" of completing his conception of history that was to be subsumed by the title *Dawn of Historical Reason.*[261] Unfortunately, this work never appeared. Consequently, where Ortega did not fulfill the "objectivities" that he spoke of in his letter to Curtius, he did fulfill, in the 1930s, his earlier demand—conceived while a student at Marburg—for the systematization of his philosophical works, as, at this point in his intellectual development, a fundamental coherence in his philosophical thought had been established.

Ortega was a prolific writer: magazine and newspaper articles and essays of general cultural interest constituted the bulk of his writings. His philosophical works are not as seminal as those of his intellectual forebears, but they do make a contribution to the intellectual tradition from which his thought emerged in that he succeeded in fusing the philosophical perspectives of phenomenology, historicism, and existentialism into a systematic philosophy of man, society, and history. Had he been able to pursue further the central ideas in *Man and People,* in another planned book—particularly his idea, "study of the general structure of human life," and his concept of the intersubjectivity of the "I" and the "Others" in the social world—he might have placed his viewpoint of phenomenological-existential-historicism in a broader theoretical analysis of the social sciences; the essential foundation of such a point of view is visible in his philosophical writings.

During Ortega's lifetime, the intellectual current in Spain shifted more toward the mainstream of European thought. He was, in many ways, the primary thinker through whom European ideas were disseminated in Spain. "Philosophy," he said at one point, "is not only a function in the philosopher's own life, but also a doctrine he brings before the public."[262] In this sense, in as much as Ortega's writings reflected a marked interest in cultural matters and his efforts toward reaching a wide (and often "select") audience, we may view Ortega as having been a twentieth-century *philosophe*. On the other hand, in that he developed a systematic explanation of man and the world, Ortega was definitely a philosopher in the traditional European sense of the word.

Some commentators[263] characterize Ortega's philosophy as formulating the viewpoints of "objectivism," "perspectivism," "ratio-vitalism," and, occasionally, "existentialism." If we place Ortega in the context of the intellectual tradition in which he developed, we find that while the existentialist perspective explicitly exists in his philosophical outlook, the viewpoints of "objectivism," "perspectivism," and "ratio-vitalism" do not convey, nor do they sharpen focus on, the fundamental issues in his philosophical thought. Triangulating his thought in its broader European intellectual context, we find, rather, that his philosophy—as a systematic explanation of real-

ity, man, society, and history—contains the viewpoints of existentialism, historicism, and phenomenology. Within the general position of
these standpoints, Ortega maintained that his philosophical attitude
was a reaction to the tradition of rationalism and to the positivistic
tradition of the natural sciences. To Ortega the abstract concepts of
the rationalistic system of idealism and the "natural truths" offered
by the natural sciences were inadequate for rendering the concrete
realities of man, society, and history. The multiple manifestations of
the experiences an individual and collective individuals undergo could
not be comprehended, according to him, within a rational or a meta-
scientific system. In Ortega's view, man is the actor who actively
engages in the "circumstances" of his drama and thereby is not a
spectator who looks out on the drama of the historical process. Metaphysical systems that attempt to view the individual in a detached
manner as being either merely a physical organism or as an organism
whose essence reflects the primacy of mind over matter, he argued, fail
to grasp the unsystematic variety of human experience and its historical
expression.

In this sense, then, the abstract logic of rationalism and the empirical logic of the natural sciences are much too concerned with the lawful and general principles of reality, whereas the philosophy of human
life, social reality, and history concerns itself with the individual, the
"unique." The knowability of human existence and historical forms,
therefore, is not constituted by the formulation of general laws or
principles; rather, it consists in the comprehensive perception of the
variety of the particular manifestations of these historical forms of human existence. This kind of philosophy of life, social reality, and history—which is aimed toward an understanding of the very essence of
man—for Ortega is a form of knowledge, because its subject matter
embodies human life in its totality and in its variation. In so far as
this point of view focuses on the "unique" individual and his "circumstances," Ortega's philosophical attitude appears to have closer affinities to the "cultural" or "human sciences" than to the natural sciences
or to the logic of rationalism.

It is thus to Ortega's philosophy of human life that we now must
turn.

Chapter II

Ortega's Philosophy of Human Life: The Historicity of Human Reality

The general synthetic function of systematic philosophies of history—both rationalistic and positivistic—as philosophies of reality and as unifying principles mediating between epistemology and social and political philosophy, has been to provide a universal principle of coherence for reality, man, and society. The function served by these systematic principles of coherence was to link the fundamental principles of reality with the fundamental characteristics of human society, so that men may guide their behavior by a general principle that is accessible to all and, thus, may make the way they relate to one another meaningful by aligning them with the ultimate "workings of nature." This coherence for man and society has entailed: first, a unitary explanation of reality, so that it may yield general principles; secondly, an absolute basis for characterizing human society so that the general principles of reality may be relevant to the variation in which men relate to one another; and finally, a necessary linkage between these general principles of reality and this absolute basis of human behavior. In short, these systematic philosophies of reality and history involved a unity embodying an overall plan of "nature" and human society.

In view of this function, Ortega's rejection of systematic explanations of reality, history, and society was, in effect, the dissolution of the coherence provided by these universal points of view. For by breaking up reality into the "natural sciences" and the "human societies," or the natural and the historical, Ortega, emphasizing the historical and the societal as the appropriate associative realms toward understanding human life, dissolved the crucial link of the fundamental principles of reality with the general characteristics of human society as formulated by the positivistic and the rationalistic systematic points of view. The "natural sciences," for him, were as inadequate for rendering the concrete nature of reality as the conceptual approach. Whether the philosophical system was rational or scientific was irrelevant—it was still a system—and systems, he contended, are abstract and static and this makes them the very antithesis of "human life." In this way, Ortega dissociated the faculty of apprehending the "living experience" from the faculty of reason as allegedly the only faculty producing valid knowledge of reality. The faculty of reason, for him, which had as its objects general ideas beyond particular phenomena, registered no ascertainable reality and produced no valid truths about the most fundamental reality—"human life." Ortega launched out against the primacy attached to what he calls "the faith in reason" and singled out Descartes, with his "clear and distinct ideas," as primarily responsible for the idealists' assertion that the attainment of uniformity lay in grasping the rational principles which held the world together.[1]

In his *Discourse on Method*,[2] Descartes prescribed the deductive method as the necessary approach in seeking true knowledge. To accomplish truth, one has to set out with a group of propositions or self-evident principles. With these principles as a point of departure, Descartes began with what he believed to be the most relatively simple, clear, intuitively known, self-evident proposition—the well-known *"cogito, ergo sum"*—and proceeded deductively to other more complex but equally certain propositions. Hence true knowledge is one that begins from the very self-evident first principles, from which all the rest are deduced. By doubting all things of reality,[3] Descartes concluded that there was one thing whose reality might not be doubted, namely: the fact that he existed. His contention was that he was unable to doubt his own existence, because doubt itself would be impossible if he did not exist. For to doubt involves thinking, and to think means to be.[4] From this subjective epistemological standpoint of recognizing the existence of the "self" as indubitable, the Cartesian universe extends to comprise a physical world as well. The physical world is mirrored by the clear and distinct ideas within the "cogito," and, hence, to understand the construction and operation of the reality of this world, one needs only to consult the ideas within oneself.

By extending this Cartesian rationalism from the realm of nature to history, Ortega argued, nineteenth-century idealism had affirmed Descartes' general principle of mind over matter and resulted in man being locked up in his own ego under the false assumption that reason possessed the key to cognizable reality. "For philosophical idealism since Descartes," he said, "man is reduced to *une chose qui pense, res cogitans*, thought or ideas. The world has no reality of its own, it is only an ideated world."[5] Ortega argued further: "To this man [Des-

cartes] there is no problem that cannot be solved. He assures us that
in the universe there are no *arcana*, no unconquerable secrets before
which humanity must stop itself in defenseless terror. . . . Finally,
man is going to know the truth about everything."[6] Ortega was not
convinced of Descartes' conclusions and absolute assertions about
the ability of the faculty of reason to reveal any valid truths of
reality. This revolt against reason by Ortega does not suggest that he
saw only negative factors in the resurgence of reason in the seventeenth century. For, during the Middle Ages, reason was something
like a paradise lost and, through Descartes, became paradise regained.
The seventeenth century ushered in a new era when sorely needed and
"man, having fallen," he said, "is born again."[7] Rather, the main
thrust of Ortega's argument seems to have been directed against
Descartes' faith in the primacy of reason to the point that Descartes
attempted to generalize natural truths primarily on the basis of rational, abstract concepts:

> The world of reality and the world of thought are each—
> accordingly—two cosmoses that correspond to one another;
> each compact and continuous, in which nothing is abrupt,
> isolated, or inaccessible, but rather such that from any of its
> points we may, without intermission and without leaping,
> pass to all other points and contemplate the whole. Man,
> then, with his reason may submerge himself tranquilly into
> the abysmal depths of the Universe, certain of extracting
> from the remotest problem, from the closest enigma, the
> essence of truth. . . . [8]

Such oversureness, as he saw it, is without foundation. Rationalism,
for Ortega, which is based on abstract reason, tries to save truth but,
in turn, renounces the most fundamental principle of reality—"life."
Convinced that truth is absolute and unchanging, the rationalists, he
explained, fail to grasp reality.[9] "Pure reason has, then," he said, "to
surrender its authority to 'vital reason.'"[10] "Vital reason" serves as a
practical function in life for Ortega, in that it is dynamic and relativistic, and, if we wish to ascertain reality and natural truths, is to
be substituted for "pure," abstract reason. Thus, natural truths are,
for him, relative in that they are viewed from the perspective of each
individual human life.

Ortega also relegated the natural sciences to the practical level as a
function of life. For, in attempting to grasp reality, he argued, the
natural scientists deal with general laws and thus completely bypass
particular phenomena. Such notions as "laws of nature," "uniformity,"
and "physical reason" are the contributing factors for their failure to

see the concrete individual fact of human life. In confronting reality
Ortega placed the natural sciences aside, in an attempt to understand
the fundamental features of reality and to get at an understanding of
"things," in a manner similar to Kant and Husserl. If the particularity
of reality was to be understood, according to this point of view, then
the general principles of the natural sciences could not be applied to
understand the varieties in the human realm. "Physical science," he
maintained, "can throw no clear light on the human element. Very
well! This means simply that we must shake ourselves free, radically
free, from the physical, natural, approach to the human element. . . .
Man cannot wait any longer. He demands that science illuminate for
him the problems of humanity."[11] The natural sciences, as empirical
disciplines, deal with the existence of the world of objects which are
accessible to us through sensory perception. This aspect of empirical
science only presents us with the positivistic perspective of knowledge.
To explain reality, the natural sciences, in their concern with the existence of objects in natural phenomena, aim at discovering the general
concepts or the natural laws under which these objects may be subsumed. In order to understand the relationship between human life
and reality, therefore, man must liberate himself from what Ortega
called "the terrorism of the laboratory." To avert compounding the
ontological distinction he felt should be made between a philosophy
of physical nature and a philosophy of human nature, Ortega claimed
that "man has no nature." Man must free himself from the shackles of
the natural scientists, he explained, for they are too involved with
general, abstract "concepts of nature" and "man has no nature."[12]
In this sense, the generalized interpretations of the natural scientists
(as was the case with the rationalists), according to Ortega, exclude
the most essential element of reality—the life of man.

Although Ortega has denaturalized man, a question still remains
for us and that is: if man has no nature, then what does he have?
"Man has history," is his reply.[13] "Man lives," he says, and, as a "living being," man relates to other "living beings" so that vital, operative
factors are in motion—the "living experience of man."[14] Having borne
out Ortega's departure from the universal perspective of reality we
find that his dictum, "man in a word has no nature; what he has is
. . . history," completes the alienation of man from nature and nature
from man.[15] History, for Ortega, "sensu stricto" constitutes "human
history."[16] This abrupt separation of man and nature, in addition to
his rejection of rational concepts as producing any valid knowledge
of reality, reaffirms Ortega's denial of universal, fundamental principles of reality and, thus, aligns him on the humanistic side of the
"natural sciences—human sciences" dichotomy.

Reality, for him, consists in the individual fact of life and history, as the manifestation of living individuals and human society, brings into view this fundamental fact.[17] Ortega's concept of "human life" as the fundamental principle of reality is somewhat similar to Dilthey's *Lebensphilosophie* and to the *Lebenswelt* of Husserl.[18] By the term "life," Ortega means the "life of each one of us."[19] Hence, the basic reality that is human life is the life of an individual together with the lives of other individuals. "I am I and my circumstances" and this "radical reality," as he conceived it, is the human predicament of modern man.[20] What does Ortega mean when he speaks of the "I"? Does he mean that man first of all exists and then, in addition, he is or acquires something called "I"? No, he means that man is "I," myself, I am this man and that this being is mine.[21] "Radical reality" refers to the sense of being the "root" or the "basic" reality. That is to say, Ortega took the point of view that everything that in any sense may be said to take part in reality must appear within the life of the individual—whether it is my life, his life, or your life.[22] As he says:

> . . . we must go back to an order of ultimate reality, to an order or area of reality which, for being radical [of the root] does not allow any other reality underneath it, rather, is to be the basic reality on which all others must by necessity appear. This radical reality . . . is our life, human life. Whenever I speak of "human life," unless I make a special exception, you must avoid thinking of someone else's life; each one of you should refer it to your own life and try to make that present to you . . . but you must always understand that by this expression I refer to the life of each individual and not to the life of other individuals nor to a supposed plural and common life. What we call "the life of others"—the life of one's friend, of one's sweetheart—is already something that appears in the scenario that is *my life*, the life of each one, and, therefore, supposes that life.[23]

The life of the individual, then, has to be the concrete identity it is rather than some abstract or imaginary being. We find that while Ortega has split man off from nature, he has tried, nonetheless, to understand human life in terms of concrete physical realities. Through his discussion of man's relation to external reality (man's "circumstances") we discover that man, by dint of his unique individuality, has an essence that is peculiarly his own. The result is that man is not only split off from nature but is also separated from the concrete physical objects of nature (i.e., plants, animals, stones, etc.). In this connection Ortega's distinction between man and nature, "human life," and "things," is analogous to similar assertions made by Heidegger in *Sein und Zeit*. The basic ontological difference between man and "things" (the term used by Ortega to describe the physical entities of reality) is established in the fact that "things" *exist* and man *lives*. Ortega agreed with the existentialist viewpoint that the existence and the essence of entities are interrelated in reality, although he selected to establish his own basic distinction between this essential relationship of existent entities and his notion that "things" *exist* and man *lives*.[24] Ortega was in accord with the standpoint that the essence of an object in reality lies in its existence and contributes to this position the view that the essence of the being of man lies in the vital dimensions of his life. The expressions "to exist" and "existence," for him, are inadequate in describing man's mode of being. "Man," he explained, "who is always 'I'—the I that each of us is—is the only being that does not exist, but *lives* or is alive. Precisely all the other things that are not man, not 'I,' are the things that *exist*, because they appear, arise, spring up, resist me, assert themselves in the ambit that is my life."[25] Hence, to *exist* and to *live* are the primary ways through which both the concrete physical objects of phenomena and man partake in reality, thereby drawing the distinction between the life of man and the existent realities of physical objects and plants that are not human.

This point of view bears a certain resemblance to the postulate that an act is directed toward an object. If all human acts are directed toward some object then all acts, according to Ortega, emanate from something—namely, the individual "ego." "My action toward the object," he said, "is what I call capturing it, conceiving it, comprehending it."[26] A real "thing" like a stone, for him, is such that it is essentially hidden to itself. In this way, the stone is necessarily indifferent to its own being, or, more precisely, it is in such a way that it is incapable of existence without that "radical reality," human life. This "radical reality," as pointed out earlier, consists in being the "basic" or the "root" of all other realities and is not to be taken to suggest some "transcendent" reality. The world of reality, for Ortega, is constituted by each one of us in the "transcendental" nature of all our acts. In this sense "radical reality," which has an immanent "transcendental" manifestation in reality, is to be differentiated from the term "transcendent." This distinction between "transcendent" and "transcendental" goes back to Kant and recurs in the thought of Husserl, Heidegger, Sartre, and Merleau-Ponty, as well as in the thought of Ortega. "The word 'transcendental,'" according to Kant in *Prolegomena to any Future Metaphysics*, "does not signify something passing beyond all experience but something that indeed precedes it a priori, but that is intended simply to make knowledge of experience possible. If these conceptions overstep experience, their employment is termed 'transcendent,' which must be distinguished from the immanent use, that is, use restricted to experience."[27] "On calling it [human life] 'radical reality,'" Ortega said, "I do not mean that it is the only reality, nor even that it is the highest, most respectable or most sublime or supreme reality, but simply that it is the root of all other radical realities in the sense that they—any of them—in order to be reality to us must somehow make themselves present or, at least, announce themselves, within the shaken boundaries of our human life."[28]

Man, thus, lives in an actively disclosing way. The disclosure concerns first and foremost man himself. It is his own being that man basically understands. This understanding, for Ortega, does not belong to the common life of man in general, rather it belongs to each unique individual.[29] For it is only within his own factual existence that man can fathom: "I am I and my circumstances." This individuation of man's being is that which makes man what he is. If man's "circumstances," for Ortega, connote any situation toward which an act may be directed by the "I," then it serves, for the most part, as a condition rather than as a denial of man's freedom of action. That is to say, once it is established that freedom entails choice, then a choice must be made with respect to the variety of possibilities which arise out of the "circumstances" of man. To create his destiny so that he may be "the novelist of himself," Ortega maintained, man "must choose among these possibilities."[30] "Therefore," he said, "I am free. But, understand it well, I am free *by coercion*, whether I want to be or not."[31] The conditions of freedom evolve within given alternatives and freedom of action thereby results in the ability to choose and act under whatever confronting "circumstances" may arise. Thus, for Ortega, how a man is himself is very much determined by the way in which he allows his being to be his. Man has not freely chosen his "circumstances"; nevertheless, he can freely take over his being as his own responsibility and allow it to disclose itself as uniquely his. "Man's destiny, then," he said, "is primarily action. We do not live to think, on the contrary: we think in order that we may succeed in surviving."[32] For once given his life, man's being or essence becomes an ever-changing reality. As his essence is characterized in conjunction with the conditions of his "circumstances," for Ortega, individual man is placed into and is delivered over to the being which is his and which he has to be. In this way, the burden of action and making decisions is placed onto man as the very essence of his being is an ever-changing reality, in the making, and his ability to be *this* or *that* being is contingent upon his actions and thus conveys how man, for Ortega, is basically different from animals and stones:

> This life that is given to us is given to us empty, and man has to go on filling it for himself, occupying it. Such is our occupation. This is not the case with the stone, the plant, the animal. Their being is given already to them predetermined and resolute. The stone, when it begins to be, not only its existence is given to it, but its behavior is also determined for it beforehand—namely, to be heavy, to gravitate toward the earth's center. Similarly, the animal is given its repertory, moves, without intervention on its part, governed by its instincts. But man is given the necessity of having to be doing something always, upon pain of succumbing, yet what he has to do is not present to him from the outset and once and for all. Because the most strange and most confounding thing about this circumstance or world in which we have to live consists in the fact that it always presents to us, within its inexorable circle or horizon, a variety of possibilities for our action, a variety in the face of which we are obliged to choose and, therefore, to exercise our freedom. The circumstance—I repeat—the here and now within which we are inexorably inscribed and imprisoned, does not at each moment impose on us a single act or activity but various possible acts or activities and cruelly leaves us to our own initiative and inspiration, hence to our own responsibility.[33]

Existentialist philosophers are noted for their emphasis on freedom of action and the necessity for man to choose what he is to be; it is apparent, from the above statement, that Ortega also comes out of this intellectual tradition. This being the case, the essence of man's being takes on a dual characteristic in Ortega's philosophy of human life, the differentiation between the internal trait of man—the "I"—and its external manifestation within the environment of "things." He views the "I" both as constituting and as being constituted by the tangible reality of the world. Life as the confrontation of the "I" with its environment—an environment in which there are various possibilities—places man outside himself. As we saw, "possibility" connotes, for Ortega, that which is potential actuality (from the viewpoint of man's "circumstances"). From this point of view of the circumstantiality of life, taking into account the fact that the "I," as the basic reality, is not sufficient unto itself, the realization of this factor of life spurs man into action and thereby confronts him with external reality.[34] Man not only is a being-that-lives but, more precisely, is a being-that-lives-in-the-world. Hence, for Ortega, man does not look out upon an external world from the isolation of his ego, for his "circumstances" contribute in defining his being as much as the "I."[35] "No," he said, "life is not to be only my mind, my ideas; it is the very contrary . . . to *live* means having to be outside of myself, in the absolute outside which is the circumstance or world: it is having, like it or not, constantly and incessantly to confront and clash with whatever makes up that world; minerals, plants, animals, other men. There is no getting out of it."[36] Thus, continual confrontation with his "circumstances" is the essential factor that prevents man from being locked in his ego. Man must act in life and, under such conditions, the living experience is a "task" and man is what the potential possibilities of his finite being exhibit him to be.

The essential finitude of man is experienced at the very heart of life itself. "Life is anguish," he remarked, "and enthusiasm and delight and bitterness and innumerable things."[37] At a certain point during his living experience, man, for Ortega, may plunge into the mood of anxiety—as if he were "between the sword and the wall"—when the black void of human life (death) rears its frightful head. "Death," he said, "is certain, there is no escaping it! Could there be less choice?"[38] Like Heidegger, Ortega viewed the reality and the fact of death as essential in revealing the very essence and contingency of man's being. For, in the face of "possible death," to experience life as being also implies an awareness of the possibility of life as not being. The acceptance of death, therefore, as a possible here-and-now discloses the radical—basic—finitude of human life.[39]

The perceptible factual occurrence of death also characterizes human life as an occurrence of time as well as reality. As man becomes aware of the reality of death, through experience, his finiteness discloses itself essentially in time:

> Our vital knowledge of other men and of ourselves is an open knowledge that is never stable. . . . Our vital knowledge is open, floating because the theme of this knowledge, life, Man, is already in itself a being ever open to new possibilities. Our past undoubtedly weighs on us; it inclines us to be more this than that in the future, but it does not chain us nor drag us. . . . Life is change; it is at every new moment becoming something distinct from what it was, therefore, it never becomes definitely *itself*. Only death, by preventing any new change, changes man into the definitive and immutable him-

self . . . from the moment we begin to be, death may inter-
vene into the very substance of our life, collaborate in it,
compress and densify it, may make it urgency, imminence
and the need of doing our best at every instant.[40]

It may be said, then, that time is in man, for the events in men's
lives are related by their position in time. "I am I and my circumstances," as the starting-point of the human condition, also expresses
the fact that the living experience of the individual is something that
takes place temporally as well as in spatial reality. What does "I am I
and my circumstances" imply, then, in this sense? If we consider
Ortega's emphasis on man as a being-that-lives-in-the-world, it seems
to suggest something like a purpose, an end. Ortega, however, did not
have a specific end in view. "I am I . . . " is not to suggest a temporality transcending the concrete experience of life. On the contrary, life
"is not cosmic time," he said, "which is imaginary and therefore infinite, but limited time, time which comes to an end, time which is
the true and irreparable time."[41] The here-and-now of the individual
is his primary concern. Thus, in his circumstances, man is earth-bound,
time-bound, and is a radically finite being.

As the temporality of man is very much a part of the here-and-now,
man's being-in-the-making, for Ortega, is a "happening" toward the
future. The future is not-here-yet and the past is no-longer-here and
these two features—the not-here-yet and the no-longer-here—tend to
permeate the very center of man's being as their positions are related
to one another in time. As death relates to man's internal finitude,
the past and present relate to his finitude in its external, temporal
manifestation. The present—the here-and-now—is understood to be
that moment during which the past and future are divided.[42] The life
of the present moment—when "some men are born and when some
men die"—in its very essence "is boxed in," Ortega said, "between
other lives which came before or which are to come after. . . ."[43] As
all human acts are considered to be directed toward some object,
Ortega viewed the future as the more important aspect of temporality because it is the "open area" toward which man directs himself
and in which man may manifest his own being.[44] Man directs himself
toward the future and, acting thus, takes upon himself the inheritance
of the past and thereby orients himself to his actual and present predicament. In short, the present originates from the past so as to engender the future.

Ortega's schematization of the past, present, and future is sustained
in the unity of a temporality that is peculiar in the experience of the
vital dimensions of man. For through the living experience, "man goes

on being and un-being." To both go-on-being and not-being means, for Ortega, to go through the experience of living.[45] The temporal experience of living hence is not structured in a one-dimensional progression. Rather, as a continual process of being and not-being, it has to be viewed from the three-dimensional perspective of past, present, and future. Man reflects upon the past as he is continually confronted with the situation of having to make conscious decisions with respect to the present and the future. As we have seen, life, death, free choice, and finiteness dwell together in the living experiences of men. Such precarious possibilities have the potential for presenting man with alarming experiences and, for this reason, make life "a task" or—to use Ortega's more dynamic phrase—"make it a drama." Having drawn upon a Shakespearean metaphor, Ortega viewed the whole world as a stage (the "circumstances"), and all the men of this world are its actors; each man has his entrance ("some men are born") and his exit (and others "who die"). But, Ortega argues, the expression "life is a drama" is not simply a metaphor. It is an implicit process within the dynamic reality of man, whose character and essence is basically different from the existence of "things." The essential feature of the reality of life "is not like the reality of this table," he explained,

> which consists merely in being here, but is made up of the fact that each one must go on doing for himself, moment after moment, in a perpetual tension of affliction and hardship, without ever having complete security within himself. Is not this the very definition of drama? Drama is not a thing which is there—it is not in any real sense a thing, a static being—but drama happens, it occurs—that is, it is the happening of something to someone, it is that which is happening to the protagonist while it is going on.[46]

We do not have to look too closely to discern that Ortega's notion of life as a "happening" is similar to the "*Geschehen*" of Heidegger's "Dasein." For the specific mode of motion of "Dasein," for Heidegger, in its "Existence" is its *Geschehen*. However that may be, life as a "happening" is an essential addition to Ortega's vocabulary as it embodies the central focus of his philosophy of life. For this process of happening, which describes man's essence (a being that goes-on-being) as a "drama," also defines his "authentic" being as he veers toward the potentialities of the future from the point of view of the here-and-now.[47] Man's choice and "destiny," then, are contemporaneous—embedded in the here-and-now. Accordingly, the contemporaneity of man presupposes the authentic temporality of man:

> The past is the moment of identity in man, the inexorable
> and fatal. But, for the same reason, if man's only *Eleatic*
> being is what he has been, this means that his authentic
> being, what, in effect, he is—and not merely "has been"—is
> distinct from the past, and consists precisely and formally in
> "being what one has not been," in *non-Eleatic* being. And
> since the term "being" is occupied irresistably by its tradi-
> tional static signification, one should agree to liberate oneself
> of it. Man is not, save that he "goes on being" this and that.[48]

"Authentic being," thus understood, has its essential weight not solely in the past, nor in the future, but in man's here-and-now—the present in its reflective connection with the past. Hence, as an "authentic
being" man is as contemporary as he is historical, and thereby the
historicity of man makes explicit the temporal manifestations of his
vital dimensions.

In this way, the temporality of man reveals itself as the subjective
structure of life—the "I" that goes-on-being—at the same time that
life's objective structure makes its appearance through history (for
"man has history"). Through the "I" and its "circumstances," Ortega
balanced off the principle of individual variety with his philosophy of
human life. However, by considering man to be an historical being
occasioned by his temporality, Ortega began to pursue a line of
thought that would eventually take him to the standpoint of establishing a principle of coherence for the realities of man, society, and history; this theme would be borne out through Ortega's philosophy of
human society and his theory of generations. For life, as the process
of happening and the temporality of man, makes implicit the assumption that "man goes on being" and thus has a discernible principle of
coherence. By way of his temporality—which involves his relations to
past, present, and future—man's very essence is historical. Temporality is to time as historicity is to history and both meet in man.

Chapter III

The Phenomenological Dimensions of Man and the Social World

Once human life is established as the fundamental standpoint of reality, for Ortega, "we are *ipso facto* given two terms or factors that are equally primary and, moreover, inseparable: Man who lives, and the circumstance or world in which man lives."[1] As already indicated, everything which in any sense may be taken as partaking in reality, for Ortega, must appear within the life of the individual. The basic distinction between man and "things" in reality is established by him in the fact that "things" *exist* and man *lives*. We also find that "things" are not the only physical entities in reality which are "situated in relation to me" and which must "arise, spring up, resist me [and] affirm themselves in the ambit which is my life."[2] For Ortega, "man lives" and, as a "living being," relates to "the other living beings." "All realities," for him, "must in some way make themselves present, or at least announce themselves within the shaken boundaries of our human life."[3] Hence, the basic reality of human life is constituted by associating the life of an individual with the lives of other individuals as well as situations that pertain to the confrontation of the individual with the existent realities of physical objects. In other words, "I am I and my circumstances," as a philosophical standpoint, is expanded to include the other "I's" and their "circumstances" as well as the empirical realm of "things."

At this point of our analysis, we have discussed human reality from the viewpoint of the "I" and its "circumstances." In accordance with this viewpoint, man—as a being-that-lives-in-the-world—does not perceive the world from the isolation of his ego, for the very essence of his being is to live in an actively disclosing manner. Being-in-the-world, for Ortega, we find, has a dual characteristic: as it relates to "I am I," being-in-the-world functions as being-for-itself; as it relates to "my circumstances," being-in-the-world functions as being-for-and-with-others. "Our world," he said, "the world of each one of us, is not a *totum revolutum*, but is organized in 'pragmatic fields.' Each thing belongs to one or some of these fields, in which it articulates its *being-for* with that of others, and so on successively."[4] The philosophical standpoint of "I am I and my circumstances" makes implicit for the essence of the individual, then, both the functions of being-for-itself and being-for-and-with-others. Within the framework of the former, it is his own being that man basically understands; in the circumstance of the latter, the confrontation of the "I" with "others" places man outside himself. Like Kant and Husserl, Ortega posited the fact that "all men live in one and the same world." "This is the attitude that we may call," he said, "the natural, normal, and everyday attitude in which we live; and, because of it, because of *living with* others in a presumed world—hence *our* world—our living is *co-living, living together*."[5]

For Ortega, as we saw, all human acts—which emanate from the individual "ego"—are directed toward some object. Like Kant, he maintained that there is no object of reality qua reality which is beyond our experience. The world (the "radical reality" of the "I"), for him, is a visible, tangible, empirical world, but everyone is not able to perceive it (i.e., those in the state of blindness). In spite of the facts that most individuals do have vision and that the "radical reality" of the "I" is constituted as being an empirical reality, everyone, according to Ortega, still is unable to discern all of the qualities of an object. In such cases, for Ortega, a basic understanding of the limitations of our knowledge of reality is the most that we can strive toward, and this kind of approach is the route taken by his analysis of the "I" and its physical structure. The issue of bodyness, for him, and its association with consciousness is often obscured by the fact that although the body is a physical structure with clearly delineated features, the consciousness process of the "I" is instead the consequence of an inner reflective process that is not easily discernible from without. For if the individual, after having grasped the internal essence of his being and consciousness, attempts to unite this very consciousness in the full sense of its inwardness with a physical structure which is composed of biological, physical, and chemical properties, then the individual will, according to Ortega, certainly encounter a great number of difficulties in understanding the whole nature of his being. These difficulties, Ortega argued, usually stem from the fact that the "I" attempts to connect its consciousness with its own body rather than with the body of "others" first. The "I," as a living being, would find it exceedingly difficult to dissect and examine the physical and chemical properties of its own brain. Hence, the dissected organs of other men are essential for a basic understanding of the nature of man, and the "I," after having examined and studied the anatomy of the "other," is cognizant of the fact that its body is similar to the bodies of other "I's."

In this connection, as there is an objective and subjective structure of the life of the individual—by way of the "I" that goes-on-being-in-the-world—the subjective consciousness of the "I" also is constituted by an internal and an external dimension. The internal dimension of the individual is composed of the intuitive, reflective, consciousness process of the mind, whereas the external dimension is made up of the physical characteristics of the individual—namely, man's body. "Two things," he said, "are always present at once and inseparably: the body that we touch, and our body with which we touch it. It is, then, a relation not between a phantom and ourselves, as in pure vision, but between a foreign body and our own body . . . we become aware that our environment, or the patent world, is composed, above all and fundamentally, of presences, of things that are bodies. And they are so because they come into contact with the closest thing to man that exists, to the I that is each of us—namely: his body. Our body brings it about that all other bodies are bodies and that the world is a body."[6] The ontological perspective of the human body, for Ortega, is the vital manifestation of man's spatial-temporal dimensions in human interactions. The body-of-man is part and parcel of the here-and-now that makes the "circumstance" of the "I" earthbound, time-bound, and radically finite:

> Man is, then, above all, someone who is in a body and who in this sense—but please note, only in this sense—is only his body. And this simple but irremediable fact is going to determine the concrete structure of our world and, with it, of our life and destiny. Man finds himself shut up in his body for life. . . . The body in which I live infused, shut up, inexorably makes me a spatial person. It puts me in a place and excludes me from all other places. It does not permit me to be ubiquitous. At each moment it fastens me to one place like a nail and exiles me from everything else. Everything else, that is, the other things in the world, are in other places, and I can only see them, hear them, and sometimes touch them from where I am. Where I am, we call *here*. . . .
>
> I can change my place, but whatever place it may be, it will be my "here." Apparently *here* and I, I and *here*, are inseparable for life. And since the world, with all the things in it, must *be for me* from "here," it automatically changes into a

perspective—that is, its things are near to or far from *here*, to right or left of *here*, above or below *here*.[7]

The "radical reality" of the "I" of the individual is rooted in the "here" of his body and the "now" of his present, and the finitude of his here-and-now is the spatial-temporal dimension in which his attention is focused on the essence of the "radical reality" of his life. This being the case, man is unable to grasp completely the essence of his being solely from the parochial perspective of the existent reality of his own body. Man is capable of understanding the internal features of his being through consciousness, according to Ortega, but cannot fully apprehend the physical nature of his body, as it is difficult for any individual to dissect and examine the anatomic features of himself.[8] Thus, the "other" (and the body of the "other") is essential, as he saw it, for assisting in defining and in understanding the existence of the "I" and its being as well as understanding more of the "other." "The relation of mine with the other," according to Ortega, "is the starting point for two different though connected lines of progressive concretion or definition. One consists in that I am coming to know, gradually, at best, more about the other, to know him better; I decipher in more detail his physiognomy, his gestures, his acts. The other consists in my relation with him becoming active, in my acting on him and he on me. In practice, the former usually follows upon the latter."[9] In this manner, then, for Ortega, the discovery of the "body of the other," as an object in reality, is indeed a reverse revelation of the "I" and its being. The being which is subsequently revealed to the "I" is revealed as being-for-and-with-others. This component of being-for-and-with-others is an integral part of being-in-the-world and being-for-itself and, thereby, provided Ortega with the phenomenological perspective through which he developed his idea of individuals interacting in human society. As he said:

> This means that the appearance of the Other is a fact that always remains as it were at the back of our life, because on becoming aware for the first time that we are living, we already find ourselves, not only with others and among others, but accustomed to others. Which leads us to formulate this first social theorem: Man is a *nativitate* open to the other, to the alien being; or, in other words: *before each one of us became aware of himself*, he had already had the basic experience that there are others who are not "I," the Others; that is to say, again, Man, on being a *nativitate* open to the other, to the *alter* who is not himself is a *nativitate*, like it or not. . . . Being open to the other, to others, is a permanent and

constitutive state of Man, not a definite action in respect to
them. The definite action—doing something with them, be it
for or *against* them—supposes this previous and inactive state
of openness. This state is not yet properly a "social relation,"
because it is not yet defined in any concrete act. It is simple
co-existence, matrix for all possible "social relations." It is
simple presence within the horizon of my life—a presence
which is, above all, more compresence of the Other, singular
or plural.[10]

The notion of the social world as a "horizon" connotes, for Ortega,
in a manner quite similar to that of Husserl, the context in which the
experience of human interaction (among "I," and "We," and "Other")
occurs. The various "I's" constitute the fundamental units of the
structure and content of the social world. "Husserl says very well,"
Ortega remarked, "the meaning of the term *man* implies a reciprocal
existence of one for the other, hence, *a community of men, a society*."[11] Through his description of reality, as we saw previously,
Ortega postulated the distinction between "things" (i.e., plants,
stones, and animals) and man through the fact that "things" *exist* and
that man *lives*. By dint of his unique individuality man has an essence
that is peculiarly his own, which means that man, for Ortega, is not
only split off from nature but is also separated from the tangible
physical objects of nature—plants, stones, minerals, and the like. All
individual human acts, for him, are directed toward some object and,
as such, the actions of the individual are manifested in accord with
the nature of the objects toward which they are directed and in accord
with their physical, spatial context. If the object is a stone, the individual's actions would be "unilateral"; if the object is an animal, on the
other hand, the individual discovers that his actions would be manifested toward an anticipated reaction by the animal to which they are
directed:

> It is now time, when we are passing through without taking
> notice of this formal structuration of the world, for us to cast
> a glance at its content, at the things that appear in it, show
> themselves, issue, arise, in short ex-ist, in it, in order to dis-
> cover which among them we can and must call social and soci-
> ety. . . . In fact, the things in the world are found by ancient
> tradition classified as minerals, vegetables, animals or humans.
> Ask yourselves, each of you, if your own behavior in the pres-
> ence of a stone can be considered as social. Evidently, it can-
> not. . . . We know that a stone is not aware of our action on
> it. . . . Our action does not evoke any corresponding action on

> its part upon or toward us. It has absolutely no capacity for any action. . . . But as soon as we begin dealing with an animal; the relation changes. If we want to do something to an animal, our plan of action is affected by our conviction that I exist for the animal and that it expects some action of mine on it, prepares for it, and prepares its reaction to this expected action of mine. There is, then, no doubt that, in my relation with the animal, the act of my behavior toward it is not, as it was in the case of the stone, unilateral; rather, my act, before being performed, when I am planning it, already calculates with the probable act of reaction on the animal's part, in such a manner that my act, even in the state of pure project, moves toward the animal but returns to me in an inverted sense, anticipating the animal's reply.[12]

We find this sort of transcendental reflection—by way of actions, responses, and reciprocal responses—to be fundamental in the kind of descriptions made by Ortega of the social world. In this connection, he did not designate animals as being "things," for "things" *exist* and, according to him, animals *co-exist* (the latter state of condition is somewhere between *existing*, as in the case of stones, and *living*, as with man). "In distinction from the stone and the plant," Ortega said, "the animal appears to me as a thing that responds to me and in this sense as something that does not simply exist for me but that, since I also exist for it, *co-exists* with me. The stone exists but does not *co-exist*."[13] With an animal as an object toward which an individual may direct his acts, there is more of a reciprocal response than there is with stones and other inanimate objects. Individual man and an animal, according to Ortega, exist-for-each-other but not to the same degree as between man and man, as the latter relate to one another as being-with-and-for-the-other. Yet the question remains: what kind of behavior can be constituted as being social and what are the contingencies implicit in this behavior? The contingency, for Ortega, relates to the fact that social behavior entails interaction between individuals, in contrast to acts between men and animals—for he views human life as the ultimate reality—and this human interaction has to be reciprocal. It is a kind of reciprocity of action that can only arise and occur between individual men:

> Can we recognize a social fact in the relation of a man with an animal? That we cannot, heedlessly, determine. . . . Of the contents of the world that only remain for us to analyze are the things that we call "men," "other men."

> . . . Does not the word "social" immediately point to a real-
> ity consisting in the fact that man conducts himself in con-
> frontation with other beings which, in their turn, conduct
> themselves with respect to him—therefore, to actions in which,
> in one way or another, the reciprocity intervenes in that not
> only am I a broadcasting center of actions toward another be-
> ing but that other being is also a broadcasting center of actions
> toward me, and, for the reasons expressed, in my action there
> must already be an anticipation of its action, my action reck-
> ons with it because its action also reckons with mine;—in
> short, to say the same thing in another way, that the two
> actors mutually respond to each other, that is, they corres-
> pond? [14]

This being the case, it is essential that the "I," in order to understand more about itself, relate to the body of the "other" as being
more than merely an object. At this point Ortega asks: "How do these
things that I call 'other men' appear in my vital world?" [15] From the
point of view of the "radical reality" that is the life of each one of us,
by means of a response on the part of Ortega to his own question, we
find that it is essential to experience the "other man" as a person with
an inner essence of his own rather than as an object. Pursuant to the
initial encounter with the body of the "other" as an object of reality,
according to Ortega, continual confrontation between the "ego" and
the "alien ego" contribute to the "circumstances" and behavior
through which the man is able to relate to the "other" as a person,
with an inner being, like himself. Ortega explained:

> Certainly, in the environs that my horizon encloses, appears
> the *Other*. The "other" is the other man. With sensible pres-
> ence, all that I have of him is a body, a body that displays its
> peculiar form, that moves, that manipulates things before my
> sight, that in other words exhibits external or visible "be-
> havior" . . . though there are present to us only a figure and
> some bodily movements, in or through this presence we see
> something that is essentially visible, something that is pure
> inwardness, something that each of us knows directly only of
> himself: his thinking, feeling, desiring, operations that, by
> themselves, cannot be presences to other men; that are non-
> external and that cannot be exteriorized directly because they
> do not occupy space or possess sensible qualities, for these
> reasons they are, in front of all the externality of the world,
> pure inwardness. [16]

For Ortega, as we discussed earlier, the "radical reality" of the "I" and its "circumstances" is an empirical reality and, to this extent, the individuals and objects of reality are entities which are experienced by us. But, at the same time, we find that these very individuals and objects are composed of certain qualities which are beyond our immediate experience. As the physical structure of man's body is characterized by Ortega to be distinct from and independent of man's inner reflective consciousness process, the same case may be made with man's understanding of and relation to the "others." That is to say, man discerns the physical structure of the body of the "other" but understands very little of the latter's inner consciousness. Through the body of the "other," the "I" perceives and understands more of its own physical features; through the awareness of its own inner consciousness process, on the other hand, the "I" attempts to understand more about, although to a lesser extent, the inner reflective process of the "other." Moreover, there are external cues (i.e., behavior and expressions) that might convey to the "I" the nature and quality of the "inwardness" of the "other." "All co-existence," Ortega said, "is a co-existence of two inwardnesses, and the extent of it is precisely the extent to which these two inwardnesses in one way or another become present to each other. . . . Now, when a body is the *sign* or *signal* of an inwardness that is as it were contained and shut up inside it, this means that the body is *flesh*, and this function of signalling its inwardness is termed 'expression.'"[17] As a result, the "other"—as a physical entity and as a person—must also be perceived through the context of its "I" and its "circumstances," by the "I" that is the percipient, and thereby becomes a kind of totality that is peculiar to itself as "other." Hence, from this ontological perspective, the way in which the body of the "I" appears to the "other" and the way in which the "other's" body is visible to the "I" are fundamentally the same. Whatever may be considered to be appropriate for the "I," in the personal sense of being-for-itself, also may be considered to be appropriate for the "others" who are existent in the world and "circumstances" embracing the "I." By experiencing the "others" as "other men," according to Ortega, the "I" understands and relates to them as units that are analogous to the "I" and that are inextricably connected, as fundamental units of reality, to their "circumstances" as well. This interaction is manifested in such a manner that the "I," for Ortega, apprehends the world-about-the-"others" and the world-about-the-"I" as one and the same world—from an objective, empirical standpoint—that differs in each individual case only insofar as it affects consciousness differently. For we all perceive reality through our sense perceptions, albeit our individual perceptions of this very reality are registered differently. For Ortega, as we have seen, I am the only one who is an "I." All the other "I's" are similar to objects (in the sense that they are perceived solely as physical organisms) and, once viewed as being "an *other* person" (that is, a being perceived as possessing both a body and an "inwardness," an *other* "I"), are referred to as the "others." My own place in this world—in time and in space—is related to my "I" and my body. When the "ego" (which is my "I") encounters an "alien ego," therefore, it is essential for it (the "ego") to transcend itself and thereby make it possible to attempt meaningfully to understand and to perceive that there are other "egos," or "I's." The "other," as "I," according to Ortega, is an "ego" that possesses a similar quality of consciousness, "inwardness," and "solitude"; an ego that will be related to as possessing both primary and secondary qualities and whose fundamental essence and structure is also encountered as existent within the "I." Thus, for Ortega, in order to attempt to enter this sphere of the "other's inwardness," it is essential to strive toward attaining the transcendental attitude. "In this sense of radical reality," he explained,

> . . . "human life" means strictly and exclusively the life of each individual, that is, always and only my life. This X that lives it and that I am accustomed to call "I," and the world in which that "I" lives, are patent to me, present or compresent, and all of this—being I who I am, and this being my world, and my living in it—all these are things that happen to me and solely to me, or to me in my radical solitude. If, by chance—I added—appears in this my world something that must also be called "human life" apart from mine, you may be absolutely sure that it will be "human life" in another sense, neither radical nor primary nor patent, but secondary, derivative, and more or less latent and hypothetical. Now, when bodies of human form appear and are present to us, we observe in them as compresent other quasi-I's, other "human lives," each with its own world, which, as such, does not communicate with mine. What is decisive in this step and in this appearance is that when my life and everything in it, on being patent to me, on being mine, have immanent character —hence the truism that my life is immanent to itself, that it is all within itself—the indirect presentation, or compresence, of the alien human life startles and confronts me with something transcendent to my own life, and which, therefore, is in it without properly being.[18]

It is through the mediacy of a human world, then, that the "I" and the "other," as collective "human lives," communicate. The "radical reality" of the "I," as the "inwardness of human life," is unique to the individual "I" and, in so far as it is possible, relates transcendentally to the "I" of the "other." The consciousness of the "I" is thus separated from the consciousness of the "other" by the very distinction that separates in the first instance the "I's" consciousness of its own body, secondly, the distinction that separates the body of the "I" from the body of the "other," and, finally, the distinction that separates the "other's" body from its consciousness. On the other hand, the bodies of the "I" and the "other," as existent physical structures in the common world of "human lives," are necessary "broadcasting centers," as Ortega put it, between the consciousnesses of the "I" and the "others." In this connection, the relation between the bodies of the "I" and the "other" is a relation of transcendental exteriority. "What is certainly patent in my life," he said, "is the notification, the signal, that there are other human lives; but since human life in its radicality is only *mine*, and these will be lives of others like myself, each the life of each, it follows that, because they are others, all their lives will be situated outside of or beyond or *trans*-mine. Hence they are transcendent."[19]

Expressed in this way, man, as a being-who-lives-in-the-world and as a being-for-and-with-others, is an empirically finite being who has to transcend the finitude of his "radical reality." As we have seen, from the perspective that we may view as being existentialist, Ortega maintained that in order for man to transcend the determinacy of his being and attain individual consciousness he has to make free choices and decisions. From an ontological point of view, Ortega is making a case, like Husserl, for the necessity of entering the transcendental attitude so that man may bring himself closer to an understanding and consciousness of the experience of the "other." The phenomenological and existentialist viewpoints are thus linked together, for man is an empirical, finite, concrete, and unique being in his particular "circumstances," who is decisively placed within the spatial-temporal context of the world of his here-and-now, and it is from this perspective that man transcends his "radical reality" in its every detail.[20] Although he took issue with the "abstract analogical transposition" of Husserl's "transcendental reduction," Ortega's phenomenological approach to the importance of transcending individual experience—as the fundamental basis for understanding the very experience of reality—is still very much in the tradition of Husserl and of students of the phenomenological method of the latter, Heidegger, Sartre, and Merleau-Ponty. When Ortega presented the ontological ramifications of reality, it is evident that he considered the human body to be connected to the totality that he called "human life" or "radical reality" and, as such, to be the foundation of its "vital structure." To be precise: the body is a body of an individual in so far as it exists in the indissoluble unity of its "radical reality." But, he commented, "what do we mean when we say that an Other is before us, that is, an other like myself, another Man?" "For this implies," he continued,

> . . . that the new being—neither stone nor plant nor merely animal—is I, *ego*—but at the same time is other, *alter*—that it is an *alter ego*. This concept of *alter-ego*—of an I that I am not but that is precisely another, hence not-I, has every appearance of being like a square circle, the prototype of the contradictory and impossible. And yet the thing itself is indubitable. There, before me, is another being that appears to me as being also an I, an *ego*. But so for I, *ego*, means for us no more than "human life," and human life, we said, is properly, originally, and radically only the life of each of us, hence, *my life*.[21]

To some minds it would seem to be an obvious fact that a man is able to understand "others," in their being and essence, both as like himself and as other than himself. From a phenomenological viewpoint, however, this fact is a problem which is neither obvious nor easy to explain and it is a problem whose solution was viewed differently by both Ortega and Husserl. The solution to this problem, for Husserl, was found in his notion of *Einfühlung*[22] ("empathy," or, literally: "feeling oneself into another"). Husserl's concept of the *Einfühlung* in *Lebenswelt* is somewhat similar to Hume's idea of "sympathy," and its philosophical function (as a "transcendental theory of experiencing someone else") was to establish, as completely as possible, a way of presenting the "other" to us. Ortega rejected the suppositions inherent in this solution to the problem because the notion of *Einfühlung* assumes that the "other" is "analogous" to my "I"; it is assumed, for him, that it is a "double" of my "I" and still does not serve the function of explaining the most difficult question —namely, how is it possible that this "double" of myself continues to appear to me as constituting the "other"? The main thrust of Ortega's argument is directed against Husserl's formulation, in his *Cartesian Meditations*, of the *alter ego* as being "an analogue" of the ego.[23] According to Husserl:

> *What is specifically peculiar to me as ego, my concrete being as a monad*, purely in myself and for myself *with an exclusive ownness*, includes [my] every intentionality and therefore, in particular, the intentionality directed to what is other.

> . . . In this pre-eminent intentionality there becomes consti-
> tuted for me the new existence-sense that goes beyond my mo-
> nadic very-owness; there becomes constituted an ego, not as
> "I myself," but as mirrored in my own Ego, in my monad.
> The second ego, however, is not simply there and strictly pre-
> sented; rather is he constituted as "alter ego"—the ego indi-
> cated as one moment by this expression being I myself in my
> ownness. The "Other," according to his own constituted sense,
> points to me myself; the other is a "mirroring" of my own
> self and yet not a mirroring proper, an analogue of my own
> self and yet again not an analogue in the usual sense.[24]

This position, according to Ortega, is much too abstract and contra-
dictory, as he contended:

> Observe how Husserl is obliged—in order to proclaim what
> is the Other in his most simple and primary character, hence,
> without yet obliging so as it is determined which Other, but
> in general and in the abstract, the Other—observe how he is
> obliged to employ constant contradictions: the Other is I al-
> though he is an I; but an I that is not I, hence some other
> thing different from my I, which of course, is well known to
> me. He tries in view of this, to express that strange reality
> which is the other by saying that it is not "I" but is something
> "analogous" to my I—but that it is not analogous either, for
> the reason that, in the long run, it contains many components
> that are identical with me, hence with "I."[25]

The solution of "an analogical transposition or projection," then,
is inadequate for Ortega, and the notion of the "appearance of the
Other" is the problem to which he extended his existentialist position of being-for-itself and being-for-and-with-others. Ortega replaced
Husserl's notion of "in [my] every intentionality," in order to clarify
the problem somewhat, with his own idea of "my life as radical reality."[26] As man is never a worldless "I"—for, as "radical reality" his
life is being-in-the-world—also he is never an isolated (other-less) "I."
"If my body is body," Ortega said, "—flesh because I am in it—in the
Other's body there must likewise be another 'I': an *alter ego*."[27]
Man understands himself as "I am I and my circumstances" and,
as such, finds himself disposed to the potential presence of "things"
and of other "I's" within his "radical reality." For Ortega, this is the
fundamental feature of being-for-and-with-others and cannot be explained as an isolated "I" that somehow discovers a way of confronting another equally isolated "I." Man does not have to find his way

to another man for, with the disclosure of his own being as being-for-and-with-others, the being of other "I's" is disclosed to him as possessing this same feature:

> Observe then: being the other does not represent an accident or adventure that may or may not befall Man, but is an original attribute. I, in my solitude, could not call myself by a generic name like "man." The reality represented by this name appears to me only when there is another being who responds or reciprocates to me. Husserl says very well: "The meaning of the term 'man' implies a reciprocal existence of one for the other, hence a *community of men*, a *society*." And conversely: "It is equally clear that men cannot be apprehended unless there are (really or potentially) other men around them." Hence—I add—to speak of man outside and apart from a society is to say something that is self-contradictory and meaningless. . . . Man does not *appear* in solitude —although his ultimate truth is solitude; man appears in sociality as the Other, frequenting the One, as the reciprocator.[28]

The "I" and the "other," then, are constituted by their appearance before each other, in the common world of society, and as each engages in reciprocal interaction. In this connection, Ortega was in basic agreement with Husserl as he attempted to reconcile the realms of "I" and "other," "solitude" and "society," by establishing the fact that a referral to the "other" (on the part of the "I") is an indispensable condition for the constitution of being-in-the-world. As we had the occasion to point out, the world for Ortega is constituted by each one of us (as being-in-the-world is the basic structure of each man's "I") and, therefore, man exists essentially for the sake of his own being as well as for being-for-and-with-others. Man apprehends the "others" as other "I's" that are disclosed in the world in a manner similar to himself, for the other "I's" have an "identical" structure of being-in-the-world, as is the case with his own "I." In this way, man's "radical reality" is a reality in which being-in-the-world is shared with other men. Therefore, in order to make explicit the transition from being-in-the-world (vis-à-vis the "I" and the "other") to society, let us now focus our analysis on the component factors that contribute to the systematic derivation of Ortega's social theory.

Within the broad spectrum of his "radical reality," man experiences other men as actually existing in the world around him. The "others," according to Ortega, are experienced both as objects and as subjects in the world. As objects, the "others" do not exist in the world as mere physical "things" of nature (i.e., plants, minerals, and stones), but as physical human entities (i.e., a body with organs, etc.). At the same time, the "others" are experienced as subjects in the world who, in turn, experience the same world experienced by my "I" and, in so doing, experience my "I" (in a manner similar to the way the "I" experiences the world and the "others" who are in it). The "I" experiences the world and "others," and therefore, as they are revealed to the consciousness of the "I," this experience is not solely an *intra*subjectively perceived phenomenon of the ego. Rather, it is an objective, "*inter*subjective world" (in the sense of "interego"), which is other than and independent of my individual perceptions. The "other" ego "appears" and is present in the world not only as an empirical and therefore tangible entity—vis-à-vis its body and actions—but is present also as an essential condition of the ego's uniformity and objectivity in the world. The objective ("intersubjective") world is one in which the "other" is existent as a sort of veritable guarantee of its (the world's) objectivity. This kind of objective world is one in which each ego must attempt to go beyond the limitations which are inherent in it as an intersubjective reality. That is to say, even though all of us may go through the same experiential process (as we perceive the objects in the world), it is essential for us to realize the important fact that our individual experiences of the world and our perceptions of its properties are different. The empirical quality of the egos of the "I" and the "other," as they appear contemporaneously in the world and as intersubjective entities, provide the necessary coherence to what might be an indefinite plurality of egos in the state of "solitude." The overall significance of the "other," then, for Ortega, is that it is an essential factor in constituting both the "radical realities" of the "I" and itself. He said,

> If, in the presence of the other, I make a demonstrative gesture pointing with my forefinger to an object that is in my vicinity and I see the other advance toward the object, pick it up, and hand it to me, I infer from this that the world that is only mine and the world that is only his seem, nevertheless, to have a common element: the object that, with slight variation, namely, its shape as viewed from his perspective and from mine, exists for both. And as this happens in connection with many things—although, sometimes, both he and I make mistakes in supposing that we share a common perception of certain objects—and as it happens not only with one other man, but with many other men, it prepares me for the idea of a world beyond mine and his, a presumed, inferred world,

common to all. This is what we call the "objective world"
facing the world of each of us in his primary life . . . —the
image of a world that, being neither only mine nor only yours
but, in principle, the world of all, will be *the* world.[29]

In this connection, and as we saw earlier, the ego of the "other"
(as in the instance of the "I") has its own acts which are directed toward an object. The observation and perception of this process would,
in turn, constitute a change in the "I's" perception of itself as it becomes aware of the different features of itself through its perception
of the acts and features of the "other" person. "Before each one of
us became aware of himself," Ortega said, "he had already had the
basic experience that there are others who are not 'I.'"[30] The behavior of the "other," according to this view, is a kind of primary
evidence of the existence of other "human lives" by way of interpret-
ing and observing the acts of the "other." This reference to human
behavior, for Ortega, is a form of grasping empirical evidence, and it
is not his intention that it should be construed as being "behavioral-
ist" in theory.[31] The presence of the "other" is salient to us through
his actions and, in this connection, Ortega maintained that it would
be difficult for man to engage actively in the "intersubjective world"
from the isolation of his ego. "From the depth of radical solitude that
is properly our life," he said, "we now and again make an attempt at
interpenetration, at *de-solitudinizing* ourselves by tentatively showing
ourselves to the other human being, desiring to give him our life and
to receive his."[32]

In the social world of being-for-and-with-others, thus, an individual
directs himself away from the possibilities that may be viewed as being exclusively his own and attempts to broaden his understanding of
himself by relating to the common world possibilities of "others."
The social world in which the individual lives—as one who is linked
with other individuals through manifold relations—is a realm that he
apprehends and interprets to be meaningful for his possibilities, his
"circumstances," and his here-and-now. It is from this standpoint that
Ortega contended that, as individuals who are rooted in our radical
realities, we must "make an attempt at interpenetration, at *de-solitudinizing* ourselves. . . . "[33] This being the case, as the spatial-
temporal dimension of man's "radical reality" is part and parcel of
his here-and-now, the reality of the social world (as the context and
mediacy through which groups of individuals interact) is also enmeshed
in his here-and-now. Through his own finitude, man's temporality
is revealed as the consciousness of the intrasubjective structure of
his life. The reality of the social world, on the other hand, reveals

itself to man as an intersubjectively structured world which is shared by the "I" with the "others." It is the spatial-temporal manifestations of this intersubjectivity that connect the "I" to the "others" and, at the same time, that sharply differentiate the world of the "I" from the social world of the "others." Each "I," according to Ortega, apprehends and interprets the reality of the social world (which is common to the "others" and in which it engages actively in reciprocal relations) as a realm through which its possibilities are organized and take place. By the same token, the "I" is aware of the fact that this very "social" world is also the realm of possible actions of the "others" and is, from their perspective, organized around them. From the outset, for Ortega, the social world is given to man as a world that is already structured and organized. As he said, "The first thing I fall foul of in my proper and radical world is Other Men, the Other singular and plural, among whom I am born and begin to live. From the beginning, then, I find myself in a human world or 'society.'"[34]

The world of social reality, as we saw, is an objective world which is common and which is accessible to the "I" and to the "others." This social world is structured around the "here" of the body of the "I" and the "now" of its present. The spatial-temporal dimension of this "here" and "now" of the "I" in the context of social reality is the tangible link between the "I" and the "others" (through the manifestations of individual interaction) and between the "I" and "people" or society (by way of individual-social-interaction). The individual interaction of the "I" with the "others," for Ortega, takes place within a world whose intersubjectivity sharply delineates the "circumstances" of the "I" from the social "circumstances" of the "others." The "I" of an individual is unique to itself, as is the case with the "I's" of other individuals in society. In spatial terms then, in this connection, according to Ortega, the "here" of the "I" is the "there" of the "others" and vice versa:

> Not only does he [the "other"] exist for me, but I exist for him. This is a very peculiar coexistence because it is mutual: when I see a stone, I see only a stone, but when I see my neighbor, another man, I not only see him, but also I see that he sees me, that is to say, in another man I always meet myself and myself is reflected in him. I am here and you are there. As the here and the there express spatial contiguity, as they are together, we can say that as you are there and I am here, we are together. But we could say the same thing about this table and those benches; this table also is here and those benches are there—they also are together.

But the strange thing in our relationship, the thing which does not happen to the table and the benches or both of them together, is that though I am here, I perceive without ceasing to be here that I am also there in you; I note, in short, that I exist for you; and vice versa; you, undisturbed over there, are at the same time here, in me; you exist for me. This is obviously a form of being together in a much more radical sense and one very different from that of one bench being next to another. To the degree that I know that I am in you, my being, my presence, my existing, is fused with yours; and in that exact degree I feel that I do not stand alone, that within myself I am not alone, but that I am with you, that I have my being with you; in short, that I am accompanied or am in a society—my living is a living with. The reality that we call fellowship, companionship or society can only exist between two objects which mutually exchange the fact of being, which are reciprocally the one or the other—I mean: I accompany you or I am in fellowship with you to the degree that you feel that you exist for me, that you are present in me, that you fill a part of my being; in short, I accompany you, I live with you or in a social relationship with you to the degree that I am you. On the contrary, to the degree that I am not you, that you do not exist for me nor for any other fellow man, to that degree you are alone, you are in solitude, and not in a social relationship or a companionship.

What a tremendous theme, this, of the polarity or the contra-position solitude-society.[35]

This "theme" of the contrast between "solitude and society," as we noted previously, is Ortega's vague manner of attempting to reconcile the uniqueness of individuality with the underlying uniformity of individual interaction in society. The "I" and the "others," for him, share in the experience of a common social world but their "spatial proximities" and their temporal consciousness are, one in the same, common and uniquely individual. The "here" of the "I" is the "there" of the "other" and, as they interrelate and communicate within the context of a common social world, the "now" of the "I" is unique to itself—by way of "I am I and my circumstances"—and, at the same time, corresponds with the "now" of the "others." Hence, in temporal terms, my "now" and their "now" also is our "now." In Ortega's philosophy of human life, as we saw, temporality is an internal structure of the individual's stream of consciousness in the connection of "I am I and my circumstances." The individual, for

Ortega, is conscious of the sensation of an inner flow of time—by way of past, present, and future—and this feature of individual consciousness provides us with the opportunity to differentiate, at this point of our analysis, between the perception of temporality as an *intra*subjective characteristic of reality and the perception of reality as being *inter*subjectively available to us. In the case of the latter, the stream of consciousness of one individual differs from that of another but both partake in the common experience of the temporal manifestations of social reality. In this context, the "now" of the "I" and the "now" of the "others" are mutual "nows" in so far as they (the "I" and the "others") are "contemporaries" in the social world. This emphasis on the spatial and temporal reality of the social world is important, for our purposes, in placing the proper perspective on Ortega's concept of the generation.

The actual experience of someone who is not "I" is existent as the experience of an objective world, of "things, animals, and others, that is external to the being of 'I.'" The objective world becomes, in this sense, the medium of communication between the "I" and the "other" and, thereby, the social context of human interaction is viewed as an important function in apprehending and perceiving reality. As Ortega said, "It is my sociality or social relation with other men that makes possible the appearance, between them and me, of *something like* a common and objective world; the world that Kant called *allgemeingültig*—'universally valid,' that is, valid for all—thereby referring to human subjects and establishing in unanimity the objectivity or reality of the world."[36] It is in this context that the subsequent consciousness process (the result of the initial confrontation of the body of the "I" with that of the "other") proceeds to what Ortega called an "I-you" synthesis—in a word, "we." At first, my "I" is the only "I" and, after the "I" confronts the "other," the next level of the consciousness process is reciprocal interaction and a reciprocal awareness of the "other" as a person like my "I." "And this is what follows from my earlier remark," he said, "when I said that the part of my world that first appears to me is the group of men among whom I am born and begin to live, the family and the society to which my family belongs—that is, a human world through which and influenced by which the rest of the world appears to me."[37] This process of the reciprocity of human interaction, for Ortega, is an important prelude for establishing what constitutes the common world and for extending the concepts of "I" and "I-you" to include concepts of "we," "society," and "social reality":

Even if there is to be living together, it is necessary to de-
part from that simple state of being open to the other, to the
alter. . . . To be open to the other is a passive thing: it is necessary, on the basis of an opening, that I may act on him and he
shall respond or reciprocate to me. . . . we live together and in
reciprocity with respect to something. The words "we live" very
well express this new reality that is the relation "we"—*unus et
alter,* I and the other together do something and on doing it *we*
are. . . . It is the first form of concrete relation with the other,
and, therefore, the first *social* reality—if we wish to employ this
word in its more common sense which is, at the same time, that
of almost all sociologists among some of the best of them, such
as Max Weber. . . .

As we live together and are the reality "we"—I and he, that
is, the Other—we come to know each other. This means that
the Other, until now an undefined man, of whom I only know,
from his body, that he is what I call my "like," my "fellow,"
hence someone able to reciprocate to me and with whose conscious response I have to calculate—as I continue to confer
with him, good or bad, this Other becomes more definite to
me and I increasingly distinguish him from the other *Others*
whom I know even less. . . . It is within the ambit of living
together that the relation "we" opens up and where the you,
or the unique human individual, appears to me. You and I,
I and you, we act on each other in frequent interaction of
individual to individual—both reciprocally unique.[38]

The process of the reciprocity of human interaction is a process
through which subjects (the "I" and the "others") take an active part
in the form of an "I-you" (or "we") synthesis and, thus, is a process
that Ortega designated as being "social."[39] As we reflect on the function of action in Ortega's philosophy of human life and as we link it
with his theory of social reality, we find that his notion of human
action is not only essential for the process of being-in-the-making but
is also crucial for his concept of being-for-and-with-others, in the
social context of the reciprocity of human interaction. "My action,
then," he said, "is social, *in this sense of the word*, when in it I reckon
with the eventual reciprocity of the Other. The other, Man, is *ab initio*
the reciprocator, and hence *is* social. He who is incapable of recipro-
cating, whether favorably or adversely, is not a human being."[40]
According to this statement, Ortega seems to suggest that a "human

being," as so defined, is one who engages in "social" interactions—one who reciprocates with another. The tangibility of human interaction, as an explicit manifestation of behavior, is concrete and functions in terms of man's "circumstances" and his relationship with "others," both of which are part and parcel of human reality (namely, "I am I and my circumstances"). Human life (and therein, reality) explains and is explained by social relations, according to this view, and social relations, as manifestations of reality, are discernible through human behavior. Hence, human interaction is subject to an objective analysis and thereby provides Ortega with his perspective of the social context and relevance of reality.

In the context of social reality, thus, man measures his "I" by what constitutes the "Others" and by what they have achieved and failed to achieve in the social world. The experience of the social world by the "I" thereby justifies and corroborates itself (as a being-in-the-world) through the experience of the "others" with whom the "I" interacts. The possibilities of man and his subsequent understanding of himself can be broadened after his encounter with the "others" in the social world that is common to all "I's." Ortega, however, also views the social world, in several aspects, as constricting rather than expanding man's possibilities. As an empirically finite being whose "radical reality" continually confronts the possibility of death, man, according to Ortega, can make efforts to transcend the determinacy of his being by making, existentially, free choices and decisions. On the other hand, man, as a social, empirically finite being who interrelates with other individuals, finds it difficult to transcend and to recoil from the process of the reciprocity of human interaction in the context of social reality and, hence, is conditioned (by society) to act with a view toward what others have done and what they are currently doing. Ortega said,

> Since this human world occupies the first boundary in the perspective of my world, I see all the rest of it, and my life and myself, across from Others, through Them. And since They never cease to act around me, manipulating things and above all talking about them, that is, operating on them, I project upon the radical reality of my life as much as I see them do and hear them say—whereupon my radical reality, which is so much mine and mine alone, remains concealed from my own eyes by a crust shaped by what I have received from other men, through their skillful maneuvers and their opinions, and I become habituated to live normally by a presumed or probable world created by them, which I am accus-

tomed to accept as authentic without further question and regard as reality itself.[41]

Although man acts in an actively disclosing way, according to this view, his individual behavior (and therefore his broader understanding of his own being) can be and is often perceived in terms of the constraints which are imposed upon him by the particular manifestations of social interaction. In view of this fact, Ortega maintained, man understands himself in his difference from the others by occasionally withdrawing from the social world to the "solitude" of his "radical reality" so as to separate his own possibilities from theirs. "Only when my docility," he said,

> or what Other Men do and say leads me into absurd, contradictory, or catastrophic situations do I ask myself how much truth there is in all this; that is to say, I withdraw myself for a moment from the pseudo-reality, from the conventionality in which I live with them, to the authenticity of my life as radical solitude. Such that to less or greater degrees and proportions and with less or greater frequency, I effectually live a double life, each one of them [of the two lives] with its own optic and perspective. And if I look around me, I seem to suspect that the same thing happens with every one of the Others. . . . There is the man who lives little more than the pseudo-life of conventionality, and there are on the other hand extreme cases in which I seem to see that the Other is energetically true to his authenticity. Between these two poles, there are all the intermediate equations, for it is a case of an equation between the conventional and the authentic, which has different figures for each of us. . . .
>
> But observe that even in the case of maximum authenticity, the human individual lives the major portion of his life in the pseudo-living of the surrounding, or social conventionality. . . . I in my solitude could not call myself by a generic name like "man"—it follows that I see the World and my life and myself in accordance with their formulas; that is, I see all this as colored by other men, impregnated with their humanity. . . . Only one aspect is clearly limited to circumstances: that this world that is humanized for me by others is not my authentic world; it does not possess an unquestionable reality; it is only more or less probable, illusory in many of its parts; and it imposes on me the duty, not an ethical but a vital duty, of submitting it to periodical purifyings so that its things shall

be rated at their true value, each with the coefficient of reality or unreality that belongs to it.[42]

There seems to be a contradiction at this point in our analysis: On the one hand, Ortega maintained that man—as a being-in-the-world—must actively engage in the "circumstances" of his world that are "outside" of himself and that prevent him from assuming the solipsistic perspective of viewing the world from the isolation of his ego. On the other hand, Ortega contended that the external social world of the "others" makes implicit the fact that man must draw upon the possibilities of his own being from whatever has been prescribed and decided and from what the "others" have achieved and failed to achieve in the social world. In order to deliver man from what he considered to be the constrictive tendency of the social world of the "others" to dominate the individual, Ortega offered the individual being-in-the-world the option of withdrawing from the social realm to the "radical solitude" of his finite being as a means of balancing off intensive introvertedness against excessive extrovertedness. Man as a being-in-the-world must engage himself in this orientation through which understanding of the self and other can occur only in relating to other human beings in the reality of the social world, for this world has possibilities not only for the "I's" and the "yous," but also for the "wes." Once given this social world that may be interpreted to signify the possible realm of action for all of us (as "all men find themselves among men"), in Ortega's view, man must discriminate between what constitutes the possibilities of the "others"—man in general in the social world—and what constitutes the possibilities that are inherent in the uniqueness of his own finite being.[43] "You are you—I mean," he said, "that you have a mode of being that is your own and peculiar to you, and that does not coincide with mine. From *you*, that is, arise frequent negations of my being—of my way of thinking, of feeling, of wanting and desiring."[44] "But what is Yours," he added, "does not exist for me—your ideas and convictions do not exist for me. I see them as alien and sometimes as opposed to me. . . . All *Yous* are such—because they are different from me—and when I say I, I am only a minute portion of the world, the tiny part of it that I now begin accurately to call 'I.'"[45] It is in this connection, he explained, that

> . . . the concrete and unique I that each one of us feels himself to be is not something that we possess and know from the outset but something that gradually appears to us exactly as other things do, that is, step by step, by virtue of a series of experiences that have their fixed order. I mean, for example—

and this is the strange and unexpected thing—we discover that
we are *I* after and by virtue of having first known the *yous*,
our *yous*, in our collision with them, in the struggle that we
called social relation.[46]

Thus, for Ortega, the individual must live neither as an isolated
"I" nor as a conformist to the common social world of the "others."
The individual, rather, must live the existence of a "unique I." That
is to say, the "unique" individual is he who lives in an actively disclosing manner and who has the ability both to come out of and to
withdraw into the possibilities of his "radical solitude"—all of which
are contingent upon the possibilities which are permitted within the
realm of the "yous" and "wes" that he confronts in the reality of the
social world. "It is in the world of the *yous*, and by virtue of them,"
he said, "that the thing that I am, my I, gradually takes shape for me.
I discover myself, then, as one of countless *yous*, but as different
from them all, with gifts and defects of my own, with a unique character and conduct, that together draw my authentic and correct profile for me—hence as another and particular *you*, as *alter tu*."[47]

At this point of our analysis, it is apparent that the term "social
world," or "society," for Ortega, is merely the term which is used to
describe the phenomenological interaction between individual "I's"
both as "unique" individuals and as social individuals. In other words,
the social world is the realm in which the interactive process of the
"I" and its "circumstances" is extended to the inclusion of other
"I's." As ultimate reality, for Ortega, is human life, social reality (as
the realm in which individual human lives are linked through social
relations) is also an essential structure of this ultimate reality.[48]
From this perspective, Ortega was concerned with the fundamental
patterns of human interaction that underlie the larger context of
social reality. The reduction of the whole of what constitutes social
reality into its component elements is the phenomenological basis of
Ortega's analysis of human society. Hence, the social relation of individuals is the distinctive unity which is defined by the reciprocal
interaction of its "unique" individual components. As he said:

> . . . the basic structure that is social relation, in which man
> moves appearing and defining himself in front of the other
> man, and from being the pure other, the unknown man, the
> not-yet-identified individual, becomes the unique individual—
> the You and the I. But now we have become aware of some-
> thing that is a constituent factor in all that we have called
> "social relation" . . . namely, that all these actions of ours
> and all these reactions of others in which the so-called "social

relation" consists, originate in an individual as such, I [myself] for example, and are directed to another individual as such. Therefore, the "social relation," as it has so far appeared to us, is always explicitly a reality between individuals, a reality formally inter-individual.[49]

The behavior and interaction of individuals in the social world, for Ortega, is a reality which is tangible and which is open to an objective analysis. This analysis is reflected through his perspective of social reality as the realm in which we may perceive and interpret the concrete functions of human interactions. The substance of Ortega's objective analysis of social relations was structured around his theories of "creative, select minorities," "mass man," and "mass society." For Ortega, "mass man" and "mass society" are manifestations of social and historical phenomena that are perceptible, in part, through the objective factor of their vast numbers and magnitude in the social world. But, he was quick to point out, the argument of sheer "quantity" is hardly an adequate and accurate explanation of the fact that "we see the multitude, as such, in possession of the places and instruments created by civilization."[50] More importantly, according to Ortega, a sharp focus on the intrinsic features of "mass man" and "mass society" would bring us much closer to discerning the essence of this concept than its external manifestations of "agglomeration" and "plenitude."[51] The philosophical dimensions of "mass man," "mass society," and "select minorities," as a theory of social relations and human interaction and as an analysis of social reality, must focus on its qualitative rather than on its quantitative characteristics. That is, while it is important and useful to make references to the quantitative factor of the concept of "masses" and the concept of "select minorities" as a descriptive means of the coherence of one group of individuals vis-à-vis another group of individuals, the qualitative feature of identifying what constitute "masses" and what constitute "select minorities" is even more essential, for Ortega, toward an understanding not only of the "unique" individuals in society but also of how these "unique" individuals are kept together as a dynamic unity. As he said:

> The concept of the multitude is quantitative and visual. Let us translate it without changing its character, into sociological terminology. Then we find the idea of social mass. Society is always a dynamic unity of two component factors: minorities and masses. The minorities are individuals or groups of individuals which are specially qualified. The mass is an aggregate of persons not especially qualified. By masses, then,

it is not to be understood, solely nor principally, "the working masses." The mass is "the average man." In this manner
what was mere quantity—the multitude—is converted into a
qualitative determination: it becomes the common social
quality, it is man as undifferentiated from other men, but as
repeating in himself a generic type. What have we gained by
this conversion of quantity into quality? Very simply this: by
means of the latter we understand the genesis of the former.
It is evident, to the verge of platitude, that the normal formation of a multitude implies the coincidence of desires, ideas,
ways of being, in the individuals who constitute the whole.
It will be said that this is just what happens with every social
group, however select it may strive to be. This is true; but
there is an essential difference.

In those groups which are characterized by not being multitude and mass, the effective coincidence of its members consists in some desire, idea, or ideal, which of itself excludes the
great number. To form a minority, whatever it may be, it is
necessary beforehand that each member separate himself from
the multitude for *special*, relatively individual, reasons. Their
coincidence with the others who form the minority is, then,
secondary, posterior to their having each adopted an attitude
of singularity, and is therefore, to a large extent, a coincidence
in not coinciding. . . . This coming together of the minority
precisely in order to separate themselves from the majority is
always introduced into the formation of every minority.[52]

This being so, it is apparent that the "masses," for Ortega, is not a
socio-economic concept in the sense of differentiating between lower,
middle, and upper classes. Nor, for that matter, is the notion of "mass
man" a political concept. The "masses," as a social phenomenon and
as an historical phenomenon, is much too inclusive a concept for
Ortega to be restricted by the confines of economics and politics.
"Public life," he said, "is not solely political, but equally, and even
primarily, intellectual, moral, economic, religious; it comprises all our
collective habits, including our fashions both of dress and of amuse-
ment."[53] How then, we ask, can we identify and define the "masses"
and the "select minorities"? What does Ortega mean by *"specially*
qualified" and "average man"? For Ortega, as we indicated previously,
it is essential that the "creative" individuals, who may constitute the
group of "select minorities," set themselves apart from the "conform-
ing majority" or "multitude."[54] In order to separate themselves from
the majority, the "select minorities" must be "qualified." To be

"qualified," for Ortega, in this sense, then, seems to suggest an explicit qualitative differentiation between the individual's perception of himself as "I" (and, therefore, as a being-in-the-world who possesses unique qualities which are creative and essentially his own) and his perception of the "masses" as the "others" (and thereby as a number of beings-in-the-world who do not discriminate their "I" from other "I's"). He said:

> At most, the mass may be defined, as a psychological fact, without the necessity of waiting for individuals appearing in mass agglomeration. In the presence of one individual person we are able to know whether he is "mass" or not. The mass is all that which sets no value on itself—good or ill—for particular reasons, but which feels itself "just like everybody," and, nevertheless, is not concerned about it; the mass man who makes no demands of himself has the pleasure of feeling himself as being identical with the rest.
>
> When one speaks of "select minorities" the habitual is apt to distort the sense of this expression, pretending to be unaware that the select man is not the petulant person who believes himself superior to the rest, even though he may not succeed in fulfilling in his person those higher exigencies. And there is no doubt that the most radical division that it is possible to make of humanity is that which splits it into two classes of creatures: those who make great demands on themselves, accumulating difficulties and duties; and those who demand nothing special of themselves, but for whom to live is to be every moment what they already are, without imposing on themselves any effort towards perfection; mere buoys that are adrift.[55]

This "radical division" of man into "two classes of creatures," to which Ortega referred, also is not to be viewed as a socio-economic division between upper and lower classes. As we saw, the distinction between "masses" and "select minorities," for Ortega, is a distinction of quality and is not confined to the hierarchic categories of economics and politics. In this connection, although Ortega was quick to declare that the "select man" is not to be interpreted as one who "thinks himself superior to the rest," the prerequisite of certain elitist qualities on the part of the "select man" makes implicit—by definition—the fact that the "select man" is superior to the "mass man." For even though Ortega contended (in his own ambiguous manner) that the "*specially* qualified select minorities" may be found (in an economic sense) to be members of the "lower classes," the probability is even greater that they would be members of the "upper classes":

> The division of society into masses and select minorities is not, therefore, a division into social classes, but into classes of men, and cannot coincide with the hierarchic separation of "upper" and "lower" classes. It is, of course, clear that in these "upper" classes, when and as long as they really are so, there is much more likelihood of finding men who adopt the "great vehicle," while the "lower" classes normally constitute individuals without quality. But, strictly speaking, within both of these social classes, there are to be found mass and authentic minority.[56]

In view of this position, it seems that the "select man" would have to be some sort of superior individual. If the "select man" (by definition a man of "genuine" quality) is to place higher demands and values upon himself, if he has refined aesthetic tastes and if he is to excel the common life of "everybody," then he must stand up and be counted, according to Ortega, so that he may set himself apart from the "masses." To accomplish this, the "select man" has to be viewed as an individual who is superior to the majority in so far as he realizes the various possibilities of his own being. Ortega's concept of the "select man," in this sense, is somewhat similar to Nietzsche's notion of the *übermensch*. For Nietzsche, the *übermensch* (over man) must free himself from the *ressentiment* of "slave morality" by setting his own standards and by creating his own values.[57] For Ortega, the "select man" must separate himself from the common values of "everybody" by placing greater demands on himself and by drawing upon the uniqueness of his "radical reality." In order to realize one's possibilities as a unique individual, as we saw, occasionally it is essential for man to withdraw from the social reality of the "others" to the "radical reality" of his "I." In such "circumstances," the individual has to ignore momentarily the objective values of the social world, according to Ortega, and must create more of the subjective values that accrue from the uniqueness of his being. This subjective withdrawal into the "solitude" of one's "radical reality" is the necessary retreat of the "select minorities" whenever they are confronted with the constraints of the "masses." As Ortega said, "The mass crushes beneath it everything that is different, everything that is excellent, individual, qualified and select. Anybody who is not like everybody, who does not think like everybody, runs the risk of being eliminated. . . . Nowadays, 'everybody' is the mass alone."[58] Ortega did not elaborate on the point of what it means to "run the risk of being eliminated," but it is apparent at this juncture that the phenomenological dimensions of his social theory of the interaction of the "I" and the "others" are mirrored in his theory of the "select minorities" ("I's") and the "masses" ("others").

Ortega's negative reaction to the idea of the domination of the individual "I" by the "others" (or, more precisely, the subordination of the "select minorities" by the "masses") echoed the fear of the "majority" that was expressed in the writings of such nineteenth-century liberal thinkers as de Tocqueville, John Stuart Mill, and Burckhardt. These thinkers witnessed what they considered to be the growing trend of the invasion by the "masses" into the various realms of life which previously had been opened exclusively to the "select few." Ortega considered this growing tendency of the nineteenth century to be very much a part of the reality of the twentieth century.[59] Burckhardt, de Tocqueville, and Mill thought that the "masses" were striving to wear the social fabric of the elite; Ortega thought that the "masses," in fact, had already forgotten "their place":

> As we shall see, it is a characteristic of the times, the predominance, even in groups whose tradition was selective, of the mass and the vulgar. Thus, in the intellectual life, which of its essence requires and presupposes qualification, one can note the progressive triumph of the pseudo-intellectuals, unqualified, unqualifiable, and by their very mental structure, disqualified.
> . . .
> This being so: there exist in society operations, activities, and functions of the most diverse order, which are of their very nature special, and which consequently cannot be properly performed without special talents. For example: certain pleasures of an artistic and refined character, or again the functions of government and of political judgment on public affairs. Previously these special activities were exercised by qualified minorities, at least by those who claimed such qualification. The mass did not attempt to intervene in them: they realized that if they wished to intervene they would necessarily have to acquire those special qualities and cease being mere mass. They recognized their place in a healthy dynamic social system.
> If we now revert to the facts indicated at the beginning, they will appear unmistakably as the heralds of a changed attitude in the mass. They all indicate that the mass has decided to advance to the foreground of social life and to occupy the

places and to use the instruments and to enjoy the pleasures hitherto reserved to the few. It is evident, for example, that the places were never intended for the multitude, for their dimensions are too limited, and the crowd is continuously overflowing; thus demonstrating to our eyes and with visible language the new phenomenon: the mass, without ceasing to be mass, is supplanting the minorities.[60]

This outcry against the fact that the "masses" were assuming more of an active role in the activities of society that previously had been reserved for the "select minorities" is not solely an outright condemnation of the domination of the latter by the "masses." It is, for Ortega, in addition, a clarion call for the "select minorities" to assert their creativity in the face of such adverse "circumstances."[61] The condition of being "select" and "qualified" is neither a right nor a privilege, according to Ortega. Rather, it is a condition of "obligation," as the "select man" must assert himself in order to attempt to realize his "vital possibilities" and, thereby, avoid the state of "inertia." Man (in general and the select man in particular), for Ortega, has no "natural rights"; indeed, he has the "obligation" to live an actively disclosing existence, which is the only meaningful effort that may actualize his "vital possibilities."[62] Once realized, then, he said, "this is life lived as a discipline—the noble life."[63] "Nobility is defined," he continued,

by the demands it makes on us through obligations, not through rights. *Noblesse oblige.* . . . The privileges of nobility are not originally concessions or favors; but, on the contrary, are conquests. And, in principle, their maintenance supposes that the privileged individual would be capable of reconquering them, at any moment, if it were necessary, and anyone were to dispute them. Private rights or *privileges* are not, then, passive possession and mere enjoyment, but they represent the profile attained by personal effort. On the other hand, common rights, such as those "of the man and the citizen," are passive property, pure usufruct and benefit, the generous gift of destiny which every man encounters and which answers to no effort whatever, unless it be that of breathing. . . .

It is irritating to see the degeneration suffered in ordinary vocabulary by a word so inspiring as "nobility." Because by coming to mean for many people hereditary "noble blood," it is changed into something similar to common rights, into a static, passive quality which is received and transmitted like something inert. But the strict sense, the *etymon* of the word

> "nobility" is essentially dynamic. Noble means the "well known," that is, known by everyone, famous, he who has made himself known by excelling the anonymous mass. It implies an unusual effort as the cause of his fame. Noble, then, is equivalent to effortful or excellent. The nobility or fame of the son is pure benefit. The son is known because his father succeeded in being. . . . The only thing left to it of the living, authentic, dynamic is the impulse it stirs in the descendant to maintain the level of effort reached by the ancestor. Always, even in this altered sense, *noblesse oblige*. The original noble places an obligation on himself, the noble heir receives the obligation with his inheritance. There is, in any case, a certain contradiction in the transfer of nobility from the initial noble to his successors.[64]

We may not agree with Ortega's definition of the *"etymon"* of the term "nobility" (or *"noblesse oblige"*), but it is evident that he was attributing a quality to the term that was synonymous with his notion of the "creative," "qualified" "select minorities." It is a quality that takes us back to his ontological focus on the "select man" and his "circumstances." The internal infusion of the conception of "obligation" impels the "select man" to strive toward the attainment of an excellence that may entail a projection into the transcendental experience (as we indicated in the case of the expanding consciousness of the "I" after its initial encounter with the "others" in the social world) and that would result in reflecting his superiority and thus would assist him in surpassing the *ressentiment* of the "inert masses." Life for the "select man," according to Ortega, "has no savor unless he makes it consist in service to something transcendental."[65] The term "transcendental," for Ortega in this context, contains more of the concrete connotation of an active, "effortful" life. As he said:

> For me, nobility is synonymous with a life of effort, always set on excelling oneself, to transcend what one is to what one proposes as a duty and an obligation. In this manner, the noble life remains opposed to the common or inert life, which reclines statically upon itself, condemned to perpetual immobility, as an external force which does not compel it to come out of itself. Hence we call mass man this kind of human being—not so much because he may be multitudinous, as because he is inert.[66]

The "select man," it seems, is the only individual capable of living the kind of life posited by Ortega in his philosophy of life and society.

"The select men," he said, "the nobles, are the only ones who are active and not merely reactive, for whom life is a perpetual striving."[67] In effect, the "select minorities" appear to be the only individuals, for Ortega, capable of realizing the "vital possibilities" of their being on placing themselves into the transcendental dimension and thereby stretching their being beyond the constraints imposed upon them by the "circumstances" of their social reality. The "masses," on the other hand, constitute the collective group of the "others" who are "reactive" as opposed to being "active" and who, as a consequence of being locked in their individual egos and the ego of *their* social world, are unable to reach beyond their constraining circumstances to the greater heights of "perpetual striving." Rather than *withdraw from* the constraining elements of the social world, the "mass man" *withdraws* from society (in lieu of withdrawing from its constraints) *into* his ego; this makes him, according to Ortega, "the actual mass man who is as much 'mass' as ever."[68] Ortega attributed this, by way of an explanation, to the fact that the "average man, following his natural disposition, has withdrawn into himself."[69] Hence, "we are in the presence," he said, "of a mass stronger than that of any preceding period, but, differing from the traditional type in that it remains hermetically enclosed within itself, incapable of allowing itself to be regulated by any order, believing itself self-sufficient—in a word, indocile."[70] This critical reaction by Ortega to what he considered to be evidence of the fact that the "masses" are "supplanting" the "select minorities," it seems, should be a criticism directed at the "select minorities," not only the "masses," for not maximizing the realization of their "vital possibilities." As he viewed the "select man" as the only person "genuinely" capable of actively engaging in the "definite possibilities" of his "circumstances," it seems, then, that Ortega should have criticized the latter more severely than he did, rather than place the burden solely on the "weak" shoulders of the "mass man." On the other hand, it appears that Ortega's elitist emphasis would have preferred to supplant the "masses" with the "select minorities." However that may be, Ortega did link his concept of "mass man," "select minorities," and "mass society" with his basic phenomenological perspective of human interaction and human life.

Previously we saw that in order to attempt to develop individual consciousness and to realize the "vital possibilities" of his being, man, for Ortega, has to absorb himself within the "circumstances" of the social world and actively interact with other individuals in this social world. The development of individual consciousness and the realization of one's "vital possibilities" also entail an occasional withdrawal from social reality into the *"solitude"* of one's self (without remaining "hermetically enclosed" and locked in the ego), with the endeavor to possess both the "unique" individuality of the "I" (against the constraints of society) and the positive process of reciprocal human interaction. Although Ortega felt that "there is no creation without withdrawal into one's self,"[71] he also maintained that the "I" has to confront actively the "others" and "collide" in the "strife" that he calls "social relations."[72] The dynamics of "*de-solitudinizing*," through the actions and the creations of the individual in the social world, then, project the realm of possibilities not only from the "I" to the "other," and vice-versa, but also from "our" social world (in the here-and-now) to their social world (in the future)—in short, from one generation to the next. The individual, for Ortega, must withdraw from the social world not solely to realize the "vital possibilities" of his own being but also to attempt to create and to actualize the "vital possibilities" of the social world through which the "circumstances" of his very being (and the being of the "others") are essentially defined. In this context, man, by engaging actively in the social reality surrounding his "circumstances," contributes substantively to the making of the essence of society and history as well as to the essence of his own being.[73] Thus, the spatial-temporality of man and his "circumstances"—by way of his life, society, consciousness of time, and history—is the subsequent focus of our line of analysis that will take us into Ortega's concept of the "generation" and its role in his philosophy of history.

Chapter IV

Historical Sociology and the Concept of Generation: Toward a Philosophy of History

In Ortega's philosophy of human life, we noted, the individual's perception of the factual occurrence of death characterizes human life as an occurrence of reality in time, for, as man becomes consciously aware of the fact of death, his finiteness is essentially disclosed in time and in space. The events in the lives of individuals are related by their position in time and, when we view the individual from the context of "social relationships," we are able to discern the fact that the temporality of social reality, for Ortega, is characterized by the existential quality of the individual's experience of the "others." In the social world, "social relationships" among individuals take the form of "fellowships." By "fellowship" Ortega conveyed the notion that in the social world, various individuals share in a common sector of time and space with one another. The objective, social world that surrounds them, as "circumstances," is a common world and the consciousness processes of the "I" are part and parcel of this common world for-and-with-"others," in a manner such that the consciousness processes of the "others" are, as well, fundamentally a part of the "circumstances" of the "I." The social world and the consciousness processes of the individual, however, are more than the experiences of other individuals that are given directly in the common, vivid present of the here-and-now. The social world, for Ortega, also contains an implicit feature of social reality that is not experienced directly (in the broader sense of immediate confrontation) by the individual—in the here-and-now—but that is contemporaneous with the life of the individual and that may subsequently be made available to him as an experience in the future. Hence, the here-and-now of the individual, as an immediate and direct experience, extends itself (both as a process of consciousness and as a perceptible factual occurrence in space) into the broader social context of living and in-

teracting as "contemporaries."[1] In this context, the explicit features
of the social reality of "contemporaries" reveal the consciousness process of a generation of individuals as a temporal process.

The temporality of the lives of individuals (as "contemporaries"
and also as what Ortega called "coevals") is central to the concept of
the generation. In this sense, ultimate reality as the reality of human
life, for Ortega, is also the explicit manifestation of time (for time is
in man as the events of his life are connected to their placement in
time) and thus provides him with the basic structure of his concept
of generation and with the basis of historic changes. The life of man,
as being-in-the-making, is life as a happening; life as a changing structure. With each fleeting moment of the here-and-now, man's inner
stream of consciousness of the flow of time relates to the fact that
his life is changing, as he grows older, and is aging with each reference
to the no-longer-here and the not-here-yet. "The most elemental fact
of human life," he said,

> is that some men die and others are born—that lives succeed
> each other. All human life, in its very essence, is enclosed in
> between other lives which came before or which are to come
> after—it proceeds out of one life and goes into one which is
> to follow. Well then, it is on this most fundamental fact that
> I establish the inevitable necessity of change in the structure
> of the world. An automatic mechanism brings with it the
> irremediable certainty that within a given unit of time the
> characters of the life drama change. . . . One need not assume
> that the actors are different: the same actors *have to* perform
> different parts. This is not to say, heedlessly, that the youth
> of today—that is, his soul and his body—is different from the
> youth of yesterday; but it is inevitable that his life should
> have a different framework than that of yesterday.
>
> Well then, this is nothing but to find the reason and the
> period for historical changes in the fact joined essentially to
> human life, that this human life always has an age [a period
> of time]. Life is time—as Dilthey already made us see and
> Heidegger repeats to us today; and not imaginary cosmic time
> because imaginary time is infinite, but limited time, time
> which grows toward an end, which is the true time, the irrep-
> arable time. For this reason man has age. Age is man's being
> always in a certain part of his limited time-span—whether it is
> to be the beginning of his vital life's time, to be the ascension
> toward the middle, to be its center, or to be approaching to-

ward its end—or, as one is accustomed to say, whether he is a child, a youth, a mature man, or an old man.[2]

This being so, the no-longer-here, the here-and-now, and the not-here-yet meet in man by way of his consciousness of the internal flow of time. Society's position in time, for Ortega, is reflected through the concept of the generation (in its particular manifestations) and within the historical process (in its general manifestations of change). That is to say, the structure of society (which is taken here to connote a collection of individuals who interact with one another and whose essences are continually being defined within a dynamic process, for life is fundamentally change) is such that its temporal reality is also a fusion of past, present, and future. It may be said, then, that Ortega's concept of generation is the principle through which the no-longer-here, the here-and-now, and the not-here-yet come together in the temporal reality of the social world. Thus, when Ortega referred to one's "life time" as consisting of youth, maturity, and old age, we are able to discern that: in the first instance, his concept of generation is a horizontal reference to living individuals as being "contemporaries"; and, secondly, it refers to the vertical differentiation, in age, between youth, maturity, and old age—in short, as being "coevals." "This means that every historic present, every 'today,' to be precise, involves three distinct times," he explained,

> three different "todays." Or, to say it another way; that the present is rich in three great vital dimensions, those who live together dwelling with others in it, whether they wish it or not, joined with one another and, by force of circumstances, on being different, in essential hostility to one another. "Today" is for some individuals twenty years; for others, forty; for still others, sixty; and this, being three such distinct ways of life, which must be the same "today," abundantly declares the quality of being dynamic, the conflict, and the collision which constitute the background of historic material and of all present day living together. And in the light of this observation, one sees the ambiguity which is hidden in the apparent clarity of a date. [Nineteen thirty-three] seems a single time, but in 1933 there lives a boy, a mature man, and an old man, and that set of numbers is tripled in three different meanings and, at the same time, embraces all three: it is the unity of three different ages in one historical time.
>
> We are all contemporaries, we live at the same time, in the same atmosphere—in the same world—but we contribute to

their forming in very different ways. This way only coincides with coevals. Contemporaries are not coevals: it is urgent to distinguish in history between that which is contemporary and that which is coeval. Dwelling in the same external and chronological time, they live together in three distinct vital periods of life. . . . The concept of generation does not primarily imply more than these two things: to be of the same age and to have some vital contact.[3]

Ortega's view of the three distinct "life times," as manifestations of the concept of generation, consists in his notions of "coevals" (which refers to the interaction of individuals of approximately the same age) and of "contemporaries" (which is a reference to the interaction between all individuals of whatever age) and their appositeness with regard to time and to space.[4] As the active engagement in the social world is important for both the development of the individual and society, the inner dynamics of "vital" human interaction, for Ortega, are also important insofar as the concept of generation has any significance in illuminating the human condition. But "there still remains on this planet," he said, "human groups which are isolated from the rest of the others. It is evident that the individuals in those groups who are of the same age as we are do not belong to our generation because they do not participate in our world."[5] Although, from a theoretical perspective, Ortega considered every living individual as being a component element of the generation of "contemporaries" and "coevals," he qualified this conception by excluding those "isolated" individuals who do not actively take part in the "circumstances" of their social world. Yet we ask ourselves: how do we characterize those individuals who do engage actively in the "circumstances" of their reality but whose social worlds are different from those of other groups of individuals? They may be of the same age as these other groups of individuals and their activities are contemporaneous, but the "vital contact" of one group of individuals who belong to a particular social setting does not necessarily interact with that of another social group, as their social worlds are different in space, though not in time. This question takes us into the wider ramifications of Ortega's concept of the generation as we discuss the larger social world of "contemporaries." In short, we are about to discuss the much broader historical implications of Ortega's concept of generation.

As we had the occasion to discuss in our analysis, consciousness processes and the social world of individuals—in the general context of spatial and temporal reality—are not limited to the direct experiences of individuals in their common social world and in the here-and-now. In this connection, Ortega's concept of generation makes implicit the notion that the social worlds which are contemporaneous with one another but which are not directly experienced as common "vital contacts" do have the potential of some interaction in the future, for as "contemporaries" there is always the possibility, though never necessary, of some kind of individual interaction in the "circumstances" of the not-here-yet. If there is no common direct experience by way of the interactions of social worlds, there is still the common experience of the consciousness processes and the link between older, contemporary, and future generations. For as each generation has its own peculiar spatial dimension, also it "has a dimension in historic time," according to Ortega; that is, "in the melody of the human generations, it comes directly after another of its kind, as the note of a song sounds in relation to the way the previous note sounded."[6]

We find, then, that Ortega added to his notion of the three distinct "life times" (by way of "contemporaries" and "coevals" as the fundamental uniformities within a particular generation) his metaphysical, rhythmic theme of the "melody of the human generations." It is the "melody of the human generations" that functions as the unifying principle of the generations in general, in contrast to the generation in particular. In the particular context of the social world of the generation, "social relations" between "contemporaries" are more immediate and direct. As the concept of the generation is expanded to incorporate the different social worlds of groups of individuals who do not engage in immediate and direct experiences, Ortega described these individuals as "coexisting contemporaries." The various individuals, in the latter case, have to enter the transcendental attitude in an effort to go beyond the immediate "circumstances" of their social world, in an attempt to understand the social world of other individuals. This kind of consciousness process takes place on a horizontal level of collective individuals, as the "coexisting contemporaries" relate indirectly to one another with the realization that each generation and each social context has a unity which is peculiar to itself, in addition to the realization of the common experience of the historical relevance of the "melody of generations" in its general manifestations. "In the 'today,'" he said, "in every 'today,' various generations coexist and the relations which are established between them, according to the different condition of their ages, represent the dynamic system of attractions and repulsions, of concurrence and polemic, which at any given instant constitutes the reality of historic life."[7]

In this connection of the awareness of the groups of individuals of "coexisting contemporaries" should be considered the internal consciousness, within the social world of a particular generation, of the social reality of generations that are neither actually nor potentially accessible to its direct experience. In this situation, the groups of individuals, in their attempt to understand other generations, will have to adopt the transcendental attitude (as in the case of expanding the consciousness of the "I" after its encounter with the "others") not only so that they may go beyond the immediate "circumstances" of their own social world, but also so that they may extend beyond their here-and-now.[8] Each group of individuals, according to Ortega, has to extend itself beyond the social reality of its particular generation by relating to the social world of its predecessors and to the social world of its successors. In the social realm of the former (the no-longer-here), the individual groups in the here-and-now would have to be conscious of the world of the "others" of whom they might have knowledge and whose previous actions might in fact influence their own actions, but with whom there had been no individual interaction. The social realm of the latter (the not-here-yet) is the world of the "others" of whom the individual groups in the here-and-now have vague and inadequate (if any) knowledge, but upon whom they may exert some influence through their own individual actions and through their here-and-now. Thus, for Ortega, each group of individuals goes through the consciousness process of the temporal dimensions of past, present, and future within the perspective of their respective generations. Man, therefore, is an historical being. He continued:

> This reveals a keen intuition that the life of man is inserted into a broader process, within which it represents a race course. The individual is ascribed to his generation, but the generation is not just anywhere—utopian and timeless—but set between two definite generations. The same as in our individual lives the act which we are now performing, and therefore, the person we now are, assumes an irretrievable part of the specific time which our existence is going to endure, thus each generation represents an essential, irretrievable and not transferrable piece of historic time, of the vital trajectory of humanity.
>
> For this is what makes man substantially historical: this is why I told you . . . that life is the opposite of the utopian and timeless—it is having to be in a certain "here" and in a unique "now" for which there are no possible substitutes. The present of human destiny, the present in which we are living—better said, the present in which we are our being, understanding by that our individual lives—is what it is for the reason that on it

> rests the weight of all the other presents, all the other genera-
> tions. If those presents which are now the past, if the struc-
> ture of life in those generations had been something else, our
> situation also would be different. In this sense each human
> generation carries within itself all the previous generations, and
> is like a contraction of universal history. And in the same
> sense it is necessary to recognize that the past is here in the
> present, that we are its summary, that our present is made out
> of the material of that past, which past, therefore, is actual
> [present]—is the heart, the hidden core, of the present.
>
> It does not matter, then, whether a new generation applauds
> or hisses the previous generation—whether it does one thing
> or another, it carries the previous generation within itself.[9]

This perspective of the external dynamics of generational change
and continuity—vis-à-vis the individual—is central not only to Ortega's
philosophy of human life as a "happening" but also to his notion that
the temporal changes within the structure of human life are part and
parcel of the momentum within the historical process. That is, the
temporal structure of the "circumstances" of the social world confronts the individual as a tangible fact with which he must confer; it
faces him as a reality in which he must attempt to realize his "vital
possibilities." The consciousness process of time in the individual is
perceived as being continuous and finite. The life of an individual,
according to Ortega, is limited by the fact of death and, as such,
heightens the individual's perception of his existence and the fact that
the social world was a part of reality before he was born and will remain a part after he dies. Hence, the individual's awareness of this
fact and his knowledge of the inevitability of death makes temporal
reality, for man, finite and continuous. This internal consciousness of
the temporal changes within the individual coupled with an awareness
of the external manifestations of change within the social world—
through generational changes—suggests that Ortega's concept of the
generation is a concept of historical methodology:

> The concept of the generations, converted into a method of
> historical investigation, consists in nothing more than project-
> ing that structure across the past. Everything else which is not
> this is to renounce discovering the authentic reality of human
> life in every period of time—that is the mission of history.
> The method of the generations permits us to see that life
> from within itself, in its actuality. History is virtually to con-
> vert that which has already passed into that which is present.
> For this reason—and not only metaphorically—history is to

> relive the past. And as living is nothing else but actuality and the present, we have to transmigrate from the actuality and the present which are ours to those of the past, looking at them not from without, not as living experiences which have been, but as those which persist in being.[10]

Ortega's view of history as a "reliving of the past" in the present bears a certain resemblance to Croce's notion that "all history is contemporary history."[11] From the vantage point of the present, historical knowledge reconstitutes the lived-experiences of the dead by the living. To this notion, Ortega contributed his concept of the generation and of "contemporaries-coevals." The "theme of history," in this sense, is the story of the present in the light of the past. The concept of the generation, then, as a methodological concept, is not only the structure within which historical analysis can be attained but is also the structure through which various individuals interact in social situations, which pertains to Ortega's philosophy of man, society, and history. The concept of the generation is "the visual device," he says, "through which historical reality, vibrant and genuine, is made visible. At any given moment a generation is one and the same thing as the structure of human life."[12] Within the spectrum of the generations, each individual may become more conscious of his here-and-now as he becomes more aware of the past and the fact that his actions may, in turn, exert a certain amount of influence on future generations. As we have seen, the individual, for Ortega, has no choice other than to accept the given of the physical features of his being and the "circumstances" of his "I." The individual can, however, attempt to carve the essence of his being by actively engaging in the world that surrounds him with an effort toward realizing his "vital possibilities"—which are also rooted within the generation of his here-and-now. The "ideas and convictions" that the individual inherits from the past are revealed to the present in a different dress and are tailored to fit the individual of the here-and-now through the guise of what Ortega calls the "spirit of the times."[13] Ortega employed the term "spirit of the times" as a referral to the tendency of the generations—the "world in force" in the social world—to provide present ideas, convictions, and actions with the ideas, convictions, and actions of the past:

> In every moment man lives in a world of convictions, the greater part of which are the convictions common to all men who live together in their epoch: it is the spirit of the times. This we have called the world "in force," the ruling world, in order to indicate that it has not only the reality which our convictions lend to it, but also that it imposes upon us,

whether we like it or not, as the most essential ingredient in our circumstances. Just as man finds himself within the body which has fallen to him by chance and must live in it and with it, so he finds himself with the ideas of his time, and in them and with them—even though it be in the peculiar fashion of contending against them—he must live. This world in force— that "spirit of the times"—toward which and in the function of which we live, in view of which we decide our most simple actions—is the variable element of human life. When it changes, so does the argument of the human drama change. Important modifications in the structure of human life depend much more on this change in the world than on the change of characters, races, etc. And as the theme of history is not human life, which is a subject of philosophy—but the changes, the variations in human life—we will have to maintain that the primordial factor of history is the world which is "in force" in each period.

But the world changes with every generation because the previous generation has done something in the world, has left it more or less distinct from the way it was found. . . . The profile of the world is different and so, in consequence, is the structure of life.[14]

As the "theme of history" consists in unfolding the transitions and variations in human life, it is apparent that Ortega viewed his concept of generation to be the fundamental concept, or the "new science," of history. The actual successions of generations are "visible" and function as a fundamental framework within which we may approach historical reality. For, he contended, "it is history which, by constructing past reality up to the very moment of our present, establishes the actual and effective series of the generations. Such a task is not even completed, it has not even been initiated: it is this which, in my judgment, the new science of history is going to undertake."[15] History, as the process through which the "series of the generations" are connected, is also a kind of phenomenological process within which the individual apprehends himself and becomes conscious of his "I," of "others," of his past and his here-and-now (for "man has history"). For Ortega:

And as the consciousness of the *you* shapes and nourishes the consciousness of the *I*, so in this superlative sense of the awareness of *you*, of the *other* who is an aged member of society, recovers for the man of the present higher consciousness of his exclusive *I*.

"Historical sense" is a sense indeed—a function and an organ to perceive the distance as such. It represents the idea which makes it possible for man to escape from himself and, at the same time, by retroflexing, to have the ultimate clarity and understanding that an individual man can acquire for himself; and, then, having to discover, in order to become aware of former generations, the assumptions from those who lived in the past and, therefore, their limits, to discover by repercussion the tacit assumptions on which an individual, himself, lives and on which he maintains inscribed his existence. He knows, then, by means of a circuitous way which is history, his own limits, and this is the only stipulated manner for man to transcend them.[16]

To Ortega, as we saw, ideas and convictions—by way of the "spirit of the times"—emerge and develop within the context of a generation, and as the successions of generations of past, present, and future are linked through the continuum of the historical process, the variety in the ideas of individuals is inextricably connected to its particular social and historical context, and to the historical process as a whole Thus, in order to analyze and thereby attempt to understand the variety and depth of contemporary ideas, Ortega clamored for the historical perspective; for it is "the historian," he maintained, who "must, for any idea belonging to a certain time, find its source, that is, he must seek another idea coming out of some former time. This strictly means to search for the direct, precise, and unquestionable influence exercised by one individual—either personally or through his work—upon another individual."[17] It is the function of history and of the historian to place ideas and events into their appropriate social and historical context. Through this function, then, according to Ortega,

. . . this is a regulative principle of impregnable strength and one that represents the condition for the possibility of an historical science. There are no spurious ideas that spring up suddenly, in the minds of men, without precedents or previous filiation. History is perfect continuity. Every idea of mine comes from another idea of mine or from the idea of some other man. There is no spontaneous generation. *Omnis cellula e cellula.* The reader should try to imagine an idea which does not come from some other idea and which does not move toward another, that does not flow into another idea. *Coming from* and *going toward* are constitutive attributes of every idea. For this reason, it is essential for every idea to have a spring of water, a source, and the mouth of a river, an outlet, which are hydraulic images of firm stability.[18]

The historical nature of human reality and social thought sheds light upon Ortega's notion that "there is no spontaneous generation," for the "series of the generations" function through the continuity of the historical process. Social thought and the ideas of individuals reflect "the minds of men" together with the particular generations within which they develop and, if constituted as "coming from" and "going toward," they are part and parcel of the "happening" of the historical process.[19] As we have seen, man's being-in-the-making, for Ortega, is a "happening" toward the future. The present grows out of the past and, as the reality exigent to man, veers toward the future. This "historical sense" of continuity, between "the minds of men" and the succession of generations, recalls for us Ortega's assertion that the individual cannot live solely within the isolation of his ego (whether he is a "mass" or a "select" man). Social thought in general and the ideas of individuals in particular, by their very essence, do not develop and expand within the solipsistic vacuum of the "I." As a being of the social world, the individual and his ideas are influenced very much by the historical context and the very social world through which they emerged, and, by the same token, are formed by the past. From this point of view, according to Ortega, "it would be a 'crass error' to presume that we can think about anything in 'absolute' independence of the human past" of what has been "thought, felt," and "desired" by man in the past.[20] Thus, feelings, desires and the thoughts of men are as historical as man is himself. He said:

> Thinking, then, renounces defining, at least directly, anything that pretends to be absolute, and resolves to investigate the one and only reality unquestionably given to it: such subjective facts of thinking, desiring, feeling as having happened have occurred at some time and at some place, that is to say, historical facts. "Pure" or absolute thought gives way to historical thought.
>
> Thus historical thought proceeds with respect to human phenomena—philosophy, law, society, arts and letters, language, religion—the same thing began with the natural sciences, as established in the works of Kepler and Galileo, when they proceeded to bring together empirically the simple facts of material phenomena.[21]

From this perspective, man, time, thought, and society are disclosed in reality as being essentially historical. Man is not born at some place and moment in general, for Ortega; rather he is born at a particular moment in time and at a particular place in space.[22] Human life has a beginning and an end and, on entering the world, man enters a social world that is given to him in conjunction with the historical process of its time dimension. In this sense the concept of "age" (or the number of years that an individual lives his life), according to Ortega, "is not the essence of mathematics, but of vital life."[23] "Age, then," he said, "is not a date, but a 'zone of dates'; and it is not only those born in the same year who are the same age in life and in history, but those who are born within a zone of dates."[24] As "age" is the "essence of life," the very essence of life itself is inextricably interwoven into the actions of man and in his social and historical context. Man thus (as a unique individual and as a member of the social world) makes history through his actions as his very being is historical. As we saw, for Ortega, "man has no nature . . . what he has is history." For, he says, "man is the entity that makes itself . . . the causa sui."[25] History, then, is the process through which the essence of man is made, both as an individual and as a social being. For as an individual being, man goes through the stream of consciousness of an internal "happening" as an historical process; as a being-that-lives-in-the-world, man experiences the succession of generations as an external "happening" within the historical process. It is in this connection that Ortega viewed the "theme of history" and "historical thought" as proceeding "with respect to human phenomena."

The influence of historicism on the historical thought of Ortega becomes more apparent as he attempted to dispense with the validity of a reality solely based upon "material phenomena," or what he called "physico-mathematical reason," by reducing human reality to the facts of history. This notion of historical reality, however, is not "absolute" and does not consist in a process which is isolated solely by the facts of its events. For "an isolated fact," he said, "although of the most enormous calibre, does not explain any historical reality; it is necessary to integrate it into the total framework of a type of human life. The rest is a chronicle's dead data."[26] Like Croce, Ortega viewed history qua history as being "contemporary" and "living," whereas mere facts are relegated to the realm of "dead chronicle."[27] History, through the succession of generations, not only provides us with the basic features of man at a particular time and at a particular place, but also provides us with "a regulative principle" of coherence for human phenomena. The unity of the past and the present in history, for Ortega, is a reality which is identified with the experiences of individuals. The contemporaneity of history, then, is a dynamic process that is ever changing and that is continuously absorbed by the past. The relations that past events bear to other events and to the present are significant in that they are continually changing and, according to Ortega, the function of the philosopher (and, in this connection, the historian, for "man has history") is not only to describe and analyze the past but also to attempt to understand these relations in conjunction with human life. Ortega thus dismissed "pure reason" and the "natural sciences" ("physico-mathematical reason") as being devoid of any authentic knowledge of human life. He said:

> It could be injurious were physico-mathematical reason, in its crude form of naturalism or in its beatific form of spiritualism, to confront human problems. By its very constitution it could do no more than search for man's nature. And, naturally, it did not find it. For man has no nature. Man is not his body, which is a thing; nor is he his soul, psyche, conscience, or spirit, which is also a thing. Man is not a thing, but a drama —his life, a pure and universal happening which happens to each one of us and in which each one in his turn is nothing but happening. . . . Existence itself is not a "fact" which is given to him and regulated like a stone, but . . . on encountering the fact that he exists, on existence happening to him, all that he encounters or all that happens to him is not something for which there is any remedy other than to act in some way in order not to cease existing. . . . Life is a gerundive, not a participle: a *faciendum*, not a *factum*.[28]

If human life is "not a thing" and "has no nature," if it is a *"faciendum"* and not a *"factum,"* then, according to Ortega, "it is necessary to resolve for ourselves, to think of it [human life] in terms of categories and concepts that will be *radically* distinct and that will make clear for us the phenomena of matter."[29] The "concepts and categories" to which Ortega referred as being *"radically* distinct" are concepts and categories that are similar to those postulated by Dilthey, in his *Einleitung in die Geisteswissenschaften,* for the purpose of distinguishing between the natural sciences (*Naturwissenschaften*) and the human or cultural sciences (*Geisteswissenschaften*). Ortega said:

> It will be said that, corresponding to what has been observed, the more stress placed on the resistance of the human phenomenon to physical reason [or science], the more prominent became another form of science opposed to this: facing the natural sciences, in effect, there arose and developed the so-called sciences of the spirit, the moral or cultural sciences. To this I reply, promptly, that these sciences of the spirit—

> *Geisteswissenschaften*—have not thus far been successful in
> moving the European to believe in the way that the natural
> sciences succeeded.[30]

The cultural sciences, he thought, will convey the appropriateness of
their realm and function in regard to human life (in contrast to the
"phenomena of matter") once it is clearly established and demonstrated that "physico-mathematical reason" and the natural sciences
"have shown themselves to be insufficient to explain the human element."[31] For Ortega, the "abstract concepts" of rationalism and the
"natural truths" offered by the natural sciences are inadequate for
rendering the unique and concrete realities of man and history. The
natural sciences and "physico-mathematical reason," as systems, he
contended, fail to grasp the unsystematic variety of human experience
and its historical expression.[32] The life of the individual is the "experience of life," and this very "experience of life," according to
Ortega, "is the life of each one of us."[33] The "experience of life,"
for him, however, is not to be considered solely as an experience
which is unique to the individual in particular but is construed also
as an experience which unifies the lives of individuals in general by
way of the historical time dimensions of society—through the succession of generations—and its relation to the here-and-now of the "I."
"The experience of life," he said, "is not made up only of the experiences that I personally have had, of my past. It is also integrated by
the past of my predecessors, that the society in which I live trans-
mits to me. Society consists primarily in a repertory of usages, intellectual, moral, political, technical, of play and pleasure . . . the determination of *what* at each moment society *is going to be* depends
on what it has been, the same as in the individual life."[34] Thus, the
"experience of life" has both individual and collective characteristics
as well as a fundamental historical manifestation. The temporal dimensions of simultaneity, succession, and process are inherent in
human life and history, for Ortega, and these temporal dimensions,
by their very nature, are concerned with the lives of individuals both
as unique and as collective beings. For "history," he said, "is the reality of man. He has no other. Through history he has made himself
such as he is."[35]

The knowability of historical reality, therefore, is not constituted
by the formulation of general laws or principles of the natural sciences; rather, it consists in the comprehensive perception of the
variety of the particular manifestations of the historical process. In
this sense, historical reality is tangible and knowable, for its subject
matter is human life in its variation and in its totality. History centers

on the "circumstances" of human life with a particular focus on the "I" of the individual and thereby, according to Ortega, must be relegated to the realm of the cultural sciences rather than be subsumed under the realm of "physico-mathematical reason" with its general schema of natural phenomena and the abstract concepts of mathematics. This distinction between the cultural sciences and the physical and mathematical sciences—which had been ushered in at the turn of the century by such historicist thinkers as Croce and Dilthey with their emphasis on the relativistic features of reality—confronted Ortega with the task of explaining for us how we are to apprehend the relations between human life, experience, and history once the coherence of the natural sciences and "physico-mathematical reason" is superseded by his notion of the variety in human and historical reality. In short, Ortega replaced the physical and mathematical sciences, as the principles of unity, with history, as the principle of diversity, so that the historical perspective of reality heightens our perception and understanding of the varieties in human reality. "Physico-mathematical reason," for Ortega, must be supplanted with what he calls "vital" or "historical reason." For "it is advisable," he said, "to take due note of the strange mode of knowledge, of comprehension, represented by this analysis of what, concretely, our life, that of the present, is. . . . In short, the reasoning, the *reason*, that sheds light here consists in a narration. Facing pure physico-mathematical reason there is, then, a narrative reason. In order to comprehend anything human, be it personal, or collective, it is necessary to tell its history. . . . Life only returns a small degree of transparency in the presence of *historical reason*."[36] For Ortega, as we saw, "man has no nature . . . he has history"; this notion at once denaturalizes and historicizes man's very essence and, thus, "historical reason" becomes the cognitive paradigm for apprehending human reality:

> The characterization of knowledge as historical magnitude . . . does not claim to defend it solely as a paradigm in which, with motive of applying it to the particular case which is knowledge, it attempts an operation of general consequence that reports my philosophical labor for some years under the title of "historical reason." It discusses, in effect, carrying to its ultimate and radical consequences, the assertion that the specific human reality—the life of man—has an historical consistency. This compels us to "denaturalize" all the concepts relating to the integral phenomenon of human life and to subject them to a radical "historicization." Very little that man has been, that he is or will be, has been thus, is thus or

will be thus once and for all, but he *has come to be thus* one day and another day *will cease to be thus*. Permanence in the forms of human life is an optical illusion originated in the crudeness of the concepts with which we think, in virtue of which ideas that only abstractly would defend applying to these forms are used as if they were concrete and, therefore, as authentically representing reality. . . . Whosoever desires to understand man, who is a reality *in vía* [*on the road*], a being substantially alien, has to throw overboard all the immobile concepts and learn to think with notions that are continually moving.[37]

This being the case, human reality is revealed through the "vital" interaction of individuals in historical reality. Through the epistemological standpoint of "I am I and my circumstances" man, in order to realize the "vital possibilities" of the essence of his being, lives in an actively disclosing manner. The process of the realization of the "vital possibilities" of man—through the "circumstances" of his being—as a being-in-the-making and as a being-that-goes-on-being-in-the-world is described by Ortega as constituting a "happening," for "being is in man," he explained, "mere *happening, happening* to him."[38] This process of "happening," which Ortega ascribed to man as an "authentic" being-that-goes-on-being-in-the-world, is an historical process and, as such, identifies man as an historical being. The individual's consciousness of his temporality in the present—as "man lives in view of the past," according to Ortega—is manifested as he veers toward his "vital possibilities" in the future. The "I's" consciousness of the time process, for Ortega, then, is as historical as the external manifestations of its "circumstances"—vis-à-vis the succession of generations in time by way of the past, present, and future—for both (the "I" and its "circumstances") are fundamentally historical as concrete experiences of reality. As he said:

> Man invents for himself a program of life, a static form of being, that responds satisfactorily to the difficulties planned for him by circumstance. He essays this figure of life, attempts to realize this imaginary character he has resolved to be. He embarks on this essay illusioned and creates, completely, the experience of it. . . . But on experimenting with it the limits of this vital program make apparent its insufficiencies. It does not resolve all the difficulties, and it creates new ones. The form of life first appeared in the forefront, through its shining face: for this reason it was the illusion, the enthusiasm, the delight of its promise. Presently, one sees the back part of its limita-

tion. Then man conceives of another vital program. But this second program is confirmed, not only in view of the circumstances, but also in view of the first. Therefore, in the second vital program, the first continues to be active and is preserved in order to be avoided. Inexorably, man avoids being what he was. On the second project of being, after the second experience of depth, follows a third, framed in the light of the second and the first and so on. Man "goes on being" and "unbeing"—living. Man goes on accumulating being—the past: he goes on making a being in the dialectical series of his experiences. This dialectic is not of logical reason, but is necessarily of historical reason—it is the *Realdialektik* of which Dilthey dreamt somewhere in an inside corner of his papers, the man to whom we owe more than anyone else the idea of life and, who is, to my mind, the most important thinker of the second half of the nineteenth century.[39]

It is quite evident, at this point, that Ortega was indebted to Dilthey for his idea of human life as ultimate reality and his concept of "historical reason." The "authentic being" of man that "goes-on-being" and "un-being," for Ortega, is historical, and the dynamic interaction between the "I" and its "circumstances," between man and society and through the continuity of past, present, and future in the succession of generations, is historical. The temporality of human life is revealed to man as the subjective structure of his consciousness of the time process—as the "I" that "goes-on-being"—at the same time that the objective structure of human life is manifested through the historical process. The objective structure of life, as we observed in the above statement, is a continuum of "circumstances" that are operative and that are connected not by a dialectical process of logic but by the "dialectical series" of the experiences of the individual—namely, the process of history. For the dialectic of the experiences in human "circumstances," according to Ortega, is linked by a principle of uniformity which is embedded in history, not in logic. At this juncture, Ortega raised the question: "In what consists this dialectic that will not tolerate the facile anticipations of logical dialectic? This is," he continued,

what one has to find out on the basis of facts. One must inquire into what is this series, what is its subject matter, and in what consists the nexus between the successive stages. This investigation is what would be called history were history to propose this as its objective, were it, that is to say, to convert itself into historical reason.

Here, then, awaiting our study, lies man's authentic "be-ing"—stretching the whole length of his past. Man is what has happened to him, what he has done. Other things could have happened to him or have been done by him, but what effec-tively has happened to him and has been done by him con-stitutes an inexorable trajectory of experiences that he carries on his back as the vagabond the bundle of all he possesses. Man is this pilgrimage of being, this substantial emigrant. But this desired sense of placing limits on what man is capable of being is meaningless. In this initial unlimitation of his possi-bilities, properly for one who has no nature, there is only one fixed line, pre-established and given, that may orient our course; there is only one limit: the past. The experiences al-ready formed of life narrow man's future. If we do not know what he is going to be, we know what he is not going to be. Man lives in view of the past.

In short, *man, in a word, has no nature; but he has . . . history*. Expressed differently: what nature is to things, his-tory, as *res gestae*, is to man. . . . Man finds that he has no nature other than what he has himself done.[40]

From this point of view, then, the dialectic of the experiences in the lives of individuals is the historical process within which it ad-vances itself toward actualizing the "vital possibilities" of man's being. The past imposes certain constraints on individual action; however, as "man has history," the future suggests a kind of freedom for one to attempt to realize one's own "vital possibilities." The reality of human life, thus, for Ortega, is the historical reality of the present. The real-ity of the present retains the reality of the past within its very struc-ture and, as an ever-changing moment in time, is part and parcel of the past and the future. He said:

Here, then, is how in our present political attitude, in our political being, all the human past that is known to us per-sists. That past is past not because it happened to others but because it forms part of our present, of what we are in the form of having been: in short, because it is *our* past. Life as reality is absolute presence: one cannot say that *there is* any-thing if it is not present, of this moment. If, then, *there is* a past, it must be as something present, something active in us now.[41]

This being the case, Ortega was in accord with Croce's notion that "we know that history is in all of us and that its sources are in our breasts."[42] According to this view, the reality of history and human life is not the recording of "chronicle's dead data" of the past, but is the "vital," living action of the present, which is one with the past and the future.[43] History is not something that we possess (for "man is not a thing"); rather, it is *what we are*. In this connection, then, the historicization of man and the historicization of reason disclose the historical process of time and consciousness as evolving from its principle of variety toward a principle of uniformity. For Ortega, the function of "historical reason" is to perceive and to register the tangible facts of historical reality through the demonstrative process of how the present originates from the past so as to engender the future. In conjunction with the historicization of man, "historical reason," for Ortega, is the medium that circumscribes and eventually supplants "physico-mathematical reason" as the unitary principle of ultimate reality—human life, and thereby "historical reason" is viewed as possessing, at once, the principle of diversity and unity. Hence, history is rationalized and reason is historicized, as is the case with man:

> Man asks himself: what is this singular thing that remains to me, my life, my disillusioned life? How has it come to being nothing but this? And the answer is the discovery of the human trajectory, of the dialectical series of his experiences. . . . Man alienated from himself encounters himself as reality, as history. And, for the first time, he sees himself compelled to occupy himself with his past, not from curiosity nor in order to find normative examples, but because he *has no* other thing. Things are never done seriously but when, truly, they are absolutely necessary. For this reason, the present hour is the time for history to re-establish itself as historical reason.
>
> Until now history has been contrary to reason. In Greece the two terms "reason" and "history" were opposed. And until now, in effect, hardly anyone has been concerned to search in history for its rational substance. At most, there has been the desire to carry to it [history] a strange reason not its own, as with Hegel, who injected into history the formalism of his logic, or Buckle, his physiological and physical reason. My purpose is strictly the reverse. It attempts to find in history itself its original, autochthonous reason. Hence the expression "historical reason" must be understood in all the rigor of the term. Not an extrahistorical reason which appears to fulfill itself in history but, literally, *a substantive reason constituted by what has happened to man*, the revelation of

> a reality transcending man's theories and which is himself,
> the self underlying his theories.
>
> Until now what we have had of reason was not historical
> and what we have had of history was not rational.
>
> Historical reason is, then, *ratio*, *logos*, a rigorous concept.
> It follows that there should not arise the slightest doubt about
> this. In opposing it to physico-mathematical reason there is
> no question of granting a license to irrationalism. On the con-
> trary, historical reason is still more rational than physical
> reason, more rigorous, more exigent.[44]

Through this description of "historical reason" it is apparent that
Ortega, like Dilthey, Windelband, Rickert, and Croce, had set before
himself the task of liberating history and man—the "cultural sciences"—
from the unifying principles of the physical and mathematical sciences.[45] Ortega was in accord with the general position of positing
the difference between nature (or the natural sciences) and history.
To Windelband, the natural sciences aim to formulate general laws
and are concerned with knowledge of the universal, whereas the objective of history is the description of individual facts and its concern
is with knowledge of the individual. Both are sciences: the former
nomothetic and the latter *idiographic*. Rickert carried Windelband's
distinction between the natural sciences and history another step by
drawing the further distinction between the general principles of the
natural sciences as nonvaluing principles and the individualizing tendencies of history as putting forward values. Rickert maintained that
the physical world really consists of individual facts and does not, in
itself, consist of general laws. The natural sciences arbitrarily con-
struct generalized principles and thereby cannot really represent reality. History, on the other hand, does consist of individual facts and,
as such, really constitutes reality.

Ortega was in accord with the general position of Windelband and
Rickert establishing the fundamental differences between the natural
sciences and history, but he went beyond this position and Rickert's
contention that history consists of individual facts with his notion of
"historical reason." From the point of view of "historical reason,"
for Ortega, the essence of history does not consist solely of individual facts; rather it consists in the development of the "dialectical
series" of the experiences of individual beings. Isolated individual
facts are "dead," disconnected and meaningless outside of the rubric
of the dynamic reality of man and his "circumstances." The function
of historical thought (as "historical thinking proceeds with respect to
human phenomena") is the manner in which the mind of the historian,

as a mind rooted in the reality of the present, apprehends and perceives the process through which this very mind has emerged into existence through the mental processes of the past. For "there are no
spurious ideas that spring up suddenly, in the minds of men, without
precedents or previous filiation."[46] In this connection, Ortega's historical thought came close to Dilthey and Croce.

To Dilthey, historical facts provide the historian with the opportunity to relive, in his own mind, the spiritual activities which had
originally created them. History, in itself, is life, and historical knowledge is the attempt to understand the inward experience of life and
its subject matter. "Here," he said, "the concept of the human studies
is completed. . . . The mind can only understand what it has created.
Nature, the subject matter of the natural sciences, embraced the reality which has arisen independently of the activity of the mind. Everything on which man has actively impressed his stamp forms the subject matter of the human studies."[47] Although Ortega shared several
of his ideas with these thinkers, he did make some distinctive contributions of his own. His reference point was not only to the separate
realms of the "cultural sciences" and the "natural sciences" and what
the former can do and what the latter cannot do, and vice versa. It
seems that by the term "historical reason" he was suggesting something further: namely, that history has its "autochthonous" reason;
history is in a realm of its own. Ortega's notion of history's "autochthonous" reason establishes for history its autonomy from both
the abstract concepts of philosophy and the logic of "physico-mathematical reason." History is autonomous in that history alone consists
of the essence of human reality and historical knowledge provides us
with the essential understanding of this human reality. Every concept "claiming to represent human reality," he says, "every concept
referring to human life, specifically, is a function of historical time."[48]
History is living and, thus, is contemporary. In this sense, Ortega's
historical thought bears a striking resemblance to that of Croce. All
history is contemporary history, for Croce, and, as such, provides the
historian with self-knowledge of the living mind. Croce identified
philosophy with history as he viewed the historical process to be the
expression of the "inseparable syntheses of individual and universal,"[49]
and, thereby, history, as the synthesis of the individual and the universal, is the most complete form of knowledge. For Croce, "history
is thought" and, in this connection, the term history is synonymous
with the notion of philosophical history. History goes on in the mind
of the historian as he identifies himself with the events of the past
that he is studying and actually relives them as he thinks them
through. History "is in all of us."[50] Philosophy, too, has its "origin

in life, and we must," Croce said, "refer them [history and philosophy] back to life if we are to give a satisfactory interpretation of their propositions, we must plunge them into life again to develop them and to find in them new aspects."[51] In this manner, Croce defined philosophy as the methodology of history and thereby established the identity of philosophy with history. "The *whole of history*," he said, "is the foundation of philosophy as history, and to limit its foundation to the *history of philosophy* alone, and of 'general' or 'metaphysical' philosophy, is impossible, save by unconsciously adhering to the old idea of philosophy, not as methodology but as metaphysic, which is the fifth of the prejudices that we are enumerating."[52]

Ortega extended Croce's concept of the contemporaneity of history to include his ontological analysis of man's "authentic being" and the "drama" of man's life as a "happening." The life of the individual, as being-in-the-world, is disclosed to him as finite in the face of death. Man is born at one time and place and dies at another. For Ortega, as we saw, man "*has come to be thus* one day and another day will *cease to be thus*."[53] The points in between this "beginning" and "end" constitute at once the very essence and the vital possibilities of his being. Birth and death signal the "beginning" and the "end" of the "series of experiences" within each individual human life, so that through time man's life as a "happening" is one of "coming from" and "going toward." The process through which man has "come to be thus" and will "cease to be thus" is characterized by the connection of the succession of the "series of experiences" of man in the spatio-temporal realm of his "circumstances." The here-and-now of the individual—vis-à-vis birth and death—is located between the boundaries of past and future. Temporality, thus, is at the very "root of man's radical reality" and thereby reveals the historicity of his being. Man "has history," in view of the temporality of his being, and the essence of his being is continuously defined within the process of becoming. In this connection, for Ortega, not only is the contemporaneity of history the reliving of the past in the present, but also it signifies a context of events which stretch through the past, the present, and the future. In short, the historicity of man's contemporaneity is the constant interplay among the events of the past, present, and future. It is this ontological dimension of man and society (by way of his theory of generations) that Ortega contributed to his notion of "historical reason" and to Croce's idea that "all history is contemporary history." History, man, reason, and time are inextricably intertwined into the dynamic, vital dimension of human life. The historical process—as the "dialectical series of man's experiences" through his past, present, and future—is, according to Ortega, "a substantive reason" that is constituted by "what has happened to man" and, as such, has its own principle of coherence by way of the dynamics of "historical reason," for it does not rest upon the *absolute* goals" that impose a kind of unity on history, as the "logic" in Hegel's system and the "positivism" in Comte. As an historical concept, "historical reason" is dynamic for, we saw, "every concept referring to a specifically human life is a function of historical time."[54] On the other hand, a philosophy of history that is concerned primarily with *absolute* goals," he argued, "is taken out of the historical process and made timeless. . . . Hegel and Comte succeeded in discovering a meaning in the past, but at the cost of relating the past to something ultrahistorical, to a *pleroma* or 'plenitude of all times' which for the same reason that they are fulfilled they cease to be in time and in space."[55]

To Ortega, the rational truths of the logic of abstract concepts and the natural truths offered by the natural sciences were inadequate for rendering the active and concrete realities of man and history. Through his notion "I am I and my circumstances," as we have seen, Ortega posited human life—the "radical reality" of the "I"—as ultimate reality. As "man has history," he viewed the reality of life to consist in the active experiences "of what, concretely, our life is in the present."[56] This being so, "history is a system," he said, "the system of human experiences linked in a single, inexorable chain."[57] It is in view of this "chain of being" in the experiences of individuals that Ortega rejected the notion that we can have an "absolute" and "final" history or philosophy of reality. For him, reality is life and history in its dynamic variety and uniformity in the present. In this connection, Ortega attempted to develop systematically for history a science of the present somewhat similar to that which Kant had constructed for the physical and the mathematical sciences and to what Dilthey had attempted with his *Critique of Historical Reason*.[58] The contemporaneity of man and history as the fundamental traits of temporal reality projects, for Ortega, this reality of the present as being an historical reality. Ortega went beyond the notion of "history as contemporary history" to incorporate into his viewpoint the idea that the reality of human life and history is a "system of human experiences" and, as such, is the "science" of man as well as the "science of the present." As Ortega said, "The science of history must be grounded in a thorough knowledge of man; but knowledge of man must in its turn, at least partly, proceed from history."[59] History thus becomes what Ortega termed the "systematic science of the present." By supplanting the principles of coherence of the physical and the mathematical sciences with that of his concept of "historical reason," Ortega attempted to resolve the dilemma of the duality of the principle of variety and the principle of uniformity of reality as he relegated the unity of both principles to be served best by the function of "historical reason." In short, the historicization of reason and man is what is constituted by "historical reason" as it systematizes the relations of the principle of diversity with the principle of unity. It is "scientific," for Ortega, in that history is the concrete, "vital," and dynamic process through which man goes-on-being and through which man's ever-changing "I" and "circumstances" are existent, tangible, and visible as the present emerges from the past and veers toward the future:

> History is the systematic science of that radical reality which is my life. It is, then, a science of the present in the most rigorous and actual sense of the word. If it were not a science of the present, where would we encounter that past which one can ascribe to it as a theme? The opposite interpretation, which is customary, is the equivalent to making of the past an abstract, unreal thing that remained lifeless just where it happened in time, when the past is the live and active force that sustains our today. There is no *actio in distans*. The past is not there, at the date when it happened, but here, in me. The past is I—by which I understand, my life.[60]

In this description, we are able to perceive that Ortega's concept of history as "the science" of present reality is the "inexorable chain" of his philosophy of history. The temporality of the life of man is revealed through the subjective structure of his "radical reality" (which is a being-that-goes-on-being), as the objective structure of human life is manifested in time and in space through the historical dimensions of past, present, and future. By actively engaging in the "circumstances" of his "I," man carves out the "vital possibilities" that are unique to his essence as being-in-the-making. By the same token, man's actions are actualized in the present and thereby are fused with the actions and the here-and-now of "others" into the dynamics of the historical process. In this way, the spatial and temporal manifestations of man's being are linked with the historicity of his being, for his life is a "happening" in a reality that is by its very nature historical. The phenomenological perspective of Ortega is thus at one with his existentialist and historicist points of view. The synthetic function of these perspectives is actualized in the actions of man, in society, and in history, and it is the fusion of these points of view that took Ortega beyond his intellectual forebears. It is within the fusion of these perspectives that Ortega contributed his philosophy of man, society, and history to the history of intellectual history. Although Ortega would probably deny this assertion, in the process of rejecting the validity of the metaphysics of the systematic explanations of reality by the physical and mathematical sciences, he in fact created his own metaphysical system, as we discern, through his epistemological standpoint, the explicit postulate: the real is the historical; the historical, the real.

Notes

Introduction

1. "Datos Biográficos de José Ortega y Gasset," in the Archives of the Ortega family (Madrid: Bárbara de Braganza 12, compiled in 1964); hereafter cited as "Datos Biográficos."

2. Ibid.

3. Ibid.

4. *El Imparcial* (Madrid), 14 March 1904, p. 3.

5. José Ortega y Gasset, *Los Terrores del Año Mil: Crítica de una Leyenda* (Madrid: Establecimiento Tipográfico de El Liberal, 1909).

6. Ibid., pp. 3-4, 7-10, 20-24, 35.

7. José Ortega y Gasset, *Obras Completas*, 6th ed., 11 vols. (Madrid: Revista de Occidente, 1962-65, 1969), 2:118.

8. *El Imparcial*, 19 January 1908, p. 1.

9. José Ortega y Gasset, "Cartas de José Ortega y Gasset a Navarro Ledesma," Archives of the Ortega family (Madrid: Bárbara de Braganza 12, 28 May 1905, p. 4; 16 May 1905, p. 6; 16 May 1905, p. 7; 5 May 1905, p. 1. Hereafter cited as "Ortega a Ledesma." These "Cartas de Ortega a Ledesma" appear with the "Cartas de Navarro Ledesma a José Ortega y Gasset" as "Cartas Inéditas a Navarro Ledesma" and as "Dos Cartas a Ortega y Gasset" in *Cuadernos*, no. 66 (1962):3-23.

10. Paul Honigsheim, "The Time and the Thought of the Young Georg Simmel," in *Georg Simmel: A Collection of Essays with Translations and Bibliography*, ed. Kurt Wolff (Columbus: Ohio State University Press, 1959), p. 172.

11. "Ortega a Ledesma," 28 May 1905, p. 9.

12. Ibid., 9 August 1905, pp. 5-6, 8.

13. Ibid., pp. 8-9; "I am weary of Leipzig which is a very ugly town, extremely common, and conspicuously industrial. I am thinking of spending next September in Berlin. . . ." Ibid., 27 August 1905, p. 2; Ortega y Gasset, *Obras*, 8:26.

14. "Datos Biográficos"; Ortega y Gasset, *Obras*, 8:26-32; Honigsheim, "Young Georg Simmel," pp. 168-70; Ortega y Gasset, *Obras*, 8:30.

15. Ortega y Gasset, *Obras*, 8:20, 34; José Ortega y Gasset, "Epistolario entre Miguel de Unamuno y José Ortega y Gasset," *Revista de Occidente* 2, no. 19 (1964): 30 December 1906, 10; 27 January 1907, 12. See also Francisco Giner de los Ríos, "Carta a Ortega," *Revista de Occidente* 3, no. 23 (1965), 13 May 1911, 125-33.

16. Ortega y Gasset, *Obras*, 6:383 n.

17. "Datos Biográficos."

18. Manuel Tuñón de Lara, *La España del Siglo XX* (Paris: Librería Española, 1966), pp. 30-38.

19. Rafael Marquina, "El Bautista del 98," *La Gaceta Literaria* 5, no. 99 (1931):4-5; Hans Jeschke, *La Generación de 1898*, trans. from German to Spanish by Y. Pino Saavedra (Santiago: University of Chile, 1946), pp. 53-58. On the question of the "Spanish problem" and the concept "generation of '98," see Carlos Blanco Aguinaga, *Juventud del 98* (Madrid: Siglo XXI de España Editores S.A., 1970), pp. 3-38. Another good account is Pedro Laín Entralgo, *España como Problema*, 2 vols. (Madrid: Aguilar, 1956), 2:9-63; 407-46.

20. Raymond Carr, *Spain: 1808-1939* (Oxford: Clarendon Press, 1966), pp. 384-86.

21. Antonio Azorín, *La Generación de '98* (Madrid: Renacimiento, 1913), pp. 25-28, 72-89.

22. Jeschke, *La Generación de 1898*, p. 60.

23. Guillermo Díaz-Plaja, *Modernismo Frente a Noventa y Ocho*, 2nd ed. rev. (Madrid: Espasa Calpe, S.A., 1966), pp. 14-20.

24. Juan López-Morillas, *El Krausismo Español: Perfil de una Adventura Intelectual* (México: Fondo de Cultura Económica, 1956), pp. 114-20, 20-29, 142-52, 169-75.

25. Ibid., pp. 15-30, 20-29, 24, 59.

26. Karl Christian Friedrich Krause, *Le Système de La Philosophie*, trans. from German to French by Lucien Buys, 2 vols. (Leipzig: Otto Schulze, 1892), 1:16-22, 135-40; Clay MacCauley, *Karl Christian Friedrich Krause: Heroic Pioneer for Thought and Life* (Berkeley, Calif., 1925), pp. 8-52. See also Krause, *The Ideal of Humanity and Universal Federation* (Edinburgh: T & T Clark, 1900), pp. 3-84; Vicente Cacho Víu, *La Institución Libre de Enseñanza: Orígines y Estapa Universitaria (1860-1881)* (Madrid: Ediciones Rialp, S.A., 1962).

27. MacCauley, *Krause*, pp. 11-19.

28. Ibid., pp. 18-19.

29. López-Morillas, *El Krausismo*, pp. 96-98, 176-80. Carr, *Spain*, 302-3; Juan López-Morillas, *Hacia El 98; Literatura, Sociedad, Ideología* (Barcelona: Ediciones Ariel, 1972), pp. 138-59; Julián Sanz del Río, *Sanz del Río (1814-1869), Documentos, Diarios y Epistolarios*, ed. Pablo de Azcárate (Madrid: Editorial Tecnos, 1969). See, in particular, Clara E. Lida, *Anarquismo y Revolución en la España del XIX* (Madrid: Siglo XXI de España Editores, S.A., 1972), pp. 99-109, 111-68.

30. Gumersindo de Azcárate, *Giner de los Ríos 1839-1914: La Cuestion Universitaria, 1875* (Madrid: Editorial Tecnos, 1967), pp. 80-82.

31. Ibid., pp. 77-82; Carr, *Spain*, pp. 469-70.

32. Azcárate, *Giner de los Ríos*, pp. 77-80; MacCauley, *Krause*, p. 19.

33. López-Morillas, *El Krausismo*, pp. 83-106.

34. Ibid., p. 175; Ortega y Gasset, *Obras*, 8:21.

35. *Faro* (Madrid), 23 February 1908, p. 18.

36. Ibid., 8 March 1908, pp. 25-26.

37. *El Imparcial*, 27 September 1909, p. 3; Ortega y Gasset, *Obras*, 1:64; López-Morillas, *El Krausismo*, p. 9; Laín Entralgo, *España como Problema*, 2: 462, 408-9. See also "Epistolario entre Unamuno y Ortega," 30 December 1906, pp. 7-8.

38. Laín Entralgo, *España como Problema*, 2:408-9, 462.

39. Ibid., *El Imparcial*, 19 July 1908, p. 3.

40. Antonio Azorín, *La Voluntad* (Madrid: Caro Raggio, 1920), pp. 237-43.

41. Ortega y Gasset, *Obras*, 4:481; Eugenio d'Ors, *Cinco Minutos de Silencio* (Valencia: Editorial Sempere, 1925), pp. 9–17.

42. "Datos Biográficos."

43. Ibid.; Ortega y Gasset, *Obras*, 8:26.

44. *España* (Madrid), 20 May 1915, p. 10; see also Ortega's long critical review, in 1917, of Max Scheler's book *The Genius of War and the German War*, in *Obras*, 2:192-223.

45. Ortega y Gasset, *Obras*, 1:311. For an interesting comparison between Ortega's theory of the novel and Lukács's, see Georg Lukács, *The Theory of the Novel*, trans. Anna Bostock (Cambridge: The M.I.T. Press, 1971); see also, Frances Weber, "An Approach to Ortega's Idea of Culture: The Concept of Literary Genre," *Hispanic Review*, 32 (1964):142-56.

46. Ortega y Gasset, *Obras*, 1:328.

47. Ibid., 1:324.

48. Friedrich Nietzsche, *The Use and Abuse of History*, trans. Adrian Collins (New York: Bobbs-Merrill Co., 1957), p. 17.

49. Ortega y Gasset, *Obras*, 1:362-63.

50. Ibid.

51. Garcia Mercadal, *Ideario de Costa* (Madrid: Biblioteca España Nueva, 1932), pp. 278-79.

52. Ortega y Gasset, *Obras*, 1:361-64, 324, 318, 324-28, 318-19.

53. Ibid., 3:60, 74, 81.

54. Ibid., 3:152.

55. Ibid.

56. Tuñón de Lara, *La España*, p. 185.

57. "Datos Biográficos."

58. Ortega y Gasset, "Propósitos," *Revista de Occidente* 1, no. 1 (1923):2-3.

59. Ortega y Gasset, "Epistolario Entre José Ortega y Gasset y Ernst R. Curtius," *Revista de Occidente* 1, nos. 6, 7 (1963), 12 December 1923, pp. 329-30.

60. Ibid., pp. 12, 15-16, 18-20, 330-31, 334, 337-39.

61. Ortega y Gasset, *Obras*, 8:24-25. See also 6:304-12.

62. *El Sol* (Madrid), 23 February 1923, p. 1; 10 March 1923, p. 1. The Residencia de Estudiantes was a kind of international house. It provided lodging for Spanish and foreign university students and an atmosphere in which such lectures took place. Ortega and Unamuno also invited David Baumgardt, from the University of Berlin, to present a lecture on Moses Maimonides. See David Baumgardt, "Looking Back on a German University Career," *Leo Baeck Institute, Year Book* (London: East and West Library, 1965), 10:261-64.

63. Carr, *Spain*, pp. 564-91; Stanley G. Payne, *Politics and the Military in Modern Spain* (Stanford: Stanford University Press, 1967), pp. 197-203, 224-25.

64. Tuñón de Lara, *La España*, p. 232.

65. "Datos Biográficos."

66. *El Sol* (Madrid), 15 November 1930, p. 1.

67. Carr, *Spain*, pp. 598-603; Stanley G. Payne, *Falange: A History of Spanish Fascism* (Stanford: Stanford University Press, 1961), p. 9.

68. "Datos Biográficos"; José Ortega y Gasset and Juan Díaz Del Moral, *La Reforma Agraria y El Estatuto Catalán: Discursos Pronunciados En Las Cortes Constituyentes* (Madrid: Revista de Occidente, 1932). The political objectives of "La Agrupación al Servicio de la República" are outlined on page 1.

69. Ortega y Gasset, *La Rectificación de la República* (Madrid: Revista de Occidente, 1931), pp. 14-20; *La Rendición de las Provincias y la Decencia Nacional* (Madrid: Revista de Occidente, 1950), pp. 35-37; *Obras*, 3:51-62; Ortega y Gasset, *La Reforma Agraria*, pp. 119-238.

70. Carr, *Spain*, pp. 603-40.

71. Ibid., pp. 609-30.

72. Edward E. Malefakis, "The Parties of the Left and the Second Republic," *The Republic and the Civil War in Spain*, ed. Raymond Carr (London: Macmillan, 1971), p. 28. See also Carlos M. Rama, *La Crisis Española del Siglo XX* (México: Fondo de Cultura Económica, 1960), pp. 105-8.

73. For an excellent analysis of Spain's party system, see Juan J. Linz, "The Party System of Spain: Past and Future," *Party Systems and Voter Alignments*, ed. Seymour M. Lipset and Stein Rokkan (New York: The Free Press, 1967), pp. 219-28, 231-64.

74. "Datos Biográficos."

75. Ibid.

76. Tuñón de Lara, *La España*, pp. 512-14.

77. Ortega y Gasset, "Letter from José Ortega y Gasset to Mr. Walter P. Paepcke," *Revista de Occidente*, Aspen Institute for Humanistic Studies, 25th Anniversary Year (1974), 26 October 1949, p. 12.

78. "Datos Biográficos."

79. "Ortega y Curtius," 14 April 1949, p. 14; 26 April 1949, p. 15.

80. "Datos Biográficos."

81. Ibid. On his trip to Darmstadt, in 1951, Ortega met Heidegger.

82. Ibid. See Arnold Toynbee, "Sobre Una Interpretación de Ortega," *Revista de Occidente* 2, no. 15 (1964):356-57. See also Ortega's *Una Interpretación de la Historia Universal: En Torno a Toynbee*, Ortega y Gasset, *Obras*, 9:13-229.

Chapter I

1. Ortega y Gasset, *Obras Completas*, 6th ed., 11 vols. (Madrid: Revista de Occidente, 1962-65, 1969), 9:360.

2. Hans Liebeschütz, "Hermann Cohen and His Historical Background," *Leo Baeck Institute, Year Book* (London: East and West Library, 1968), 12:6-10.

3. Melvin Richter, *The Politics of Conscience: T.H. Green and His Age* (Cambridge: Harvard University Press, 1964), pp. 165-90.

4. Herbert Spiegelberg, *The Phenomenological Movement: A Historical Introduction*, 2d ed., 2 vols. (The Hague: Martinus Nijhoff, 1965), 1:235.

5. Georg G. Iggers, *The German Conception of History: The National Tradition of Historical Thought from Herder to the Present* (Middletown: Wesleyan University Press, 1968), pp. 128-73.

6. Ortega y Gasset, *Obras*, 8:29-31.

7. Thomas E. Willey, "Back to Kant: The Revival of Kantian Idealism in Germany, 1870-1914" (Ph.D. diss., Yale University, 1965), p. 175; Hans Liebeschütz, *Das Judentum im Deutsch Geschichtsbild von Hegel bis Max Weber* (Tübingen: J.C.B. Mohr/Paul Siebeck, 1967), p. 20.

8. Iggers, *German Conception*, p. 148.

9. Ernst Cassirer, *The Problem of Knowledge* (New Haven: Yale University Press, 1950), pp. 11-13; Willey, "Back to Kant," p. 10; Maurice Mandelbaum,

History, Man, and Reason: A Study of Nineteenth Century Thought (Baltimore: Johns Hopkins University Press, 1971), pp. 289–98.

10. Willey, "Back to Kant," pp. 107–10. Henri Dussort, *L'École de Marbourg* (Paris: Presses Universitaires de France, 1963), pp. 44–59.

11. Alice Stériad, *L'Interprétation de la Doctrine de Kant par L'École de Marbourg* (Paris: V. Giard & Briere, 1913), pp. 64–87; Jules Viullemin, *L'Héritage Kantien et la Révolution Copernicienne: Fichte, Cohen, Heidegger* (Paris: Presses Universitaires de France, 1954), pp. 133–41.

12. Ernst Cassirer, "Hermann Cohen," *Social Research* 10, no. 2 (1943): 224.

13. Viullemin, *L'Héritage Kantien*, pp. 143–47; Willey, "Back to Kant," pp. 154–58; Iggers, *German Conception*, pp. 144–47.

14. Stériad, *L'Interprétation de la Doctrine de Kant*, pp. 144–48.

15. Ibid., pp. 83–91; Cassirer, "Hermann Cohen," p. 226; Ortega y Gasset, *Obras*, 8:273, 9:587.

16. Stériad, *L'Interprétation de la Doctrine de Kant*, pp. 90–94.

17. Ibid., pp. 99–105.

18. Immanuel Kant, *Critique of Pure Reason*, trans. Norman Kemp Smith (New York: Macmillan, 1963), p. 20.

19. Stériad, *L'Interprétation de la Doctrine de Kant*, pp. 21–29, 146–48, 173–219.

20. Liebeschütz, "Hermann Cohen," pp. 3–34; F. H. Heinemann, "Jewish Contributors to German Philosophy," *Leo Baeck Institute, Year Book* (London: East and West Library, 1964), 9:168–78.

21. Stériad, *L'Interprétation de la Doctrine de Kant*, pp. 87–98, 117–32; Viullemin, *L'Héritage de Kant*, pp. 195, 198–208.

22. Ortega y Gasset, *Obras*, 8:27, 2:559, 6:383 n. 2.

23. Ibid., 4:403–4 n.

24. Ibid., 4:25.

25. Ibid., 2:558–59, 8:20.

26. Iggers, *German Conception*, pp. 147–49. See also Wilhelm Windelband and Heinz Heimsoeth, *Lehrbuch der Geschichte der Philosophie* (Tübingen: J. C. B. Mohr/Paul Siebeck, 1957), pp. 583–622.

27. Maurice Mandelbaum, *The Problem of Historical Knowledge* (New York: Liveright Publishing Corp., 1938), pp. 119–22. See Ortega's preface to the Spanish edition. Heinrich Rickert, *Ciencia Cultural y Ciencia Natural*, trans. Francisco Romero with a foreword by Rickert (Buenos Aires: Espasa-Calpe Argentina, S. A., 1945).

28. Heinrich Rickert, *Science and History: A Critique of Positivist Epistemology*, trans. George Reisman (Princeton: D. Van Nostrand Co., 1962), p. xv.

29. Mandelbaum, *Historical Knowledge*, p. 122.

30. Some commentators maintain that Dilthey's concept of *Geisteswissenschaften* could be traced to John Stuart Mill's notion of the "Logic of the Moral Sciences" in his *Logic*. See Mill, *A System of Logic: Ratiocinative and Inductive*, 5th ed., 2 vols. (London: Parker, Son & Bourn, 1862), 2:409–550. See also Hajo Holborn, "Dilthey and the Critique of Historical Reason," *Journal of the History of Ideas* 11, no. 1 (1950):98–99; Rickert, *Science and History*, p. xv; Carlo Antoni, *From History to Sociology*, trans. Hayden V. White (London: Merlin Press, 1962), pp. 16–18.

31. H. A. Hodges, *The Philosophy of Wilhelm Dilthey* (London: Routledge & Kegan Paul, 1952), pp. 222–26, 240–48, 211–12; Wilhelm Dilthey, *Gesammelte*

Schriften, 12 vols. (Leipzig-Berlin: B.G. Teubner, 1923-36), 7:86-88, 117-20, 147-48; Rickert, *Science and History*, pp. xiv-xix.

32. Hodges, *The Philosophy of Wilhelm Dilthey*, pp. 239-50, 304-6.

33. Wilhelm Dilthey, *Patterns and Meaning in History: Thoughts on History and Society*, ed. with an intro. by H.P. Rickman (New York: Harper & Brothers, 1962), p. 73.

Although Ortega aligned his philosophy of life with Dilthey's *Lebensphilosophie*, there are other representatives of the vitalist tradition, such as Goethe, Schopenhauer, Burckhardt, and Nietzsche, who should be mentioned in this context. A composite assessment of the vitalist tradition and of Ortega's relation to these thinkers is a dimension not treated here. For comparisons, see especially Arthur Schopenhauer, *The World as Will and Representation*, trans. E.F.J.Payne, 2 vols. (New York: Dover Publications, 1969), 1:245, 251-55, 275-85, 2:349-52, 439-46, 568-74, 634-39; Friedrich Nietzsche, *The Will to Power*, trans. Walter Kaufmann and R.J.Hollingdale (New York: Random House, 1968), pp. 22, 184, 272-75, 298-300, 312-344, 351-60, 451-52; Jacob Burckhardt, *Force and Freedom: Reflections on History*, ed. James Hastings Nichols (Boston: Beacon Press, 1964), pp. 79-103, 140-152. See also Karl Löwith, *From Hegel to Nietzsche: The Revolution in Nineteenth-Century Thought*, trans. David E. Green (New York: Doubleday & Co., 1967), pp. 2-28, 315-23; Karl Löwith, *Jacob Burckhardt: Der Mensch Inmitten Der Geschichte* (Lucerne: Vita Nova Verlag, 1936), pp. 11-61, 92-96, 324-348; and Friedrich Meinecke, *Historism: The Rise of a New Historical Outlook* (London: Routledge & Kegan Paul, 1972), pp. 373-495.

34. Dilthey, *Patterns and Meaning in History*, pp. 73-82, 85-94, 97-112, 122-25.

35. Hodges, *The Philosophy of Wilhelm Dilthey*, pp. 114-26; Dilthey, *Gesammelte Schriften*, 7:141-43, 148-52, 191-204, 258.

36. H.A.Hodges, *Wilhelm Dilthey: An Introduction* (New York: Oxford University Press, 1944), p. 32.

37. Ortega y Gasset, *Obras*, 6:171-72.

38. Ibid., 5:26, 35, 44-45; 7:103-4.

39. Ibid., 5:33-34.

40. See especially Karl Popper, *The Poverty of Historicism* (New York: Harper & Row, 1964), pp. 39-159; see also Friedrich A.Hayek, *The Counter-Revolution of Science: Studies on the Abuse of Reason* (Glencoe: The Free Press, 1952), pp. 11-102.

41. Robert N. Beck and Dwight E. Lee, "The Meaning of Historicism," *The American Historical Review* 59, no. 3 (April 1954); 568; see Georg G. Iggers, "The Dissolution of German Historism," *Ideas in History: Essays Presented to Louis Gottschalk By His Former Students*, ed. Richard Herr and Harold T. Parker (Durham: Duke University Press, 1965), pp. 288-329. See also Meinecke, *Historism*, pp. 235-511; Karl Mannheim, *Essays on the Sociology of Knowledge* (London: Routledge & Kegan Paul, 1952), pp. 84-133; Carlo Antoni, *L'Historisme*, trans. Alain Dufour (Geneva: Librairie Droz, 1963), pp. 1-10, 113-25; Ernst Troeltsch, *Der Historismus und seine Probleme* (Tübingen: Scientia Aalen, 1961), pp. 1-11, 102-30, 200-220, 417-20, 493-530, 596-632.

42. Mandelbaum, *Historical Knowledge*, pp. 88-89. See also Ortega's claim that "historicism and positivism of the nineteenth century passed over every eternal value in order to salvage the relative value of each epoch." Ortega y Gasset, *Obras*, 7:285.

43. Quoted in Hodges, *Wilhelm Dilthey: An Introduction,* pp. 33-34.

44. *Aesthetics: As the Science of Expression and General Linguistics (Estetica come scienza dell'espressione e linguistica generale,* 1904); *Logic: As the Science of the Pure Concept (Logica come scienza del concetto puro,* 1905); *Philosophy of the Practical: Economic and Ethic (Filosofia della practica, economia ed etica,* 1909); and *History: Its Theory and Practice (Teoria et Storia della Storiografia,* 1916). See also his *La Storia Come Pensiero e Come Azione* (Bari: Gius, Laterza & Figli, 1939), trans. into English by Sylvia Sprigge as *History as the Story of Liberty* (New York: Meridian Books, 1955). The emphasis here is placed primarily on Croce's earlier formulation of historicism in *Theory and History of Historiography,* written in 1912 and 1913, where the focus is toward defining philosophy as a method of history. Since Ortega was more familiar with this earlier work, he gave less emphasis to Croce's *History as Thought and as Action,* written in 1938, which called for an inquiry into "the relation between the writing of history and practical action." Croce, *History as the Story of Liberty,* p. 5. In *History as Thought and as Action* Croce returned to the subject matter of *Theory and History of Historiography* (which had been continued in his *History of Italian Historiography in the Nineteenth Century* as well as in several other shorter essays) "to add new considerations" that were characterized by "further studies" and that were "stimulated by new experience of life." Croce, *History as the Story of Liberty,* p. 5. See also Croce, *Philosophy, Poetry, History: An Anthology of Essays,* trans. with an intro. by Cecil Sprigge (London: Oxford University Press, 1966), pp. 13-31, 77-85, 121-212, 497-634.

45. Benedetto Croce, *Philosophy of the Practical: Economic and Ethic,* trans. Douglas Ainslie (London: Macmillan, 1913), p. 15.

46. Benedetto Croce, *Aesthetics: As the Science of Expression and General Linguistics,* trans. Douglas Ainslie (New York: Noonday Press, 1963), p. 1.

47. Ibid., p. 4.

48. Ibid., pp. 5-6.

49. Ibid:, p. 4.

50. Ibid., p. 22.

51. Benedetto Croce, *History: Its Theory and Practice,* trans. Douglas Ainslie (New York: Russell & Russell, 1920), pp. 60-61.

52. Ibid., p. 61.

53. Croce, *Philosophy of the Practical,* p. 33.

54. Croce, *History: Theory and Practice,* pp. 94-107; Hodges, *Wilhelm Dilthey: An Introduction,* pp. 33-34. See Ortega's preface to Émile Bréhier's *History of Philosophy,* where he identified philosophy with history. "Philosophy," he said, "is thus the history of philosophy and vice versa." Ortega y Gasset, *Obras,* 6: 418. See also Ortega's aspiration concerning the interpenetration of history and philosophy: "I hope, for very concrete reasons, that in our age the curiosity for the eternal and invariable which is philosophy and the curiosity for the inconstant and changeable which is history, for the first time, join one another and embrace." Ibid., 7:285.

55. Spiegelberg, *Phenomenological Movement,* 1:168-75.

56. Ibid., 1:5.

57. Edmund Husserl, "Philosophy as Rigorous Science," *Edmund Husserl: Phenomenology and the Crisis of Philosophy,* trans. Quentin Lauer (New York: Harper & Row, 1965), p. 82.

58. Quoted in Spiegelberg, *Phenomenological Movement,* 1:5.

59. Husserl, "Philosophy as Rigorous Science," pp. 71-107.

60. Marvin Farber, *The Foundation of Phenomenology* (Albany: State University of New York Press, 1943), pp. 16-19, 24-60; Spiegelberg, *Phenomenological Movement*, 1:92.

61. Edmund Husserl, "Phenomenology," *Encyclopedia Britannica*, 14th ed.; Edmund Husserl, *Ideas: General Introduction to Pure Phenomenology*, trans. W.R. Boyce Gibson (London: Macmillan, 1931). pp. 103-4.

62. Husserl, *Ideas*, pp. 107-9.

63. Edmund Husserl, *The Idea of Phenomenology*, trans. William P. Alston and George S. Nakhnikian (The Hague: Martinus Nijhoff, 1964), pp. 18-19.

64. Ibid., pp. 11, 33-36, 43-47.

65. Ibid., pp. 35, 43-44.

66. Ibid., pp. 45-49.

67. Ibid., p. 37.

68. Farber, *Foundation of Phenomenology*, pp. 522-28; Husserl, *Ideas*, pp. 89-117; Edmund Husserl, *Cartesian Meditations*, trans. Dorion Cairns (The Hague: Martinus Nijhoff, 1960), pp. 18-26.

69. Husserl, *Ideas*, pp. 93-99; idem, *Cartesian Meditations*, pp. 46-53.

70. These unedited, unpublished manuscripts have been compiled by Iso Kern and have been published recently in the series *Husserliana* (15 vols.). Edmund Husserl, *Zur Phänomenologie der Intersubjektivität*, *Husserliana*, ed. Iso Kern, vols. 13, 14, 15 (The Hague: Martinus Nijhoff, 1973). We had the fortunate opportunity of access to earlier proofs, at the Husserl Archives, the University of Louvain. References made here are to the pagination of these early proofs, which corresponds to the recently published volumes.

71. Husserl, *Cartesian Meditations*, pp. 130-39.

72. Ibid., pp. 82-88.

73. Ibid., p. 89.

74. Ibid., pp. 89-106, 120-31.

75. Ortega y Gasset, *Obras*, 8:32-35, 40-41.

76. Ibid., 8:40-41, 43.

77. Ibid., 8:42.

78. Ibid.

79. Ibid.

80. Ibid., 8:47.

81. Ibid., 8:43.

82. Ibid., 1:245-61.

83. Spiegelberg, *Phenomenological Movement*, 1:367-84.

84. Ortega y Gasset, *Obras*, 1:244-45.

85. Ibid., 1:249.

86. Ibid., 1:253.

87. Ibid., 1:251-52.

88. Ibid., 1:253.

89. Ibid.

90. Ibid.

91. Ibid., 1:254.

92. Ibid., 1:252-53.

93. Ibid., 1:318-19.

94. Ibid., 7:335.

95. Ibid., 8:273, n.2.

96. Ibid., 3:360-64.

97. Ibid., 3:361.

98. Ibid., 3:363.

99. Ibid., 3:362.
100. Ibid., 8:273, n. 2.
101. Ibid., 8:272.
102. Ibid., 8:273.
103. Ibid., 5:545.
104. Ibid.
105. Ibid.
106. Edmund Husserl, *The Crisis of European Sciences and Transcendental Phenomenology*, trans. David Carr (Evanston: Northwestern University Press, 1970), pp. 349-51.
107. Ibid., pp. 369-78. In regard to the "problem of genesis" see Husserl, *Phänomenologie*, 14:2, 11. See also Ortega's *Idea of Principle in Leibnitz and The Evolution of Deductive Theory*, *Obras*, 8:63-351, which treats problems similar to those discussed in Husserl's *Crisis*.
108. Husserl, *Crisis*, pp. 389-95.
109. Ortega y Gasset, *Obras*, 5:546-47, n.1. Ortega's essay *History as a System* first appeared translated into English in *Philosophy and History: Essays Presented to Ernst Cassirer*, ed. Raymond Klibansky and H.J. Paton (London: Oxford, 1936), pp. 283-322. In 1936, Ortega was nominated, along with several other prominent international thinkers, to the International Committee of the journal *Actes du huitième Congrès Internationale de Philosophie*. See *Actes du huitième Congrès Internationale de Philosophie à Prague, 2-7 Septembre 1934* (Prague, 1936), pp. xxviii-xxi.
110. Ortega y Gasset, *Obras*, 8:160-61.
111. Ibid., 5:545.
112. Ibid.
113. See Husserl, *Phänomenologie*, 14:1, 8-9, 2, 11-12; idem, *Cartesian Meditations*, pp. 107-12.
114. Ortega y Gasset, *Obras*, 5:545.
115. José Ortega y Gasset, "Epistolario entre José Ortega y Gasset y Ernst R. Curtius," *Revista de Occidente* 1, nos. 6, 7 (September, October 1963):329-36, hereafter cited as "Epistolario entre Ortega y Curtius"; Ernst R. Curtius, *Französischer Geist Im Neuen Europa* (Berlin-Leipzig: Deutsche Verlags-Anstalt Stuttgart, 1925), pp. 339-44.
116. Ortega y Gasset, *Obras*, 4:510.
117. Ibid., 4:511.
118. Max Scheler, *Formalism in Ethics and Non-Formal Ethics of Values*, trans. Manfred S. Frings and Roger L. Funk (Evanston: Northwestern University Press, 1973), p. xix; Spiegelberg, *Phenomenological Movement*, 1:5; John Staude, *Max Scheler, 1874-1928: An Intellectual Portrait* (New York: The Free Press, 1967), p. 27.
119. Scheler, *Formalism in Ethics*, pp. 48-110.
120. Staude, *Max Scheler*, pp. 163-201.
121. In 1926, with respect to the affinities between the thoughts of Scheler and Ortega, Scheler remarked: "In Spain it was J. Ortega y Gasset, professor of metaphysics at the University of Madrid, who followed both my value theory and my sociological thought. I refer the reader to '¿Qué son los valores?' *Revista de Occidente*, Vol. I, no. 4 and his two works *El Tema de Nuestro Tiempo* (Madrid: Calpe, 1923) and *El Espectador* (Madrid: Calpe, 1921). . . ." Scheler, *Formalism in Ethics*, p. xxxiii. For a comparison of their notions of "love," "sympathy," and "fellow-feeling," see Scheler's *Nature of Sympathy*, trans. Peter Heath (New Haven: Yale University Press, 1954), and Ortega's *Man and People*, *Obras*, 7:70-271, and *Studies on Love*, *Obras*, 5:551-96. See also "Epistolario entre Ortega y

Curtius," *Revista de Occidente* 1, no.6, 9 March 1925, p. 333; 22 November 1929, p. 335.

122. Spiegelberg, *Phenomenological Movement*, 1:120-22.
123. Ortega y Gasset, *Obras*, 1:93-104.
124. Ibid., 1:110-11, 140, 367.
125. Ibid., 1:358-88.
126. Ibid., 2:612-20.
127. Spiegelberg, *Phenomenological Movement*, 1:367-84.
128. Ortega y Gasset, *Obras*, 6:347.
129. Ibid., 1:318.
130. Ibid.
131. Ibid.
132. Ibid.
133. Ibid.
134. Ibid.
135. Ibid.
136. See Julián Marías, *Ortega: Circunstancia y Vocación* (Madrid: Revista de Occidente, 1960), 1:377-90; Joachim Iriarte, *La Ruta Mental de Ortega* (Madrid: Editorial "Razón y Fe," 1949), pp. 35-70, 75-95; José Ferrater Mora, *Ortega y Gasset: An Outline of His Philosophy* (New Haven: Yale University Press, 1957), pp. 25-30.
137. Ortega y Gasset, *Obras*, 1:319.
138. Ibid.
139. Ibid., 1:320.
140. Ibid., 1:320-21.
141. Ibid., 1:322.
142. Ibid.
143. Kant, *Critique of Pure Reason*, p. 41.
144. Ibid.
145. Ibid., pp. 65-74.
146. Ortega y Gasset, *Obras*, 1:316.
147. Ibid., 1:317.
148. Ibid., 1:353-54.
149. Ibid.
150. Ibid., 2:286, 297, 6:308.
151. See especially Henri Bergson, *Creative Evolution*, trans. Arthur Mitchell (New York: H. Holt, 1911), xiii-xv, 4-11, 13-29, 39-55, 82-97, 103-5, 251-71.
152. Ortega y Gasset, *Obras*, 3:147-48.
153. Ibid., 3:146, 147, 155.
154. Ibid., 3:157-203.
155. Ibid., 3:157.
156. Ibid., 3:163.
157. Ibid.
158. Ibid., 3:162.
159. Ibid., 3:157-62, 198.
160. Ibid., 3:178.
161. Ibid., 3:189.
162. See Ortega's long footnote in his "Goethe From Within," ibid., 4:404.
163. Ibid., 3:179.
164. Ibid., 3:198.
165. Ibid., 3:200.
166. Ibid.
167. Ibid., 3:199.

168. Ibid. In regard to "perspectivism," Ortega in 1932 mentioned to Fernando Vela: "The theory of my philosophy is: perspectivism. But it is not 'point of view' in the idealist sense of the term, but on the contrary: it is that the view, *reality, is* also *point of view*." Ibid., 4:390. Three years earlier, Ortega acknowledged the influence of German thinkers on his own philosophy of "perspectivism": "I have managed to initiate a method which the Germans, who are prone to the elaboration of formalities, baptized for me with the name 'perspectivism.'" Ibid., 7:286. For a comparison, in this connection, see especially Nietzsche, *The Will to Power*, pp. 149-50, 155, 267-83, 294-306, 326-30, 339-40, 360.

169. Ortega y Gasset, *Obras*, 3:201.

170. Ibid., 4:404.

171. Ibid., 3:270-80.

172. Ibid., 3:272-73.

173. Ibid., 3:271.

174. Ibid.

175. Ibid., 3:272.

176. Ibid.

177. Ibid., 3:273.

178. Ibid.

179. Ibid., 3:278, 279.

180. Ibid., 3:280.

181. Ibid., 3:273.

182. Ibid., 3:277.

183. Ibid., 4:54.

184. Ibid., 4:54-55.

185. Ibid., 4:55.

186. Ibid.

187. Ibid., 4:56.

188. Ibid., 8:83, n.2, 4:52-53, 57.

189. Ibid., 4:57.

190. Ibid.

191. Ibid., 4:58.

192. Ibid.

193. Ibid.

194. Ibid.

195. Ibid., 7:309-10, 328, 335.

196. Ibid., 7:319.

197. Ibid., 7:310.

198. Ibid., 7:303, 310.

199. Ibid., 7:329 ff.

200. Ibid., 7:300.

201. Ibid., 7:301.

202. Ibid.

203. Ibid., 7:351.

204. Ibid., 7:346, 366-67, 395 ff., 402.

205. Ibid., 7:365-66, 371-74.

206. Ibid., 7:400.

207. Ibid., 7:402.

208. Ibid., 7:400.

209. Ibid., 7:371.

210. Ibid., 7:295, 299.

211. Ibid., 7:328, 355, 357.

212. Ibid., 7:312, 317, 319, 361, 371, 376.
213. Ibid., 7:317.
214. Ibid., 7:376, 394-95.
215. Ibid., 7:325.
216. Ibid.
217. Ibid.
218. Ibid., 7:394.
219. Ibid., 7:405.
220. Ibid., 7:402.
221. Ibid., 7:411.
222. Ibid., 7:417; see Martin Heidegger, *Being and Time*, trans. John Macquarrie and Edward Robinson (New York: Harper & Brothers, 1962), p. 236.
223. Ortega y Gasset, *Obras*, 7:430.
224. Ibid., 7:416; see Heidegger, *Being and Time*, p. 399.
225. Ortega y Gasset, *Obras*, 7:422.
226. Ibid., 7:431.
227. Ibid., 6:171.
228. Ibid., 6:166.
229. Ibid., 6:165.
230. Dilthey, *Patterns and Meaning in History*, p. 88.
231. Ibid., pp. 72-73.
232. Ibid., p. 72.
233. See Georg Misch, *Lebensphilosophie und Phänomenologie* (Leipzig-Berlin: B.G. Teubner, 1931), pp. 5-197, 216-37.
234. Heidegger, *Being and Time*, pp. 21-83; Herbert Spiegelberg, "Phenomenology and Existentialism," *Journal of Philosophy* 57, no.1 (1960); 62-74; Spiegelberg, *Phenomenological Movement*, 1:408-13.
235. Ortega y Gasset, *Obras*, 7:415-16.
236. Ibid., 8:271-84, 296-300.
237. José Ortega y Gasset, "Martin Heidegger und die Sprache der Philosophen," *Universitas* 7, no. 9 (1952):897-903.
238. Ortega y Gasset, *Obras*, 4:403. See also 4:541; 9:625-44.
239. *El Sol* (Madrid), 1 March 1931, p. 3; see also Ortega's article, "What is Knowledge? " 18 January 1931, p. 3.
240. Martin Heidegger, "Encuentros con Ortega y Gasset en Alemania," *Clavileño* 8, no. 39 (1956):1-4.
241. Ortega y Gasset, *Obras*, 5:44.
242. Ibid., 1:324-25.
243. Ibid., 7:289-92.
244. Ibid., 5:44; see Wilhelm Pinder, *Das Problem der Generation* (Munich: Bruckman, 1961), p. 31. See also Mannheim's notion of "The Problem of Generations," in his *Sociology of Knowledge*, pp. 276-320.
245. Ortega y Gasset, *Obras*, 5:13-167.
246. Ibid., 6:11-50.
247. Ibid., 7:73-270.
248. Ibid., 5:44; see Pinder, *Problem der Generation*, pp. 33 ff.
249. For further affinities among Ortega, Dilthey, and Heidegger, see Dilthey, "Über das Stadium der Geschichte der Wissenschaften von Menschen, der Gesellschaft und dem statt," *Gesammelte Schriften*, 5:31-73; Heidegger, *Being and Time*, pp. 41, 36.
250. Ortega y Gasset, *Obras*, 9:366, n.5. See also note 54 above.

251. Ibid., 4:143-277.

252. Staude, *Max Scheler*, pp. 35-44, 147-52.

253. Ortega y Gasset, *Obras*, 4:131.

254. Ortega y Gasset, "Epistolario entre Ortega y Curtius," 3 December 1937, p. 340. See also Ortega y Gasset, *Obras*, 5:379.

255. Ortega y Gasset, *Obras*, 9:355, n.1. See also where, in his letter to Walter Paepcke, Ortega wrote: "In my *Mission of the University* I postulate the urgent need of creating the scientific syntheses, that is, a type of scientific intellectual task which specializes in creating 'synthetic bodies of doctrines' in all disciplines in order to make possible *education in a total synthesis of human life*." Ortega y Gasset, "Letter from José Ortega y Gasset to Mr. Walter P. Paepcke," *Revista de Occidente*, Aspen Institute for Humanistic Studies, 25th Anniversary Year (1974), 26 October 1949, p. 12. Hereafter cited as "Letter from Ortega to Paepcke."

256. See the list of courses offered by Ortega at the Instituto de Humanidades that expound his thesis of *Man and People*, Ortega y Gasset, *Obras*, 7:270-72. See also Ortega y Gasset, "Letter from Ortega to Paepcke," pp. 9-10.

257. Ortega y Gasset, "Epistolario entre Ortega y Curtius," 4 March 1938, p. 4.

258. Ortega y Gasset, *Obras*, 8:61.

259. Ibid., 8:63-352.

260. Ibid.

261. Ibid., 9:83, 362.

262. Ibid., 6:395.

263. See, for example, Ferrater Mora, *Ortega y Gasset*, pp. 15-60; see also Marías, *Circunstancia y Vocación;* Julián Marías, *Filosofía Actual y Existencialismo en España* (Madrid: Revista de Occidente, 1955); José Sánchez Villaseñor, *Ortega y Gasset, Existentialist: A Critical Study of His Thought and Its Sources*, trans. J. Small (Chicago: Regnery, 1949); Alfred Stern, *Philosophy of History and the Problem of Values* (The Hague: Mouton & Co., 1952); Janet Winecoff Díaz, *The Major Themes of Existentialism in the Work of José Ortega y Gasset* (Chapel Hill: The University of North Carolina Press, 1970); Alfonso Barroso Nieto, "Ortega y Gasset y el Perspectivismo," *Verdad y Vida*, vol. 4, no. 4 (Madrid, 1946); Sabino Alonso Feuyo, "Existencialismo Español: Ortega y Gasset, Unamuno y Xavier Zubiri," *Saitabi* 5, no. 9 (1949): 54-60; José Gaos, "El Tema de Nuestro Tiempo (Filosofía de la perspectiva)," *Revista de Occidente* 1, no. 3 (October-December, 1923):374; Alfred Stern, "¿Ortega Existencialista o Essencialista?" *La Torre* 15-16 (July-December 1956):385-99.

Chapter II

1. José Ortega y Gasset, *Obras Completas*, 6th ed., 11 vols. (Madrid: Revista de Occidente, 1962-65, 1969), 6:15.

2. René Descartes, "Discourse on the Method of Rightly Conducting the Reason and Seeking for Truth in the Sciences," *The Philosophical Works of Descartes*, trans. Elizabeth S. Haldane and G.R.T. Ross, 2 vols. (London: Cambridge University Press, 1931), 1:92-94.

3. Ibid., 1:86-87, 89.

4. Ibid., 1:101-2.

5. Ortega y Gasset, *Obras*, 7:116.

6. Ibid., 6:16.

7. Ibid., 6:24.
8. Ibid., 6:16.
9. Ibid., 3:158.
10. Ibid., 3:178.
11. Ibid., 6:23.
12. Ibid., 6:24.
13. Ibid., 6:32, 41.
14. Ibid.
15. Ibid.
16. Ibid., 8:86.
17. Ibid., 5:32.
18. "We had with Husserl and Dilthey," Ortega remarked, "arrived—at last! —to a frame of mind of making a philosophy which was quietly preoccupied only with 'seeing' how things properly are, or better, with the things we see clearly and those which we do not see. . . ." *Obras*, 8:298.
19. Ibid., 5:77.
20. Ibid., 5:39.
21. Ibid., 5:108.
22. Ibid., 5:40-41.
23. Ibid., 7:99-100.
24. Ibid., 8:299, 279.
25. Ibid., 7:101.
26. Ibid., 8:252, n.3.
27. Immanuel Kant, *Prolegomena to Any Future Metaphysics*, ed. Lewis White Beck (New York: Bobbs-Merrill Co., 1950), pp. 122-23, n.2.
28. Ortega y Gasset, *Obras*, 7:100-101.
29. Ibid., 7:103.
30. Ibid., 6:34.
31. Ibid.
32. Ibid., 5:304.
33. Ibid., 7:102-3.
34. Ibid., 5:72-73.
35. Ibid., 7:100-101.
36. Ibid., 7:106.
37. Ibid., 8:297.
38. Ibid., 7:104.
39. Ibid., 5:62-63, 8:296-97.
40. Ibid., 7:186-87.
41. Ibid., 5:37.
42. Ibid., 5:35-36.
43. Ibid., 5:36-37.
44. Ibid., 7:100-101.
45. Ibid., 6:40-41.
46. Ibid., 5:31.
47. Ibid., 5:34.
48. Ibid., 6:39.

Chapter III

1. José Ortega y Gasset, *Obras Completas*, 6th ed., 11 vols. (Madrid: Revista de Occidente, 1962-65, 1969), 7:115-16.

2. Ibid., 7:101.

3. Ibid., 7:100-101.

4. Ibid., 7:130.

5. Ibid., 7:152.

6. Ibid., 7:124-25.

7. Ibid., 7:125-26.

8. For some interesting comparisons in this regard, see Edmund Husserl, *Zur Phänomenologie der Intersubjektivität, Husserliana*, ed. Iso Kern, vols. 13, 14, 15 (The Hague: Martinus Nijhoff, 1973), 14:3-10, 55-73, 108-13, 428-35; Jean-Paul Sartre, *Being and Nothingness: An Essay on Phenomenological Ontology*, trans. Hazel E. Barnes (New York: Washington Square Press, 1953), pp. 371-440; and Maurice Merleau-Ponty, *Phenomenology of Perception*, trans. Colin Smith (London: Routledge & Kegan Paul, 1965), pp. 67-206.

9. Ortega y Gasset, *Obras*, 7:150.

10. Ibid., 7:149-50.

11. Ibid., 7:148.

12. Ibid., 7:133-34.

13. Ibid., 7:135; see also Husserl, *Phäenomenologie*, 14:109-11, 116-19, 15:40-43, 45-49.

14. Ortega y Gasset, *Obras*, 7:135-37.

15. Ibid., 7:137.

16. Ibid., 7:137-38.

17. Ibid., 7:138.

18. Ibid., 7:141.

19. Ibid., 7:142; see Edmund Husserl, *Cartesian Meditations*, trans. Dorion Cairns (The Hague: Martinus Nijhoff, 1960), pp. 89-100, 104-11.

20. Ortega y Gasset, *Obras*, 5:545-47.

21. Ibid., 7:158-59.

22. See especially Husserl, *Phänomenologie*, 14:3-11, 429-33, 15:40-50; idem,.*Cartesian Meditations*, 90-92; see also Max Scheler, *The Nature of Sympathy*, trans. Peter Heath (New Haven: Yale University Press, 1954), pp. 6-50.

23. Husserl, *Cartesian Meditations*, p. 94.

24. Ibid.

25. Ortega y Gasset, *Obras*, 7:161-62.

26. Ibid., 7:161, 163.

27. Ibid., 7:163.

28. Ibid., 7:148.

29. Ibid., 7:150.

30. Ibid., 7:138.

31. Ibid., 7:140.

32. Ibid.

33. Ibid.

34. Ibid., 7:177.

35. Ibid., 5:60-61.

36. Ibid., 7:151.

37. Ibid., 7:151-52.

38. Ibid., 7:152-53.

39. Ibid., 7:174-75.

40. Ibid., 7:175.

41. Ibid., 7:177-78.

42. Ibid., 7:178-79.

43. Ibid., 7:178, 190.

44. Ibid., 7:189-90.

45. Ibid., 7:190.

46. Ibid., 7:193-94.

47. Ibid., 7:196. Ortega continued with this point by adding: "And here we have why I declared accordingly one must return to reverse, in my judgment, the traditional doctrine, which in its most recent and refined form is the doctrine of Husserl and his disciples. *Schütz*, for example, the doctrine according to which the *you* would be an *alter ego*. Well, then, the concrete *ego* comes into the world as *alter tu*, following the *yous*, amongst them—not in life as radical reality and as radical solitude, but in that design of second reality which is living together with others." Ibid. Cf. Alfred Schutz, *Collected Papers I: The Problem of Social Reality*, ed. with an intro. by Maurice Natanson (The Hague: Martinus Nijhoff, 1962), pp. 7-19, 99-106, 140-49, 207-59.

48. Ortega y Gasset, *Obras*, 7:135.

49. Ibid., 7:202-3.

50. Ibid., 7:144.

51. Ibid., 7:143.

52. Ibid., 4:145-46.

53. Ibid., 4:143.

54. Ibid., 4:143-48.

55. Ibid., 4:146.

56. Ibid., 4:146-47.

57. See especially Friedrich Nietzsche, *Beyond Good and Evil*, trans. Walter Kaufmann (New York: Vintage, 1966), pp. 203-31; Nietzsche, *The Genealogy of Morals*, trans. Walter Golffing (New York: Doubleday Anchor, 1956), pp. 154-55, 170-82; Nietzsche, *The Will to Power*, trans. Walter Kaufmann and R.J.Hollingdale (New York: Random House, 1968), pp. 100-108, 119-22, 201-4, 341-57, 434, 451-52, 493-519.

58. Ortega y Gasset, *Obras*, 4:148.

59. Ortega's critique of "mass society" and "mass culture" was not a critique of the system of capitalism but a critique of the system of democracy. His elitist aversion to "mass society" underscored the so-called dangers of the democratic majority in mass society. The general thrust of his position in the *Revolt of the Masses*, therefore, had been the focus of the criticisms of some Marxist social theorists. See, for example, Otto Kirchheimer, "Constitutional Reaction in 1932," *Politics, Law, and Social Change*, ed. Frederic S. Burin and Kurt L. Shell (New York: Columbia University Press, 1969), p. 79. "However one may evaluate this process Ortega y Gasset has called *The Revolt of the Masses*," Kirchheimer argued, "it seems clear that the condition which is interpreted either as self-limitation or as submission of the masses, depending on one's ideological attitude, belongs to the past. This socio-psychological *habitus*, doubtless still an attribute of the beginning of mass democracy, has receded as a consequence of the watershed of the Great War and of the changes connected with it. The crisis of democracy . . . has only accelerated this development."

In his study of the Frankfurt School, Martin Jay pointed out how other members of the Institute "denounced the nostalgic yearnings of elitist critics such as José Ortega y Gasset. 'The right to nostalgia, to transcendental knowledge, to a dangerous life cannot be validated,' Horkheimer wrote. 'The struggle against mass culture can consist only in pointing out its connection with the persistence of social injustice.'" See Martin Jay, *The Dialectical Imagination: A History of the Frankfurt School and the Institute of Social Research, 1923-1950* (Boston: Little, Brown and Co., 1973), p. 215.

60. Ortega y Gasset, *Obras*, 4:147.

61. Ortega is caught in a "double bind" here, very much like de Tocqueville and Marx. That is, he perceived in society the inevitability of the developing political participation by the majority but also argued that something should be done about it.

62. Ortega y Gasset, *Obras*, 4:148-49, 179.

63. Ibid., 4:165, 181-82.

64. Ibid., 4:182-83.

65. Ibid.

66. Ibid., 4:183.

67. Ibid.

68. Ibid.

69. Ibid., 4:183-84.

70. Ibid., 4:184.

71. Ibid., 5:79-80.

72. Ibid., 7:194.

73. Ibid., 5:79-80.

Chapter IV

1. José Ortega y Gasset, *Obras Completas*, 6th ed., 11 vols. (Madrid: Revista de Occidente, 1962-65, 1969), 5:36-42.

2. Ibid., 5:37.

3. Ibid., 5:37-38.

4. Ibid.

5. Ibid.

6. Ibid.

7. Ibid., 5:39-40.

8. Ibid., 5:39-40, 44-48.

9. Ibid., 5:45.

10. Ibid., 5:40.

11. Benedetto Croce, *History: Its Theory and Practice*, trans. Douglas Ainslie (New York: Russell and Russell, 1920), pp. 11, 24-28.

12. Ortega y Gasset, *Obras*, 5:55.

13. Ibid., 5:43.

14. Ibid., 5:43-44.

15. Ibid., 5:53.

16. Ibid., 6:387-88.

17. Ibid., 6:167.

18. Ibid.

19. Ibid., 6:202-4.

20. Ibid., 6:203-4.

21. Ibid., 6:184.

22. Ibid., 7:151-52, 5:37-40.

23. Ibid., 5:40.

24. Ibid.

25. Ibid., 6:33.

26. Ibid., 5:55.

27. Ibid., 5:40, 55. See also Croce, *History: Theory and Practice*, pp. 11–30.

28. Ortega y Gasset, *Obras*, 6:32–33.

29. Ibid., 6:25.

30. Ibid.

31. Ibid., 6:36.

32. Ibid.

33. Ibid., 6:37.

34. Ibid., 6:37–38.

35. Ibid., 4:125.

36. Ibid., 6:39–40.

37. Ibid., 5:538, 540.

38. Ibid., 6:40.

39. Ibid., 6:40–41.

40. Ibid., 6:41.

41. Ibid., 6:39.

42. Croce, *History: Theory and Practice*, p. 26.

43. Ortega y Gasset, *Obras*, 5:55, 6:39–40. See also Croce, *History: Theory and Practice*, pp. 11–30.

44. Ortega y Gasset, *Obras*, 6:49–50.

45. Ibid., 6:306; Hajo Holborn, "Dilthey and the Critique of Historical Reason," *Journal of the History of Ideas* 11, no. 1 (1950):94–110; Carlo Antoni, *From History to Sociology*, trans. Hayden V. White (London: Merlin Press, 1962), pp. 17–38; Heinrich Rickert, *Science and History: A Critique of Positivist Epistemology*, trans. George Reisman (Princeton: D. Van Nostrand Co., 1962), pp. 1–9, 18–30; Benedetto Croce, *Logic: As the Science of the Pure Concept*, trans. Douglas Ainslie (London: Macmillan and Co., 1917), pp. 330–55.

46. Ortega y Gasset, *Obras*, 6:167.

47. Wilhelm Dilthey, *Patterns and Meaning in History: Thoughts on History and Society*, ed. and intro. by H.P. Rickman (New York: Harper & Brothers, 1962), p. 125.

48. Ortega y Gasset, *Obras*, 5:539–40.

49. Croce, *History: Theory and Practice*, pp. 60–61; Ortega y Gasset, *Obras*, 6:40–41; see also note 54 to chapter one, above.

50. Ibid., p. 26.

51. Ibid., p. 162.

52. Ibid., p. 161.

53. Ortega y Gasset, *Obras*, 5:539.

54. Ibid., 5:539–40.

55. Ibid., 6:416–17.

56. Ibid., 6:40.

57. Ibid., 6:43.

58. Ibid., 6:186; Holborn, "Dilthey and the Critique of Historical Reason," pp. 97–100. See also p. 54 in chapter 1 above.

59. Ortega y Gasset, *Obras*, 6:195.

60. Ibid., 6:44.

Bibliography

Unpublished Materials

"Datos Biográficos" of José Ortega y Gasset in the Archives of the Ortega family in Madrid.
"Cartas de José Ortega y Gasset a Navarro Ledesma," nos. 1-11, 1905, in the Archives of the Ortega family.
"Cartas de Navarro Ledesma a José Ortega y Gasset" in the Archives of the Ortega family. (No dates; presumably 1905.)

Completed Works of Ortega

Obras Completas. Vols. 1, 2. 6th ed. Madrid: Revista de Occidente, 1963.
Obras Completas. Vols. 3, 4. 5th ed. Madrid: Revista de Occidente, 1962.
Obras Completas. Vols. 5, 6, 7. 6th ed. Madrid: Revista de Occidente, 1964.
Obras Completas. Vols. 8, 9. 2nd ed. Madrid: Revista de Occidente, 1965.
Obras Completas. Vols. 10, 11. 1st ed. Madrid: Revista de Occidente, 1969.

Works, Articles and Correspondences of Ortega not included in his Completed Works

"Epistolario entre José Ortega y Gasset y Ernst R. Curtius." *Revista de Occidente*, 1, nos. 6, 7 (1963):329-41, 1-27.
"Epistolario entre Unamuno y Ortega." *Revista de Occidente*, 2, no. 19 (1964): 3-28.
*La Rectificación de La República. Madrid: Revista de Occidente, 1931.
*La Rendención de Las Provincias y La Decencia Nacional. Madrid: Revista de Occidente, 1931.
Los Terrores del Año Mil: Crítica de una Leyenda. Ph.D. dissertation; Madrid: Establecimiento Tipográfica de El Liberal, 1909.
"Tesis Para un Sistema de Filosofía." *Revista de Occidente*, 3, no. 31 (1965): 1-8.

---

* These two works are now included in volume 11 of Ortega's completed works. References to them in this text cite the earlier form.

"Letter from José Ortega y Gasset to Mr. Walter P. Paepcke," *Revista de Occidente*, Aspen Institute for Humanistic Studies, 25th Anniversary Year (1974).

Magazines and Newspapers

Crisol (Madrid), 1931.
El Imparcial (Madrid), 1904-13.
El Sol (Madrid), 1917-33.
España (Madrid), 1914-20.
Faro (Madrid), 1908.
Luz (Madrid), 1932-33.

Commentaries

Abellán, José Luis. *Ortega y Gasset En La Filosofía Española: Ensayos de Apreciación*. Madrid: Editorial Tecnos, S. A., 1966.
———. "El Tema de España en Unamuno y Ortega." *Asomante* 17, no. 4 (1961): 26-41.
Adams, Mildred. "Ortega y Gasset." *Forum and Century* 90 (July-December, 1933):373-78.
Alluntis, J. "The Vital and Historical Reason of Ortega y Gasset." *Franciscan Studies* 15, no. 1 (1955):60-78.
Alonso Fueyo, Sabino. "Existencialismo Español: Ortega y Gasset, Unamuno y Xavier Zubiri." *Saitabi* 5, no. 9 (1949):54-60.
Antoni, Carlo. *Commento a Croce*. Venice: N. Pozza, 1955.
———. *From History to Sociology: The Transition in German Historical Thinking*. Translated by Hayden V. White with a foreword by Benedetto Croce. London: Merlin Press, 1962.
———. *L'Historisme*. Translated by Alain Dufour. Geneva: Librairie Droz, 1963.
Arjona, Doris King. "La *Voluntad* and *Abulia* in Contemporary Spanish Ideology." *Revue Hispanique* 74, no. 166 (1928):573-672.
Aron, Raymond. *Dimensions de La Conscience Historique*. Paris: Union Générale D'Éditions, 1961.
———. *Introduction to the Philosophy of History: An Essay on the Limits of Historical Objectivity*. Translated by George J. Irwin. London: Weidenfeld and Nicolson, 1961.
Azcárate, Gumersindo de. *Giner de los Ríos 1839-1914: La Question Universitaria, 1875*. Madrid: Editorial Tecnos, 1967.
Azorín, Antonio. *La Generación de '98*. Madrid: Renacimiento, 1913.
———. "Ortega y Gasset." *Juventud, Egolatria*. Madrid: Caro Raggio, 1949, pp. 117-18.
———. *La Voluntad*. Madrid: Caro Raggio, 1919.
Baroja, Pío. "Homenaje." *Indice*, October 1955, pp. 1-4.
Barroso Nieto, Alfonso. "Ortega y Gasset y el Perspectivismo." *Verdad y Vida* 4, no. 4 (1946):7-10.

Baumgardt, David. "Looking Back on a German University Career." *Leo Baeck Institute, Year Book*. London: East and West Library, 1964, 10:237-65.

Beck, Robert N. and Lee, Dwight E. "The Meaning of Historicism." *The American Historical Review* 59, no. 3 (1954):568-77.

Berger, Peter L. and Luckmann, Thomas. *The Social Construction of Reality: A Treatise in the Sociology of Knowledge*. New York: Doubleday & Co., 1966.

Bergson, Henri. *Creative Evolution*. Translated by Arthur Mitchell. New York: Henry Holt, 1911.

Bidney, David. "Anthropological Thought in Cassirer." *The Philosophy of Ernst Cassirer*, ed. Paul Arthur Schlipp. Evanston: Library of Living Philosophers, 1949, pp. 467-544.

Blanco Aguinaga, Carlos. *Juventud del 98*. Madrid: Siglo XXI de España Editores S.A., 1970.

Bo, C. "Ortega y Gasset y 'El Espectador.'" *Clavileño* 4, no. 24 (1953): 77-81.

Borel, Jean-Paul. *Raison et Vie Chez Ortega y Gasset*. Neuchâtel: La Baconnière, 1959.

Botin, A. "El Estilo de Ortega y Gasset." *Clavileño* 4, no. 24 (1953): 82-83.

Brenan, Gerald. *The Literature of the Spanish People*. Cambridge: University Press, 1951.

Burkhardt, Carl J. "Encuentro con Ortega." *Sur* 241 (July-August 1956): 179-87.

Cano, José Luis. "Ortega y El Amor." *Cuadernos Hispano-Americanos* 95 (November 1957):224-27.

Caponigri, A. Robert. *History and Liberty: The Historical Writings of Benedetto Croce*. London: Routledge & Kegan Paul, 1955.

———. *Spanish Philosophy: An Anthology*. Translated and with an introduction by A. Robert Caponigri. Notre Dame: University of Notre Dame Press, 1967.

Carr, H. Wildon. "'Time and History' in Contemporary Philosophy: With Special Reference to Bergson and Croce." *Proceedings of the British London Academy*, 20 March 1918, pp. 331-49.

Carr, Raymond. *Spain: 1808-1939*. Oxford: Clarendon Press, 1966.

Cassirer, Ernst. *Essay on Man: An Introduction to a Philosophy of Human Culture*. New Haven: Yale University Press, 1944.

———. "Hermann Cohen." *Social Research* 10, no. 2 (1943):218-22.

———. *The Problem of Knowledge: Philosophy, Science and History since Hegel*. Translated by William H. Woglom and Charles W. Hendel. New Haven and London: Yale University Press, 1950.

Cassou, Jean. *La Litterature Espagnole Contemporaine*. Paris: S.KRA, 1929.

———. "Obras de Ortega y Gasset." *Religión y Cultura* 20 (October-December 1932):449-53.

Ceplecha, Christian. *The Historical Thought of José Ortega y Gasset*. Washington, D.C.: Catholic University Press of America, 1958.

Cohen, Morris Raphael. *The Meaning of Human History*. La Salle: Open Court Publishing Co., 1947.

———. *Reason and Nature: An Essay on the Meaning of Scientific Method*. Glencoe: Free Press, 1953.

Collingwood, R.G. *Essays in the Philosophy of History*. Edited with an introduction by William Debbins. Austin: University of Texas Press, 1965.

———. *The Idea of History*. New York: Oxford University Press, 1956.

———. *The Idea of Nature*. London: Oxford University Press, 1945.

Croce, Benedetto. *Aesthetic: As the Science of Expression and General Linguistic*. Translated by Douglas Ainslie. New York: Noonday Press, 1963.
——. *History as the Story of Liberty*. Translated by Sylvia Sprigge. London: George Allen & Unwin Ltd., 1941.
——. *History: Its Theory and Practice*. Translated by Douglas Ainslie. New York: Russell & Russell, 1920.
——. *Logic: As the Science of the Pure Concept*. Translated by Douglas Ainslie. London: Macmillan and Co., 1917.
——. *Philosophy, Poetry, History: An Anthology of Essays*. Translated with an introduction by Cecil Sprigge. London: Oxford University Press, 1966.
Curtius, Ernst Robert. *Französischer Geist Im Neuen Europa*. Berlin-Leipzig: Deutsche Verlags-Anstalt Stuttgart, 1925.
——. "Ortega." Translated by Willard R. Trask. *Partisan Review* 17 (March 1950):259-71.
——. "Ortega." *Merkur* 3, no. 15 (1949):417-30.
De Kalb, Courtenay. "The Spiritual Law of Gravitation: Minority Rule as Analysed by Ortega." *Hispania* 14 (March 1931):81-88.
De Puy, Ida Blanche. "The Basic Ideology of José Ortega y Gasset: The Conflict of Mission and Vocation." Ph.D. dissertation, Stanford University, 1961.
Descartes, René. "Discourse on the Method of Rightly Conducting the Reason and Seeking for Truth in the Sciences." *The Philosophical Works of Descartes*. Translated by Elizabeth S. Haldane and G. R. T. Ross. London: Cambridge University Press, 1931.
Díaz, Janet Winecoff. *The Major Themes of Existentialism in the Work of José Ortega y Gasset*. Chapel Hill: University of North Carolina Press, 1970.
Díaz-Plaja, Guillermo. *Modernismo Frente a Noventa y Ocho*. Madrid: Espasa Calpe, S.A., 1966.
Dilthey, Wilhelm. *Gesammelte Schriften*. 12 vols. Leipzig-Berlin: B.G. Teubner, 1923-36.
——. *Patterns and Meaning in History: Thoughts on History and Society*. Translated and edited with an introduction by H. P. Rickman. New York: Harper Torchbooks, 1962.
Dujovne, León. *La Concepción de La Historia en la Obra de Ortega y Gasset*. Buenos Aires: Santiago Rueda, 1968.
Durán, Manuel. "Tres Definidores del Hombre—Masa: Heidegger, Ortega, Riesman." *Cuadernos Americanos* 90, no. 6 (1956):115-29.
Dussort, Henri. *L'Ecole de Marbourg*. Paris: Presses Universitaires de France, 1963.
Fain, Haskell. *Between Philosophy and History: The Resurrection of Speculative Philosophy of History within the Analytic Tradition*. Princeton: Princeton University Press, 1970.
Farber, Marvin. *The Aims of Phenomenology*. New York: Harper Torchbooks, 1966.
——. *The Foundation of Phenomenology*. Albany: State University of New York Press, 1943.
——. *Philosophical Essays in Memory of Edmund Husserl*. Cambridge: Harvard University Press, 1940.
Ferrater Mora, José. *Ortega y Gasset: An Outline of His Philosophy*. New Haven: Yale University Press, 1957.
——. *Studies in Modern European Literature and Thought*. New Haven: Yale University Press, 1957.

Gaos, José. "Los Dos Ortega." *La Torre* 4, nos. 15-16 (1956):385-99.
——. *Sobre Ortega y Gasset y Otros Trabajos de Historia de Las Ideas en España y La América Española*. México: Impr. Universitaria, 1957.
——. "El Tema de Nuestro Tiempo (Filosofía de la perspectiva)." *Revista de Occidente* 1, no. 3 (October-December 1923):374.
Garagorri, Paulino. *Ortega: Una Reforma de la Filosofía*. Madrid: Revista de Occidente, 1958.
——. *Relecciones y Disputaciones Orteguianas*. Madrid: Taurus, 1965.
Giner de los Ríos, Francisco. "Carta a Ortega." *Revista de Occidente* 3, no. 23 (1965):125-33.
——. *Obras Completas*, vol. 2. Madrid: La Lectura, 1916.
Granell, Manuel. *Ortega y Su Filosofía*. Madrid: Revista de Occidente, 1960.
Hayek, Friedrich A. *The Counter-Revolution of Science: Studies in the Abuse of Reason*. Glencoe: Free Press, 1952.
Heidegger, Martin. *Being and Time*. Translated by John Macquarrie and Edward Robinson. New York: Harper & Brothers, 1962.
——. "Encuentros con Ortega y Gasset en Alemania." *Clavileño* 7, no. 39 (1956):1-2.
Heinemann, F.H. "Jewish Contributors to German Philosophy." *Leo Baeck Institute, Year Book*. London: East and West Library, 1964, 9:161-78.
Hering, Jean. "Phenomenology in France." In *Philosophic Thought in France and the United States: Essays Representing Major Trends in Contemporary French and American Philosophy*, edited by Marvin Farber. Albany: State University of New York Press, 1968.
Hierro S-Pescador, José. *El Derecho en Ortega*. Madrid: Revista de Occidente, 1965.
Hodges, H. A. *The Philosophy of Wilhelm Dilthey*. London: Routledge & Kegan Paul, 1952..
——. *Wilhelm Dilthey: An Introduction*. New York: Oxford University Press, 1944.
Holborn, Hajo. "Dilthey and the Critique of Historical Reason." *Journal of the History of Ideas* 11, no. 1 (1950):93-118.
——. "Ernst Cassirer." In *The Philosophy of Ernst Cassirer*, edited by Paul Arthur Schlipp. Evanston: Library of Living Philosophers, 1949, pp. 41-59.
Honigsheim, Paul. "The Time and the Thought of the Young Simmel." In *Georg Simmel, 1858-1918: A Collection of Essays*, translated with a Bibliography and edited by Kurt Wolff. Columbus: Ohio State University Press, 1959.
Huerta, Eleazar. "Lenguaje y Literatura en La Filosofía de Ortega." *Revista Nacional de Cultura* 18, no. 114 (1956):37-43.
Hughes, H. Stuart. *Consciousness and Society: The Reorientation of European Social Thought*. New York: Random House, 1958.
Husserl, Edmund. *Cartesian Meditations*. Translated by Dorion Cairns. The Hague: Martinus Nijhoff, 1964.
——. *The Idea of Phenomenology*. Translated by William P. Alston and George Nakhnikian. The Hague: Martinus Nijhoff, 1964.
——. *Ideas: General Introduction to Pure Phenomenology*. Translated by W. R. Boyce Gibson. New York: Collier-Macmillan, 1962.
——. "Phenomenology." In *Encyclopedia Britannica*, 14th ed.
——. *The Phenomenology of Internal Time-Consciousness*. Translated by James

S. Churchill. Edited by Martin Heidegger, with an introduction by Calvin O. Schrag. Bloomington: Indiana University Press, 1964.

——. "Philosophy as Rigorous Science." In *Edmund Husserl: Phenomenology and the Crisis of Philosophy*, translated by Quentin Lauer. New York: Harper & Row, 1965.

——. *Zur Phänomenologie der Intersubjektivität. Husserliana*, vols. 13, 14, 15. Edited by Iso Kern. The Hague: Martinus Nijhoff, 1973.

Iggers, Georg. "The Dissolution of German Historism." In *Ideas in History: Essays Presented to Louis Gottschalk by His Former Students*, edited by Richard Herr and Harold T. Parker. Durham: Duke University Press, 1965.

——. *The German Conception of History: The National Tradition of Historical Thought from Herder to the Present*. Middletown: Wesleyan University Press, 1968.

Iriarte, Joaquín. "La 'Circunstancia' histórica de Ortega." *Indice* 10, no. 85 (1955):3-9.

——. "Ortega en Su Vivir y en Su Pensar." *Razón y Fe* 153, no. 698 (1956): 427-48.

——. *Ortega y Gasset: Su Persona y Su Doctrina*. Madrid: Editorial Razón y Fe, 1942.

——. "Ortega y Su Circunstancia Última." *Indice* 10, no. 85 (1955):14.

——. *La Ruta Mental de Ortega*. Madrid: Editorial Razón y Fe, 1949.

Izquierdo, Julián. *Filosofía Española: Tres Ensayos*. Madrid: Ed. Argos, 1955.

Jay, Martin. *The Dialectical Imagination: A History of the Frankfurt School and the Institute of Social Research, 1923-1950*. Boston: Little, Brown & Co., 1973.

Jeschke, Hans. *La Generación de 1898*. Translated by Y. Pino Saavedra. Santiago: University of Chile, 1946.

Kant, Immanuel. *Critique of Pure Reason*. Translated by Norman Kemp Smith. New York: Macmillan, 1963.

——. *Prolegomena to Any Future Metaphysics*. Edited with an introduction by Lewis White Beck. Indianapolis: Bobbs-Merrill, 1950.

Kern, Iso. *Husserl und Kant: Eine Untersuchung über Husserl Verhältnis zu Kant und zum Neukantianismus*. The Hague: Martinus Nijhoff, 1964.

Kirchheimer, Otto. *Politics, Law and Social Change: Selected Essays of Otto Kirchheimer*. Edited by Frederic S. Burin and Kurt L. Shell. New York: Columbia University Press, 1969.

Klibansky, Raymond and Paton, H. J., eds. *Philosophy and History: Essays in Honor of Cassirer*. London: Oxford University Press, 1936.

Kluback, William. *Wilhelm Dilthey's Philosophy of History*. New York: Columbia University Press, 1956.

Kockelmans, Joseph J., ed. *Phenomenology: The Philosophy of Edmund Husserl and Its Interpretation*. New York: Doubleday Anchor, 1967.

Krause, Karl Christian Friedrich. *The Ideal of Humanity and Universal Federation*. Edinburgh: T & T Clark, 1900.

——. *Le Système de La Philosophie*. 2 vols. Translated by Lucien Buys. Leipzig: Otto Schulz, 1892.

Krieger, Leonard. "The Autonomy of Intellectual History." *Journal of the History of Ideas* 34, no. 4 (1973):499-516.

——. "Culture, Cataclysm and Contingency." *Journal of Modern History* 40, no. 4 (1968):447-73.

——. *The German Idea of Freedom*. Boston: Beacon Press, 1957.

Laín Entralgo, Pedro. *España como Problema*. 2 vols. Madrid: Aguilar, 1956.

——. "Ortega y El Futuro." *La Torre* 4, nos. 15-16 (1956):249-70.

——. *Teoría y Realidad del Otro*. 2 vols. Madrid: Revista de Occidente, 1961.

Larraín Acuña, Hernán. *La Génesis del Pensamiento de Ortega*. Buenos Aires: Compañia General Fabril Editora, 1962.

Liebeschütz, Hans. "Hermann Cohen and His Historical Background." *Leo Baeck Institute, Year Book*. London: East and West Library, 1968, 12:3-34.

——. *Das Judentum im Deutschen Geschichtsbild von Hegel bis Max Weber*. Tübingen: J. C. B. Mohr/Paul Siebeck, 1967.

Linz, Juan J. "The Party System of Spain: Past and Future." In *Party Systems and Voter Alignments*, edited by Seymour M. Lipset and Stein Rokkan. Glencoe: Free Press, 1967, pp. 197-282.

Livingstone, L. "Ortega y Gasset's Philosophy of Art." *PMLA* 67, no. 5 (1952): 609-54.

López-Morillas, Juan. *Hacia El 98: Literatura, Sociedad, Ideología*. Barcelona: Ediciones Ariel, 1972.

——. *Intelectuales y Espirituales: Unamuno, Machado, Ortega, Marías, Lorca*. Madrid: Revista de Occidente, 1961.

——. *El Krausismo Español: Perfil de una Adventura Intelectual*. México: Fondo de Cultura Económica, 1956.

——. "Ortega y Gasset y La Crítica Literaria." *Cuadernos Americanos* 93, no. 3 (1957):97-106.

——. "Ortega, Marías y Libro-Escorzo: En Torno a Las 'Meditaciones del Quijote.'" *Insula* 12, no. 133 (1957):1-2.

Löwith, Karl. *From Hegel to Nietzsche: The Revolution in Nineteenth-Century Thought*. Translated by David E. Green. Garden City: Doubleday & Co., 1967.

Lukács, Georg. *The Theory of the Novel*. Translated by Anna Bostock. Cambridge: M.I.T. Press, 1971.

MacCauley, Clay. *Karl Christian Friedrich Krause: Heroic Pioneer for Thought and Life*. Berkeley: University of California Press, 1925.

McClintock, Robert. *Man and His Circumstances: Ortega As Educator*. New York: Teachers College Press, 1971.

Magid, H. "Concord and Liberty." *The Journal of Philosophy* 44, no. 5 (1947): 135-37.

Malefakis, Edward E. *Agrarian Reform and Peasant Revolution in Spain: Origins of the Civil War*. New Haven: Yale University Press, 1970.

——. "Parties of the Left and the Second Republic." In *The Republic and the Civil War in Spain*, edited by Raymond Carr, pp. 16-45. London: Macmillan, 1971.

——. "Peasants, Politics and Civil War in Spain, 1931-1939." In *Modern European Social History*, edited by Robert Bezucha, pp. 192-227. New York: D.C. Heath & Co., 1972.

Mandelbaum, Maurice. *History, Man and Reason: A Study in Nineteenth Century Thought*. Baltimore: Johns Hopkins University Press, 1971.

——. *The Problem of Historical Knowledge*. New York: Liveright Publishing, 1938.

Mannheim, Karl. *Essays on the Sociology of Knowledge*. London: Routledge & Kegan Paul, 1952.

Marías, Julián. *La Escuela de Madrid: Estudios de Filosofía Española*. Buenos Aires: Emece, 1959.

——. *Filosofía Actual y Existencialismo en España*. Madrid: Revista de Occidente, 1955.

——. *La Filosofía Española Actual*. Madrid: Revista de Occidente, 1948.

——. *José Ortega y Gasset: Meditaciones del Quijote, Comentario*. Madrid: Revista de Occidente, 1957.
——. *Miguel de Unamuno*. Translated by Frances M. López-Morillas. Cambridge: Harvard University Press, 1966.
——. *Ortega: Circunstancia y Vocación I*. Madrid: Revista de Occidente, 1960.
——. *Ortega y Tres Antipodas: un Ejemplo de Intriga Intelectual*. Buenos Aires: Revista de Occidente, 1950.
——. *La Teoría de Ortega y Gasset Sobre El Método Histórica de Las Generaciónes*. Madrid: Revista de Occidente, 1949.
Marichal, Juan. "La Singularidad Estilística de Ortega y Gasset." *Ciclón* 2, no. 3 (1956):11-19.
Marquina, Rafael. "El Bautista del 1898." *La Gaceta Literaria* 5, no. 99 (February 1931):5.
Marrou, Henri I. *De la Connaissance Historique*. Paris: Seuil, 1954.
Masur, Gerhard. *Prophets of Yesterday: Studies in European Culture, 1890-1914*. New York: Harper & Row, 1961.
Mercadal, Garcia. *Ideario de Costa*. Madrid: Biblioteca España Nueva, 1932.
Merleau-Ponty, Maurice. *Phenomenology of Perception*. Translated by Colin Smith. London: Routledge & Kegan Paul, 1962.
Meyerhoff, Hans, ed. *The Philosophy of History in Our Time: An Anthology*. Garden City: Doubleday Anchor, 1959.
Mill, John Stuart. *A System of Logic: Ratiocinative and Inductive*. 5th ed., 2 vols. London: Parker, Son & Bourn, 1862.
Misch, George. *Lebensphilosophie und Phäenomenologie*. Leipzig-Berlin: B. G. Teubner, 1931.
Montoro Sanchis, Antonio. *José Ortega y Gasset: Biografía por Sí Mismo*. Madrid: Biblioteca Nueva, 1957.
Nicol, Eduardo. *Historicismo y Existencialismo: La Temporalidad del Ser y la Razón*. México: El Colegio de México, 1950.
Nietzsche, Friedrich. *Beyond Good and Evil*. Translated by Walter Kaufmann. New York: Vintage, 1966.
——. *The Birth of Tragedy and the Genealogy of Morals*. Translated by Francis Golffing. Garden City: Doubleday Anchor, 1956.
——. *The Use and Abuse of History*. Translated by Adrian Collins. Indianapolis: Bobbs-Merrill Co., 1957.
——. *The Will to Power*. Translated by Walter Kaufmann and R. J. Hollingdale. New York: Random House, 1968.
Ors, Eugenio d'. *Cinco Minutos de Silencio*. Valencia: Editorial Sempere, 1925.
Ortega y Gasset, Eduardo. "Mi Hermano Jose." *Cuadernos Americanos* 87, no. 3 (1956):174–211.
Ortega y Gasset, Manuel. *Niñez y Mocedad de Ortega*. Madrid: "Clave," 1964.
Payne, Stanley. *Falange*. Stanford: Stanford University Press, 1961.
——. *Franco's Spain*. New York: Thomas Crowell, 1967.
——. *Politics and the Military in Modern Spain*. Stanford: Stanford University Press, 1967.
Pinder, Wilhelm. *Das Problem Der Generation*. Munich: Bruckmann, 1961.
Piñera, Humberto. *Unamuno y Ortega y Gasset: Contraste de Dos Pensadores*. Universidad de Nuevo León, México: Centro de Estudios Humanísticos, 1965.
Popper, Karl. *The Poverty of Historicism*. New York: Harper & Row, 1964.
Raley, Harold C. *José Ortega y Gasset: Philosopher of European Unity*. University, Ala.: University of Alabama Press, 1971.

Rama, Carlos. *La Crisis Española del Siglo XX*. México: Fondo de la Cultura Económica, 1960.

Ramírez, Santiago. *La Filosofía de Ortega y Gasset*. Barcelona: Herder, 1958.

Reding, Katherine P. "The Generation of 1898 in Spain as Seen Through the Fictional Hero." *Smith College Studies in Modern Language* 17, nos. 3-4 (1935):1-120.

Rickert, Heinrich. *Science and History: A Critique of Positivist Epistemology*. Translated by George Reisman and edited by Arthur Goddard. Princeton: D. Van Nostrand, 1962.

Ringer, Fritz. *The Decline of the German Mandarins: The German Academic Community, 1890-1933*. Cambridge: Harvard University Press, 1969.

Sánchez Villaseñor, José. *Ortega y Gasset, Existentialist: A Critical Study of His Thought and His Sources*. Chicago: Regnery, 1949.

Sartre, Jean-Paul. *Being and Nothingness: An Essay on Phenomenological Ontology*. Translated with an introduction by Hazel E. Barnes. New York: Washington Square Press, 1966.

——. *Critique de La Raison Dialectique, Précédé de Question de Méthode*. Paris: Gallimard, 1960.

——. *The Transcendence of the Ego: An Existentialist Theory of Consciousness*. Translated with an introduction by Forrest Williams and Robert Kirkpatrick. New York: Noonday Press, 1957.

Scheler, Max. *Formalism in Ethics and Non-Formal Ethics of Values*. Translated by Manfred S. Frings and Roger L. Funk. Evanston: Northwestern University Press, 1973.

——. *Man's Place in Nature*. Translated with an introduction by Hans Meyerhoff. Boston: Beacon Press, 1962.

——. *The Nature of Sympathy*. Translated by Peter Heath with an introduction by Werner Stark. New Haven: Yale University Press, 1954.

——. *Philosophical Perspectives*. Translated by Oscar A. Haac. Boston: Beacon Press, 1958.

——. *Ressentiment*. Translated by William W. Holdheim and edited with an introduction by Lewis A. Coser. Glencoe: Free Press, 1961.

Schopenhauer, Arthur. *The World as Will and Representation*. 2 vols. Translated by E. F. J. Payne. New York: Dover Publications, 1969.

Schutz, Alfred. *Collected Papers I: The Problem of Social Reality*. Edited with an introduction by Maurice Natanson. The Hague: Martinus Nijhoff, 1962.

——. *Collected Papers II: Studies in Social Theory*. Edited with an introduction by Arvid Brodersen. The Hague: Martinus Nijhoff, 1964.

——. *Collected Papers III: Studies in Phenomenological Philosophy*. Edited by I. Schutz with an introduction by Aron Gurwitsch. The Hague: Martinus Nijhoff, 1966.

Spiegelberg, Herbert. "Husserl's Phenomenology and Existentialism." *Journal of Philosophy* 57, no. 1 (1960):62-74.

——. *The Phenomenological Movement*. 2d ed., 2 vols. The Hague: Martinus Nijhoff, 1965.

Stark, Werner. *The Sociology of Knowledge: An Essay in Aid of a Deeper Understanding of the History of Ideas*. Glencoe: Free Press, 1958.

Staude, John R. *Max Scheler, 1874-1928: An Intellectual Portrait*. Glencoe: Free Press, 1967.

Stériad, Alice. *L'Interprétation de La Doctrine De Kant par L'École de Marbourg*. Paris: V. Giard & Briere, 1913.

Stern, Alfred. "¿Ortega Existencialista o Esencialista?" *La Torre* 4, nos. 15-16 (1956):385-400.

——. *Philosophy of History and the Problem of Values*. The Hague: Mouton, 1962.

——. "Unamuno and Ortega: The Revival of Philosophy in Spain." *Pacific Spectator* 8, no. 4 (1954):310-24.

Suñer, Enrique. *Los Intelectuales y la Tragedia Española*. San Sebastián: Biblioteca España Nueva, 1938.

Torre, Guillermo de. "Homenaje a Ortega y Gasset." *Ateneo* 124 (January-February, 1956):1-106.

——. "Las Ideas Estéticas de Ortega." *Sur* 241 (July-August 1956):79-89.

Troeltsch, Ernst. *Der Historismus und seine Probleme*. Tübingen: Scientia Aalen, 1961.

Tuñón de Lara, Manuel. *La España del Siglo XX*. Paris: Librería Española, 1966.

Veyne, Paul. *Comment on Écrit L'Histoire: Essai D'Épistémologie*. Paris: Seuil, 1971.

Vuillemin, Jules. *L'Héritage Kantien et La Révolution Copernicienne: Fichte, Cohen, Heidegger*. Paris: Presses Universitaires de France, 1954.

Weber, Frances. "An Approach to Ortega's Idea of Culture: The Concept of Literary Genre." *Hispanic Review* 32 (1964):142-56.

Weingartner, Rudolph H. *Experience and Culture: The Philosophy of Georg Simmel*. Middletown: Wesleyan University Press, 1960.

Weintraub, Karl J. *Visions and Culture: Voltaire, Guizot, Burckhardt, Lamprecht, Huizinga, Ortega y Gasset*. Chicago: University of Chicago Press, 1966.

White, Hayden V. "The Abiding Relevance of Croce's Idea of History." *The Journal of Modern History* 35, no. 2:109-24.

——. *Metahistory: The Historical Imagination in Nineteenth Century Europe*. Baltimore: Johns Hopkins University Press, 1973.

Willey, Thomas. "Back to Kant: The Revival of Kantian Idealism in Germany, 1870-1914." Ph.D. dissertation, Yale University, 1965.

Windelband, Wilhelm. *History of Philosophy*. 2 vols. Translated by James H. Tufts. New York: Harper Torchbooks, 1958.

—— and Heimsoeth, Heinz. *Lehrbuch der Geschichte der Philosophie*. Tübingen: J.C.B. Mohr/Paul Siebeck, 1957.

Xénopol, Alexandru D. "Natur und Geschichte." *Historische Zeitschrift* 113, no. 17 (1914):1-21.

——. *La Théorie de L'Histoire: Des Principes Fondamentaux de L'Histoire*. 2nd edition. Paris: Ernest Leroux, 1908.

Index